Football, Violence and Social Identity

As the 1994 World Cup competition in the USA again demonstrates, football is one of the most popular participant and spectator sports around the world. The fortunes of teams can have great significance for the communities they represent at both local and national levels. Social and cultural analysts have only recently started to investigate the wide variety of customs, values and social patterns that surround the game in different societies. This volume contributes to the widening focus of research by presenting new data and explanations of football-related violence.

Episodes of violence associated with football are relatively infrequent, but the occasional violent events which attract great media attention have their roots in the rituals of the matches, the loyalties and identities of players and crowds and the wider cultures and politics of the host societies. This book provides a unique cross-national examination of patterns of order and conflict surrounding football matches from this perspective with examples provided by expert contributors from Scotland, England, Norway, the Netherlands, Italy, Argentina and the USA.

This book will be of interest to an international readership of informed soccer and sport enthusiasts and students of sport, leisure, society, deviance and culture.

Richard Giulianotti, Norman Bonney and **Mike Hepworth** are respectively Research Assistant, Senior Lecturer and Reader in the Department of Sociology, Aberdeen University, Scotland.

Football, Violence and Social Identity

Edited by Richard Giulianotti,
Norman Bonney
and Mike Hepworth

London and New York

First published 1994
by Routledge
11 New Fetter Lane, London EC4P 4EE

Simultaneously published in the USA and Canada
by Routledge
29 West 35th Street, New York, NY 10001

Reprinted in 1999

Phototypeset in Baskerville by Intype, London

Printed and bound in Great Britain by
Biddles Ltd, Guildford and King's Lynn

British Library Cataloguing in Publication Data
A catalogue record for this book is available from the British Library.

Library of Congress Cataloging in Publication Data
A catalog record for this book is available from the Library of Congress.

ISBN 0–415–09837–8 (hbk)
ISBN 0–415–09838–6 (pbk)

Contents

Tables

Contributors

Eduardo P. Archetti, Department of Anthropology, University of Oslo

Gary Armstrong, Department of Anthropology, University College, London

Norman Bonney, Department of Sociology, University of Aberdeen

Hans H. van der Brug, Institute of Mass-Communications, University of Amsterdam

Alessandro Dal Lago, Department of Sociology, University of Bologna

Rocco De Biasi, Department of Sociology, University of Milan

Eric Dunning, Department of Sociology, University of Leicester

Gerry P. T. Finn, Department of Education, University of Strathclyde

Richard Giulianotti, Department of Sociology, University of Aberdeen

Mike Hepworth, Department of Sociology, University of Aberdeen

Dick Hobbs, Department of Sociology, University of Durham

Jerry M. Lewis, Department of Sociology, Kent State University

Amílcar G. Romero, TEA, Buenos Aires

AnneMarie Scarisbrick-Hauser, Survey Research Center, University of Akron

Acknowledgements

In putting together this collection, we have enjoyed help and encouragement from a variety of sources. Through its research grant (Award no. R000232910), the ESRC has provided essential financial support for our examination of football fan behaviour, the result of which is this book. We also thank the contributors, as well as all those who attended the Aberdeen University soccer conference in April 1992. Ian Pirie, the University's Conference Officer, played a big part in getting the gathering kicked-off. The staff and various students of the Department of Sociology and the Research Committee at the University of Aberdeen have maintained a regular and stimulating interest in the football research being undertaken there. Elsewhere, Pierre Lanfranchi, Richard Holt, Ian Taylor, Steve Redhead, Robert Moore and Mike Featherstone have, possibly unwittingly, given helpful advice and assistance on our behalf. At the other side of the research process, the patience, talk and humour of particular supporter groups in Edinburgh and Aberdeen have been equally important. Finally, Chris Rojek's support at Routledge in seeing through the book from its proposal stage to completion has been vital.

Richard Giulianotti
Norman Bonney
Mike Hepworth

Chapter 1

Introduction

Richard Giulianotti, Norman Bonney and Mike Hepworth

This edited collection is about football fan association and behaviour; more specifically, it is about football fan violence. It explores the inter-relations of participatory and aggressive behaviour, social identity, and the politics of public order and control, within a football context. In contradistinction to Steve Redhead's (1986) stretched claim, it is not the 'final football book' on fan violence or supporter culture generally. Rather, as its various contributors demonstrate, it is part of a series of academic texts exploring football fan culture and experience. In keeping with the overriding theme of these inquiries, our principal concern is with football-related violence. However, its cross-cultural and interdisciplinary themes provide the collection with an appreciably fresh approach to this subject.

This collection is the first major English language text to draw together a spectrum of international and methodological perspectives on football fan violence. In doing so, it is situated at the interface of transformations and continuities in football's contemporary status. Changes relate most notably to its globalization, as the world's premier spectator sport and cultural form – witnessed not only in the financial promise of the United States hosting the 1994 World Cup Finals, but also at the affective, everyday level, through football followers' heightened curiosity with, and media consumption of, the game's interpretation and performance in other nations and continents. A counterpoint to these dynamics is the most palpable, culturally shared experience of football, its public, media and governmental association with varying degrees of partisanship, rivalry and aggression among its spectators.

There has been a marked consistency in the academic ques-

tions asked of British football hooliganism, pertaining to definition, social ascription and action. Why is it that particular social
practices are designated 'football hooliganism'? Which social
groups are identified as 'football hooligans', and by whom?
Where are the clear demarcations or grey areas between particular modes of fan behaviour, in terms of fanaticism, 'hooliganism'
or generally expressive support? In addition to readdressing these
questions, in the light of current political and academic debates
on contemporary fan violence, this collection's distinctively cultural theme introduces a range of underlying, comparative inquiries. What commonalities or differences exist between expressive
young supporters in different cultural contexts? Are the bases
for these overlaps or distinctions found in actual behaviour or
secondary interpretation? What historical, political and social
forces have shaped particular cultures of club or national fan
identity? How extensive is the influence of British youth styles
and subcultures on their contemporaries abroad? Is this exchange
one-way or reciprocal? And, perhaps most importantly of all,
what effect might the State have in recognizing, repelling or
rehabilitating 'football hooligan' supporters?

The pluralist theme of this collection relates not only to the
subject matter, but also to the contributors' nationalities, academic disciplines and methodologies. The authors are from
Argentina, Norway, Italy, the Netherlands, the United States, Scotland and England. Between them, their papers broach a range
of perspectives – anthropological, psychological and sociological.
Methods deployed include qualitative studies of primary and secondary data, through fieldwork and case histories; statistical data
compilation and analysis; the application of interpretive and
figurational sociologies, and contemporary social theory.

The introductory chapter is by Richard Giulianotti. It provides
the reader with a natural history of what we continue to know as
'football hooliganism', as it has been read in British parliamentary
and sociological terms. Giulianotti seeks to demonstrate that
some models advanced to explain the general evolution of political issues do not neatly fit British 'football hooliganism'. Identifying the issue's politico-sociological genus in the mid-1960s, he
charts its course through Westminster and academe in distinctive
periods, until the present. In this way, he outlines the production
of knowledge on fan violence, and how academic contributions
have related historically to particular political and social questions

surrounding the phenomenon. Broad cultural issues have further shaped the social meaning of fan disorder, and the subsequent approach of politicians and academics. These have included the consensual, corporatist system of policy-making, predominant in the 1960s and 1970s, which sought to involve all relevant parties in decision-making; and the socially divisive New Right administration of the 1980s, invoking harsh and quick 'solutions' to fan violence and crime in general. There has also been an increasingly nationalist intervention in the political culture of football, bringing with it sniping comments across the Scottish border over the respective merits (and violent propensities) of neighbouring English and Scottish fans. Giulianotti's paper suggests that the English political endeavour of the 1990s to tone down ('deamplify') prior concern with fan violence, by referring to the effectiveness of recent legislation, duplicates the Scottish experience of the 1980s. Bearing in mind the appallingly stereotyped persona of the English fan abroad, it would appear unlikely that a culture of State-induced fan fraternity will be allowed to match that cultivated amongst Scottish international fans (cf. Giulianotti, 1993a).

The study of political and sociological inquiries into fan disorder is illuminated further by two Argentinian academics, the anthropologist Eduardo Archetti and the ethnographer Amílcar Romero. They kick off with a provocative critique of English sociological explanations of football-related violence. Arguing that a lack of field research appears generic to these studies, the authors promote a flexible, anthropological approach sympathetic to that pioneered by Armstrong and Harris (1991). Detailing four case studies, dating from 1958 ('the first death') to 1983–4 ('organized fan violence'), Archetti and Romero chart the main points on the trajectory of Argentinian football-related violence, against a terrain of military dictatorship and societal 'paramilitarization'. The essay serves to underscore the centrality of special politico-cultural and historical processes in the generation of football-related violence and hooligan identities. It also establishes the collection's theme that football culture is indicative of a given society's cognition of existential, moral and political fundamentals.

Italian sociologists Alessandro Dal Lago and Rocco De Biasi continue the critical study of English explanations of football hooliganism. They present statistical and ethnographic evidence that the class-orientated explanations of English football hooliganism, whether in terms of employment status or cultural lifeworld (cf. Dunning, this volume; I. Taylor, 1987), are incongruent to Italian football fan identity and culture. Drawing on research with AC Milan, Internazionale and Genoa supporters, they argue that the Italian *tifo* (football fanaticism) harbours strong, often conflicting intra-city and regional animosities. The most fundamental, macrocultural conflicts involve major sides divided by the *mezzogiorno* (see Dunning, this volume); but this ought not to overshadow localized rivalries such as Atalanta (of Bergamo) and Brescia, or Fiorentina (Florence) and Bologna (cf. Roversi, 1992: 56–8). Moreover, the distinctive identity of Italian football fans is further illustrated by two modes of football fan association, within each club's support. Official fan clubs are far more populous and centralized than their UK equivalents. Conversely, the tensions underlying the ambivalent relationship between the 'militant' fans, the *ultras*, and their elected club, are mirrored on a broader stage by commentators and other fans from outwith Italy confusing these supporters with 'organized hooligans'.

And if 'militant' fans mirror a 'fanatical' relationship to the club, surely they manage to strike at something more fundamental, perhaps the deeply embedded values about the game itself. In 1985, Redhead and McLaughlin briefly identified the distinctive 'casual' style and its regional rivalries; it required a further eight years for its symbolic and cultural components to be given systematic examination in print, through Richard Giulianotti's (1993b) research in Aberdeen. Gerry Finn's paper explores the value network of Glasgow Rangers casuals, by unpacking the cultures of aggression and violence rooted in Scottish and other soccer, using a societal psychological approach. Socialization processes of playing, administering and supporting the game display ambiguous and highly contextual validations of aggression and evaluations of violence. One of Finn's principal exponents of 'dirty play', the English midfielder Vinny Jones, illustrates his on-field instrumentality through an aptly hooligan metaphor:

> I think that in any walks of life, if the top man gets sorted out early doors . . . I mean if I was on me own and there's a gang of lads and they're gonna start on me, I would go in and

whack the biggest and the toughest straight away. And that's
what happened in the Cup Final.

(Vinny Jones, Wimbledon FC, *Soccer's Hard Men*)

In the pursuit of their football-related goals, players and spectators enjoy related senses of liminality: the hedonic charge readily afforded by football culture, the 'flow' sensations of immersion
in the action. Finn confronts the significance of the anti-hooligan,
'carnival' identity of Scottish international fans, and the continuing presence of club-level soccer hooligan subcultures. Each, he
maintains, is enwrapped by the sense of *jouissance*, of being 'at
one with the action', that characterizes the game's culture –
though with diametrically opposing consequences.

From Scotland we cross the border to England. The leading
British sociologist of football hooliganism is in no doubt that
any deep-seated metamorphosis in English fan culture has been
overstated. And, in a robust defence of figurational sociology, he
is equally consistent in advancing the value of the Eliasian case
in explaining the phenomenon. Eric Dunning compiles and
evaluates the latest batch of critiques on the 'Leicester School',
which seek to identify empirical and epistemological weaknesses
in its numerous researches. Some fieldwork and presentational
shortcomings are acknowledged, particularly regarding the
location of football within a community configuration, and the
repositioning of subsequent findings on an English rather than
British or pan-European stage. However, the process-sociological
perspective of Norbert Elias is retained wholeheartedly, to the
extent that its applicability to football-related disorder overseas is
also adduced. Regional and ethnic rivalries vicariously enacted
by football fans in Italy accord with the 'established-outsider'
thesis advanced by Elias (Elias and Scotson, 1965). Equally, Eliasians would further contend that the historical interplay of political
and football violence may be explained by the weak co-develop-
ment of self-control and State formation (Elias, 1982).

The major theme of the paper by American sociologists Jerry
M. Lewis and AnneMarie Scarisbrick-Hauser is the difficulty which
official reports into British stadium disasters have in addressing
football hooligan behaviour. By way of illustration they explore
the inquiries concerned with disasters at Birmingham, Bradford
and Hillsborough (Popplewell, 1985; P. Taylor, 1990). The analysts posit that the reports neglect to delineate precisely the types

of behaviour in which football fans engage on an everyday basis. More particularly, recent inquiries have failed to establish adequate distinctions between 'hooliganism' and culturally accepted modes of behaviour among fans. Such lacunae can have grave implications for supporters regularly experiencing the policy outcomes of ill-informed findings. In response, Lewis and Scarisbrick-Hauser introduce the McPhail categories for describing crowd behaviour recorded in the two most recent reports. The paper is therefore one of the first to seek a systematic and positivist understanding of soccer fan behaviour.

A similarly positivist, policy-orientated approach is promoted by the Dutch sociologist H. H. van der Brug. Outlining the historico-cultural genesis of Dutch fan subcultures, or 'Sides', van der Brug firstly recognizes a general trend towards attacks on opposing fans and players rather than referees and officials. He goes on to explore the educational level of Dutch hooligans, contrasting the findings with British research, as well as the differing antici-pation of hooligan incidents by Dutch international supporters on their travels. The association of football hooliganism and its media reportage is also documented. The scale of club-level vio-lence in the Netherlands since the late 1980s had led most of the British press to predict intense levels of violence, a 'superhooligan showdown', when England were due to play Holland, firstly at a Wembley friendly in March 1988, and then at the 1988 European Championship Finals in June, and the 1990 World Cup Finals in Cagliari. That nothing of this proportion materialized elicited few meaningful enquiries from its publicists, although a key reason lay in the understated, consensual strategy adopted by Dutch polic-ing in anticipation of these fixtures (van der Brug and Meijs, 1988). The author cautiously advocates restitutive public policies such as club/hooligan social programmes for reducing the inci-dence of match-related disorder. The proactive method of polic-ing 'away' fans *en route* to fixtures is similarly endorsed.

In Britain, a more theatrical and coercive police measure is the 'dawn raid'. Acting on the basis of 'intelligence' about individuals, acquired in the course of earlier police work, a unit of officers descends on one address or a number of domiciles, as part of a co-ordinated 'operation'. The facilitating 'search warrant' is granted by magistrates on the police expectation of discovering material evidence regarding the planning or execution of foot-ball-related violence. The controversial paper by anthropologist

Gary Armstrong and criminologist Dick Hobbs exposes a darker underside to the philosophy behind the 'dawn raid'. Spotlighting the genesis of recent, technology-led strategies in the policing of English football fans, the authors identify two principal methods which are increasingly prevalent and 'media-friendly' – panoptical surveillance of fans through closed circuit television and data-bases, and covert policing of 'hooligan' subcultures. The authors argue that these methods represent a significant departure from established policing practices, a transition sustained by the liberal left's disinclination to defend the civil rights of the hooligan 'folk devil'. The weak justification for subsequent 'dawn raids' on the homes of individuals is registered by the authors, who also note their failure to effect criminal convictions. Armstrong and Hobbs attack the underlying rationale for these tactics, the belief that by imprisoning the sinister 'generals', the hooligan residue will be left rudderless and thereby discontinue its football violence.

Continuing the critical, socio-legal analysis of football hooligan-ism, the final chapter is an extended case study of a Scottish football-related trial. Two of three men accused of attempted murder and mobbing and rioting were convicted and jailed, following disorder at a disco in Dunfermline. The convictions pivoted on the general belief that the football hooligan gang, the Hibs casuals from Edinburgh, had perpetrated the mêlée. Draw-ing on Scots Law jurisprudence and post-modern social theory, Richard Giulianotti outlines the genus of the Scottish 'soccer casual' subcultural style, and its particularly problematic relation-ships to the Scottish juridico-administrative system, which pro-motes the domestic game as 'hooligan free'. The media's portrayal of Hibs casuals, prior to the court case, as a surrep-titious, quasi-Mafia outfit is explored, as well as the events leading up to the disorder. Assessing the circumstances in which the trial took place, the gathering and presentation of evidence, and the lack of corroboration provided by the prosecution, the paper argues that the convictions were of highly dubious probity. The verdicts reflect more a diffuse state of mind on Scottish hooligan-ism than a 'reasonable' evaluation of the evidence brought before the court.

REFERENCES

Armstrong, G. and R. Harris (1991) 'Football Hooligans: theory and evidence', *Sociological Review*, 39, 3: 427–58.

Brug, H. H. van der and J. Meijs (1988) 'Dutch Supporters at the European Championships in Germany', *Council of Europe*.

Elias, N. (1982) *State Formation and Civilization: the civilizing process*, Oxford: Blackwell.

Elias, N. and J. L. Scotson (1965) *The Established and the Outsiders*, London: Frank Cass.

Giulianotti, R. (1993a) 'A Model of the Carnivalesque? Scottish football fans at the 1992 European Championship finals in Sweden and beyond', *Working Papers in Popular Cultural Studies No.6*, Manchester Institute for Popular Culture.

—— (1993b) 'Soccer Casuals as Cultural Intermediaries: the politics of Scottish style', in S. Redhead (ed.) *The Passion and the Fashion*, Aldershot: Avebury.

Popplewell, O., Lord Justice (Chairman) (1985) *Inquiry into the Crowd Safety and Control at Sports Grounds: interim report*, London: HMSO.

Redhead, S. (1986) *Sing When You're Winning*, London: Pluto.

Redhead, S. and E. McLaughlin (1985) 'Soccer's Style Wars', *New Society*, 16 August.

Roversi, A. (1992) *Calcio, Tifo e Violenza*, Bologna: Il Mulino.

Taylor, I. (1987) 'Putting the Boot into a Working Class Sport: British soccer after Bradford and Brussels', *Sociology of Sport Journal*, 4.

Taylor, P., Lord Justice (Chairman) (1990) *Inquiry into the Hillsborough Stadium Disaster: final report*, London: HMSO.

Chapter 2

Social identity and public order
Political and academic discourses on football violence

Richard Giulianotti

INTRODUCTION

Although the world's leading team sport, it was not until the 1960s that the social significance of football received substantive and separate attention from social scientists and historians (Harrington, 1968; Lever, 1969; I. Taylor, 1969). For over a decade, the major contributions focused on English fans, particularly on the subject of hooliganism, as Marxists (Ian Taylor, John Clarke, John Hargreaves, Alan Ingham), anthropologists (Peter Marsh and associates, Desmond Morris) and process-sociologists (Eric Dunning and the Leicester researchers) clashed over the nature of the football-watching experience, and more specifically the causes of these supporters' disorderly behaviour.[1] Subsequently, the most notable contributors to the English hooliganism debate have included environmental psychologists (David Canter and associates), cultural anthropologists (Gary Armstrong and Rosemary Harris), those working within the cultural studies (Richard Giulianotti and Steve Redhead) and collective behaviour fields (Jerry Lewis and AnneMarie Scarisbrick-Hauser), or upholding the tradition of urban ethnography (Dick Hobbs and Dave Robins). The initial restriction of the debate to the 'English' phenomenon has attracted commentaries on its inapplicability to other cultural settings, for example in contemporary Scotland (Richard Giulianotti), North America (Alan Roadburg) or more recently Italy (Alessandro Dal Lago and Rocco De Biasi). Meanwhile, the majority of studies of football-related violence undertaken in Europe and elsewhere have been published in relative isolation, although some have sought to test English sociological theories.

As a totality, it is apparent that these discourses have carved out an important academic niche for the sociology of football violence. Rather lamely, the conservative New Right has designated this 'the football hooliganism industry', a careerist construct which is also deemed to exist in 'race relations', and characterized by a financial reward which outstrips the seriousness of 'the problem' by some measure (*Sunday Times*, 8 August 1993). As I shall seek to demonstrate, this assertion is itself in no small way related to the current political and historical *milieu* in which 'football hooliganism' as 'social problem' is currently located, both in England and Scotland: a context now serving to promote fan disorder's perceived decline ('deamplification'), in overt contrast to prior exaggeration of its incidence and seriousness ('amplification').[2]

THE GENUS OF FAN VIOLENCE: CONTINUITY OR CHANGE?

If we switch our attention to historical developments in football culture, then the figurationalists provide a persuasive account of the game's long genealogy of disorderly and violent behaviour on and off the football field. This 'continuity' thesis appears to be as applicable to Britain as it is abroad (Dunning *et al.*, 1984, 1988; Jones, 1986), covering such traditional folk games as Cornish 'curling', Welsh 'knappan', Florentine *calcio*, or north Italian *gioco della pugna* (Elias and Dunning, 1986; Guttman, 1986; Levine and Vinten-Johansen, 1981). Notwithstanding the violent propensities of the players and spectators of these games (the two were, until formal codification, usually indistinguishable), there are problems of historical comparability here, not least in a hermeneutic sense. Did the performers really comprehend their actions as 'play' or 'violence' in our contemporary manner? One observation which points to football hooliganism's essentially modern genus relates to the uncertain, nineteenth century parentage of the ascription 'hooligan' (Pearson, 1983). Its lineage is more exactly understood as emanating from historically regular, non-rational public fears and anxieties (Stan Cohen's 'moral panics') over perceived increases in social crime and disorder, contrasting with idealized visions of the past's peaceability. Not only do these historical and cultural questions underpin Redhead's (1993a: 3) refrain, that there is no hard and fast definition of what 'football hooliganism' actually is. (Does it involve actual violence, the intention of seeking fights, or merely the desire to be publicly associated with football-related disorder?) More significantly, it introduces the archivist of fan disorder to the importance of historically specific definitions in his or her own inquiry; in short, how and when knowledge is produced on the phenomenon.

In contradistinction to the figurationalists' thesis, Ian Taylor's (1971a, 1982a and b) Marxist standpoint argues that football hooliganism has its modern origins in a pitch invasion during a televised 1961 cup-tie at Sunderland. He maintains that this reflected and gave rise to the appearance of 'oppositional' soccer 'subcultures' in Britain, amongst the young working class.[3] There are a number of drawbacks to this case also, not least of which are the empirical shortcomings of an admittedly 'speculative' analysis (Archetti and Romero, this volume). There is the further possibility of an involuntary, inverted imperialism towards other fan disorder, an ethnocentrism more fully embraced by Hobbs and Robins (1991: 559), who disparage 'adolescents slavishly copying from television the hairstyles, footwear and chanting of British fans'. Do we mine Italian and Argentinian (or even Scottish) disorder for evidence of English influences – in gang names, chants, and fashions – before the label of 'football hooligan' is stamped for export?[4] What we can say is that the term itself is British in origin, having become so globally renowned as to verge on the internationally elliptical; French, German, Italian, Spanish, Swedish and Portuguese languages all use English derivatives of 'hooligan' to represent particular types of football spectator not solely from the British Isles. And in the following, I shall attempt to sketch a natural history of football hooliganism's *definitive* form, its British variant, as it emerged as a focus of political concern and sociological inquiry. This serves to delineate the various tensions and interplays between political and sociological definitions of the phenomenon at particular historical 'moments'. Equally, it points to the evolution of increasingly international discourses on its manifestation and evaluation. Perhaps most importantly, it provides some explanation for political (and sometimes academic) discourses, attesting at one stage or another to football fan disorder's perceived ubiquity or invisibility.

FAN VIOLENCE: PERIODS OF BRITISH POLITICAL AND ACADEMIC ATTENTION

Houlihan (1991: 174–200) has argued that the history of football fan disorder as a British political issue corresponds to Downs's (1972) three stage, 'issue attention cycle':

Stage 1: A latent and continued prevalence of the prospective policy area; little or no research is undertaken, the issue being considered an adjunct to more pressing problems or inequalities.

Stage 2: Alarming discovery and excited investigation of the social phenomenon; the professions are invited to investigate its manifestations, likely causes and possible remedies.

Stage 3: An embarrassed realization of legislative costs and quick relegation from the executive's public eye; investigation is discontinued and professional concern refocused elsewhere.

The model omits critical assessment of the historical, hermeneutic and political contexts of issue selection and action. It ignores the variable extent to which the politico-administrative system can uncloak, act upon and discard any one issue without stirring effective opposition. A more detailed scrutiny of political and sociological discourses on fan disorder suggests the issue has passed through several, more complex postwar phases. Nominally, these commence with the 'prehistory' of the early postwar period until 1968; the major stages may then be differentiated as 1968–70, 1971–8, 1979–84, 1985, 1986–April 1989, and finally May 1989–present. In contrast to the model advanced by Downs and Houlihan, during each of these periods judgements of football hooliganism's political salience and social incidence were often ambiguous or equivocatory, or founded upon ideological rather than financial imperatives.

'Prehistory' to maturation: football hooliganism towards the 1970s

Corresponding with the majority of academic explanations, the political origins of 'football hooliganism' *per se* are in the mid-1960s. It was not until April 1967 that *Hansard*'s reports of the House of Commons proceedings classified 'Football Grounds (Violence and Hooliganism)' as a discrete locus of parliamentary inquiry. The early postwar period was characterized by political concern over fans' attendance at midweek fixtures, jeopardizing the maximization of working manhours and the national rebuild-ing programme. A fourteen-year hiatus separated the isolated concern over disorder among Arsenal fans queuing for 1952 FA Cup semi-final tickets, and the generally 'disorderly conduct' of a 'small minority of spectators who cause disturbances' at matches (*Hansard*, 27 January 1966). In this period, the few questions extended by Members of Parliament gradually sought to reconsti-tute the function of social control agents, from physical crowd control to arresting and raising the fines on those convicted. Pitch invasions were still interpreted favourably in the 1960s, as 'an increasing tendency of football supporters to invade the field of play in congratulations of their team' (*Hansard*, 12 May 1966).

The period 1968–70 marks the parliamentary and academic maturation of 'football hooliganism' from irregular disturbance to definitive social policy area. Attention in the Commons oscil-lated around three themes, with wider political and cultural res-onances. First, a gradual escalation in fan violence was perceived, with a concomitant rise in social unease. In February 1968, refer-ence was made to 'the growing public concern about the increase in hooliganism in football generally' (*Hansard*, 29 February 1968). Fifteen months later, through 'the continuing amount of damage caused by soccer hooligans' (*Hansard*, 1 May 1969), the issue was formalized as a threat to private property. Towards the end of the same year, during the first lengthy Commons exchange on the subject, there were early indications of spiralling Government activity (through questions on 'what further steps' would be implemented); and the origination of the 'prophecy of doom' – 'there are serious riots on the way' (*Hansard*, 20 November 1969).

Secondly, specific loci of fan disorder were identified, particu-larly through a redefinition of vandalism on football 'special' trains conveying supporters only. During one exchange, the Min-ister of Transport indicated that British Railways considered these trains cost-effective, in removing the threat of fan disorder from ordinary services.[5] Finally, the established corporatist framework of policy 'problem solving' was transferred to football hooligan-ism. Short-term abrogation of responsibility for single incidents was supplanted by a long-term fielding of demands for consulta-tive committees between the executive, police and football authorities; direct liaison with the Football League was introduced.

This period 1968–70 also heralded the first commissions of

informed inquiry into football hooliganism, through the Harrington (1968) and, to a lesser extent, the Lang (1969) Reports. The
former's most important legacy was perhaps the construction of
a table pointing to the lower-working-class background of football-
related offenders already arrested and convicted, a schema which
inaugurated a lengthy debate in sociological circles on the political economy of modern football and the class background of its
deviant subcultures (Archetti and Romero, this volume; Cohen,
1972; Dal Lago and De Biasi, this volume; Dunning et al., 1988
and this volume; Giulianotti, 1994; Hobbs and Robins, 1991; I.
Taylor, 1971a; Trivizas, 1980).

Exemplars of disorder: fan violence 1971–8

With the issue now embedded in the national and governmental
consciousness, the second period of 1971–8 marks a transition
towards some kind of policy reflexivity, in which social control
measures already implemented are evaluated for their efficacy
and practicality. First, isolated instances of fan disorder were
presented as emblematic of a generic phenomenon which
remained out of control. Disorder involving Manchester United,
Chelsea, Derby County, Glasgow Rangers and Millwall fans served
as referents to protocols for a *national* policy on football hooliganism. Only in the case of Scotland, with the subsequent legislative
support for the 1978 McElhone Report, was such a concertedly
national policy adopted.

The nascent focusing of political attention on to hooligan
exemplars was mirrored within the academic field, with social
scientific studies of fans following Oxford United (Marsh et al.,
1978) and Arsenal of London (Cohen and Robins, 1978). The
first study, rescued from the ethological by an application of
symbolic interactionism,[6] conceptualized football hooliganism as
largely harmless, metonymic and ritualized (see Lewis and Scarisbrick-Hauser, this volume; Morris, 1981). Deploying a variation
on 1960s 'labelling theory', the Oxford researchers attributed any
genuine violence to excessive social control interventions. There
have to be some doubts about the violent propensities of these
fans at this time, their club being in the Third Division and
relative newcomers to the English League. The study of Arsenal
fans provided an important ethnographic dimension to earlier
Marxist speculations on the structural role of unemployment,

urban decay and the cultivation of a middle-class image for the game, in provoking a young working-class backlash through hooliganism. The Marxist position thus came to articulate a romanticized conception of the football hooligan as subcultural agent, seeking to recapture 'magically' the communitarianism of the traditional working-class locale, abandoned by his parents, local government and the representative football club's directors (Clarke, 1978; Cohen, 1972; Hall and Jefferson, 1976; Pearton, 1986: 79–80; Shipman, 1988; I. Taylor, 1971b). Public concern with the football hooligan was deemed to be largely processed in tabloid sensationalism, which marked a broader social movement towards a right-wing populism in dealing with crime (Hall, 1978; Hall *et al.*, 1978).

Ethogenic and Marxist/subcultural discourses on fan disorder were compressed by a *Panorama* (BBC TV) documentary on Millwall fans in 1977. Although not ignoring the working-class localism of south-east London's 'home, pub and club' culture, the narrator, broadcasting psychologist Dr Anthony Clare, concentrated on the Oxford theories of militaristic 'order on the terraces':

> But within Millwall's terrace army, there are divisions. At the bottom of the hierarchy are the youngsters; they call themselves the Half-Way Line. When it comes to aggro, they imitate their elders. But as they grow older, they have a career choice to make. Some of them graduate to Treatment; they're the ones in the surgical masks. Although one of Millwall's heavy mobs, Treatment don't pick fights but they're always there when they happen. In the trench warfare of the terraces, it's F-Troop who go over the top. F-Troop are the real nutters, self-confessed loonies like Harry The Dog, who go looking for fights and are seldom disappointed . . .

Contrasted with the burgeoning political concern over young fans, these academic discourses represent both an attempt to 'deamplify' descriptions of their behaviour, and an indictment of the policy 'solutions' advanced by politicians, which, they argue, failed to address the underlying roots of 'football hooliganism'. Indeed, the parliamentary period 1971–8 witnessed the extension of some familiar and some bizarre control strategies for stemming fan violence, such as implementing segregation in English grounds; increasing the number of attendance centres; banning away fans; spraying indelible paint on fighting fans; curtailing opportunities for pre-match drinking; acting on the hypodermic transfer of violence to outside the football stadia; countering the possibility of media glorification of fan violence; and withdrawing passports from hooligans operating overseas. Finally, it should be noted that in 1974 football hooliganism's status as a policy issue was affirmed through the first lukewarm political attempt to *deamplify* its significance: even in suggesting that 'the condition has improved considerably inside grounds', the Minister for the Environment conceded that violence may have been displaced to beyond the public and media eye; that the football season was then only ten weeks old; and there had also been 'one or two sporadic outbursts' (*Hansard,* 4 December 1974).

The New Right ascendancy: a casual stroll through 1979–84

The third period of 1979–84 covers the executive transition from a corporatist framework enabling liberal democratic, dialogical government to a New Right administration, intent on the singular implementation of *laissez-faire* economic and punitive judicial policies. The era is marked by a more intense sensitization of the executive towards football hooliganism, and a growing trend towards centralization of decision-making against the offender. An official working party on football fan behaviour, involving a range of academics, was set up at the Department of the Environment and contributed a report in 1984. A liaison group for the 1982 World Cup, under the department's auspices, was retained, issuing 'mandatory measures' to be taken against hooligans by all English clubs in the season 1983–4. These enacted earlier recommendations of controlling ticket sales to secure effective segregation, as well as introducing greater custodial powers for magistrates, and raising the number of attendance centres for offenders.

If we turn our attention momentarily to the sociological contribution in this period, it is immediately apparent that investigations of British football hooliganism came to be dominated by the team of researchers at Leicester University (*inter alia* Dunning, this volume; Dunning *et al.,* 1988; Murphy *et al.,* 1990; Williams *et al.,* 1984). Funded principally by the Football Trust, the researchers offered the first systematic study to combine statistical and ethnographic data, within the guiding philosophy of

Eliasian sociology.[7] One of the central tenets of the Leicester research is that, in a broad historical setting, public expectations of more 'civilized' behaviour have percolated through the social classes; these have failed to penetrate fully the lower working classes, whose behaviour is still largely socialized subculturally, in terms of aggressive and spontaneously violent masculinity. This thesis underpins Leicester's empirical findings: that historically, greater opprobrium has come to be directed at football offenders, especially in the postwar period; and that the football hooligan subcultures of the mid-1960s have been principally manned by the lower working classes. Other research in the early 1980s produced less structural findings. Pratt and Salter's (1984: 214) open-ended conclusions on football hooliganism stated that it represented 'a meeting point for a variety of social conflicts, hostilities and prejudices'. And the first systematic, participant observation study of the *policing* of (Aston Villa) football fans, a social dynamic central to many English writers but hitherto largely ignored by them, was forwarded by an American sociologist (Lewis, 1982) – whose conclusion generally underscored the successes rather than failures of methods used in public order maintenance.

The distinctive opposition of English and Scottish fan identities became more pronounced with the accession of the Thatcher administration. Following the televised pitch invasion and battle between Rangers and Celtic fans at the 1980 Scottish Cup Final, legislation against alcohol consumption and drunkenness at football grounds was enacted in Scotland. Accordingly, Scottish politicians typically promoted the efficacy of these measures, arguing wryly for similar measures to be adopted in England.[8] In response, English media and politicians were not averse to amplifying the violent propensities of Scottish fans attending the biannual Home International at Wembley (Giulianotti, 1993a; McDevitt, 1994). By 1985, the Scots found themselves effectively penalized by a sudden Government/FA decision to switch the fixture to Hampden, after thousands of their constituents had booked accommodation for the traditional 'Wembley Weekend'. Meanwhile, the growing international reputation of English supporters for violence began to be utilized by Scottish fans travelling abroad, as a means of asserting a culturally distinctive national identity, and winning over their hosts.[9]

The newest development in the 1979–84 period was the

inflation of 'football hooliganism' to an issue of international magnitude. The first extended debate on soccer fan violence in the House of Commons followed a ministerial statement on events surrounding the France v. England fixture in February 1984, which produced thirty arrests. Recycling the Government's own law-and-order ticket, Opposition MPs pointed to prior trouble abroad involving English fans in Denmark, Holland, Luxemburg, Switzerland, and Italy, in demanding a toughening of control strategies, particularly on the issue of passports. A year earlier, the British Government had been the catalyst for a Rotterdam meeting of European ministers with responsibility for sport. The resultant Council of Europe (1985) convention agreed standards of international co-operation in policing, identifying and prosecuting football offenders. The international flavour of English fan disorder was the underlying theme of the first major sociological work devoted to football hooliganism *per se*, *Hooligans Abroad*, in which the Leicester researchers followed English fans to Spain, Germany and Denmark.

Thatcherism and the football armageddon: crisis year of 1985

1985 stands out as the apogee of executive disquiet over football hooliganism, the shift from a centralized, State interventionist approach at an international level, to a stumbling, Prime Ministerial crusade against the voguish 'enemy within'. Three major incidents of crowd disorder, two of them fatal, precipitated an administration by crisis on football (see Lewis and Veneman, 1987). The year also constitutes a subcultural high point in the 'soccer style wars' fought out by English and Scottish soccer 'casuals', the contemporary hooligan style predominant among the range of young masculine identities (Finn, this volume; Giulianotti, 1993a, this volume; Redhead, 1986, 1991a and b; Redhead and McLaughlin, 1985). In hindsight, the three main occasions of violence against fans themselves stand out as predictable, almost wilful punctuations in the hard-headed Thatcherite campaign against football hooliganism. Subsequently, the blinkered assault on crowd control was purchased at the price of bartering away the politics of environmental safety inside stadia.[10]

The first on 14 March pivoted on the pitch invasion and riot involving Millwall fans after an FA Cup quarter-final in Luton. Following the disorder, Millwall supporters pointed to the role of

low ticket allocations and subsequent overcrowding in the terraces, in precipitating earlier pitch invasions and public unrest
(*Nine O'Clock News*, BBC, 14 May). A report was obtained by the
Home Secretary from Bedfordshire's Chief Constable, and a
Prime Ministerial appointment with the Football Association
arranged. Two months later, a second parliamentary debate
(*Hansard*, 13 May) arose following the Bradford fire disaster and
the fan disorder at Birmingham on the same day. Fifty-seven
people were killed and over 200 injured at Valley Parade, as fire
engulfed the wooden main stand; a discarded cigarette had
ignited mountains of paper and other rubbish beneath, which
had been allowed to accumulate over the years. The disorder at
Birmingham, involving Birmingham City and Leeds United fans,
saw one spectator killed following the collapse of a wall, the arrest
of 125 fans, and the injury of 96 police officers and over 80
fans. A full-scale inquiry chaired by Mr Justice Popplewell was
implemented to investigate ground safety and hooliganism (Lewis
and Scarisbrick-Hauser, this volume), an association which,
claimed the Bradford MP Max Madden, caused resentment
amongst his constituents (*Hansard*, 4 June 1985; cf. I. Taylor,
1987). A fortnight later, 39 people were killed and many more
injured at the Liverpool v. Juventus European Cup Final in
Brussels' Heysel Stadium, after several pre-match charges by Liverpool fans, the attempted escape by Italian supporters and, again,
the collapse of a wall. The following week, the Prime Minister
Margaret Thatcher introduced the parliamentary debate on the
tragedy, immediately prejudging the findings of the awaited Popplewell Report, by listing several measures which the Government
would seek to implement (*Hansard*, 3 June 1985). The most
important included the reduction of alcohol's role in producing
fan violence through legislation similar to that in Scotland;[11] the
introduction of club membership schemes for spectators, with
the possible objective of banning away supporters; increasing the
number of all-ticket fixtures to the same end; and installing closed
circuit television at football league grounds. In July, the interim
report of the Popplewell Inquiry was published, which offered
support for a moderation of Government football policy. It
recommended 'urgent consideration' should be given by clubs
in England and Wales for a membership scheme to exclude away
fans; it had already been adopted by Luton Town, whose Chairman, David Evans, was a right-wing Conservative MP.

At a European level, UEFA implemented an indefinite ban on English football clubs playing sides belonging to any other national association.[12] Potentially, this measure constituted a restraint of trade according to English common law, though with lesser certainty under European Community Law (Evans, 1986). Yet such was the Government's desire to support swingeing action against clubs and their fans, that it repressed its own political instincts, of free trade and English institutional autonomy, to support this external imposition.

Academic commentators on football hooliganism have not failed to register the significance of these events, on both the nature of the phenomenon and their theorizations of its social consequence. The strongest rethinking occurred on the part of Ian Taylor (1987). In 'left realist' mode, he stated that Thatcher's social neglect was now so corrupting that the football hooligan could no longer be regarded as a morally engaging, anti-bourgeois 'resistance fighter'. Taylor dichotomized him as either belonging to the ill-educated and chauvinistic labour aristocracy; or part of the swelling young unemployed, enduring social and personal disenfranchisement.

The Heysel disaster also precipitated lengthy and important consideration from two specialists in young football fan activity, John Williams and Steve Redhead. As a postscript to Heysel, the Leicester researchers had maintained that 1985 did not inaugurate a fundamental change in English terrace culture (Dunning et al., 1988: 246–9). John Williams of the Leicester group took this a stage further, forwarding a pessimistic and darkly ironic piece on the cohabitation of English fan racism and violence with the 'Falklands spirit' xenophobia of the Thatcher Government at its zenith. This stands in some contrast to his later, partial apportionment of the 'new football cultures' (such as fanzines), which overtly eschewed violent subcultures and identities, to the renascent properties of post-Heysel soul-searching (Williams, 1991a: 180). Steve Redhead (1991a: 75) was more explicit on this point, quoting one ex-football hooligan on the collective guilt experienced by all English hooligans following Heysel, and how it altered fundamentally their perceptions of football-related violence (see Hills and Benson, 1993; Redhead, 1991b: 146). However, as with Williams, Redhead's point is made in retrospect; three months after Heysel, Redhead and McLaughlin (1985) were predicting a continuation in the intensity of regional enmities that characterized British soccer casual violence.

Meanwhile, the globalization of 'football hooliganism' was now firmly established on the academic stage, with research (some of it later published in English) being undertaken into indigenous violence in Austria (Horak, 1991), Belgium (van Limbergen and Colaers, 1989), the Netherlands (van der Brug, 1986), Argentina (Archetti, 1985) and Africa (Igbinovia, 1985). In contrast to the English reading of Rubicon into Heysel by some, the analysis of the American sociologist Lewis (1989: 28) concluded that 'the problem is not strictly an English, Belgian or Italian one, but rather is one for all international soccer authorities to focus on'.

Policy ambivalence: culminations of earlier invective, 1986-9

Subsequently, the parliamentary period 1986–9 is characterized by a quite paradoxical executive approach towards football hooliganism, giving rise to deamplification (to confirm the efficacy of existing measures) and amplification (to legitimize further legislation). The leitmotif was one of vigilance against an increasingly insidious enemy, with more sophisticated technology and policing methods to be the major exposer and weapon against match-related violence (see Armstrong and Hobbs, this volume). In the Popplewell Report (1986), the Home Office located support for a gamut of anti-hooligan innovations: the membership scheme, closed circuit television and the hoolivan (*Hansard*, 16 January 1986). That the Government regarded itself as 'on the right track' here was deemed to have been corroborated by the decline in arrests (by 47 per cent) and ejections (30 per cent) for the 1985/6 English football season (*Hansard*, 25 July 1986). The 'good behaviour' and 'positive attitude' of *British* fans at the 1986 World Cup Finals in Mexico elicited praise from the Prime Minister (*Hansard*, 17 July 1986; *pace* Williams, 1986) and, according to the Minister for Sport, 'the Mexican people and media' (*Hansard*, 23 July 1986). Yet no seismic shift in fan culture was discerned politically. The Public Order Act 1986 duly followed by the end of the year, extending magisterial powers on exclusion orders, alcohol consumption to and from matches, and proscribing the carrying of smoke bombs. The implementation of the membership scheme remained optional to clubs, thus isolating Luton's ban on away fans: Home Office minister Douglas Hogg reflected some restraint in the Cabinet by noting, 'Nobody has suggested that it would be a panacea, but we think that it is an important step forward and we hope that the football industry will carry it forward' (*Hansard*, 20 November 1986). The discretionary policy did not change following meetings with the Football League and Football Association (*Hansard*, 9 February 1987).

The deamplifying impulse was most remarkably adopted by Home Secretary Douglas Hurd, in explaining *rises* in arrests and ejections for the 1986/7 English season, due to the penetrative eye of closed circuit television and a tougher police line on racial chanting (*Hansard*, 22 July 1987). This hardly impressed the Opposition, alerted to the incongruity of the Government presiding over a disciplinarian social policy and rising levels of crime. Labour targeted police complaints about the membership scheme's impracticalities to hoist the Government on its own law-and-order petard (*Hansard*, 17 February 1988). Calling the Opposition's bluff on police support, the Government sought further dispensation for legislation through focusing upon evidence of planning and engagements in match-related disorder, such as the 'successes' of covert policing against hooligan 'generals' (see Armstrong and Hobbs, this volume), and the predicted English fan disorder at the 1988 European Championships in Germany (van der Brug, this volume). The 'survival of football as a spectator sport is in question' argued the Prime Minister (*Hansard*, 14 June 1988); 'the steps taken so far have been shown to be inadequate', confirmed her Minister for Sport (*Hansard*, 16 June 1988). The doubting Douglas Hogg then reaffirmed executive faith in the membership scheme, now to be mandatory for all English league clubs: 'The Government believe that the proposed national membership scheme will help to break the link between violence and football by excluding from grounds, and thereby deterring from travelling to matches, those who cause trouble' (*Hansard*, 12 April 1989). The scheme decreed that all football spectators at English league fixtures would require to be affiliated to the Football Membership Authority, which offered no rights of appeal to those refused, and no prospect of match attendance for the 'casual' (*sic*) supporter.

Opposition to the scheme intensified from December 1988 to the Hillsborough disaster in April 1989. A ninety-minute parliamentary debate, effectively on its viability, was opened by the Opposition, at 3.30 a.m. Backbench speakers drew upon academic commentaries by Leicester researchers (Dunning *et al.*, 1988) and Hargreaves's (1986) Marxist study of sports policy, to illustrate the disproportionate scale of the Government's response to the identified 'problem' (*Hansard*, 19 December 1988). This contrasts with Labour's earlier frontbench strategy, the 'It's not only this' approach (Cohen, 1980: 58) of Denis Howell; football hooliganism was an 'evil' not confined to the game, being a 'deep-seated malaise' and 'social disease' (*Hansard*, 16 June 1988). Petitions were organized against the scheme by supporters' clubs and presented to the House. By Easter, almost 4,000 representations had been made to the Government against the scheme; over 500,000 fans eventually signed petitions against it.

And only two days after the Prime Minister welcomed the return of English clubs to European competition for the 1991/2 season the Hillsborough disaster occurred in Sheffield. Ninety-six lives were lost in the central 'pen' in the Leppings Lane end through crowd crushing (see Lewis and Scarisbrick, this volume). The Government issued reassurances on delaying indefinitely the progress of the Football Spectators Bill, which sought to enable the club membership scheme (*Hansard*, 18 April 1989). Two days later the obstinate Prime Minister confirmed her personal intention to force the legislation through by the end of the parliamentary session (*Hansard*, 20 April 1989); but the forthcoming Taylor Report's findings would be taken into account in framing the final Act.

Academic inquiry was at its most productive during this period, with the publication of various major texts. At the time, virtually all commentators confirmed the political consensus on the seriousness and unacceptability of football hooliganism, adding that the phenomenon continued to harbour deep-seated social roots, unaddressed by contemporary policy. The Leicester researchers produced their major work on the historico-sociological roots of football hooliganism. They argued wholeheartedly that current short-term intensifications of policing and intelligence on identified 'hooligans' could only assuage the incidence of fan disorder; without long-term strategies aimed at tackling basic social divisions, football hooliganism would continue (see Dunning *et al.*, 1988; this volume). Ian Taylor (1991a: 15) conveyed a pessimistic sociological sentiment on football culture's 1980s flavour, maintaining that the experience of 'Kop End' terrace life during that same period [the 1980s] at many clubs has actually been one of rampant racism, crudely sexist banter, and of aggravation conducted by groups of young white males of little education and even less wit.

This confirmed Taylor's movement from his initial position, which had identified a radical teleology in young fan subcultures. His rather conservative solution moved outwith the Marxist confines of restructuring the political economy in both the game and its working-class habitat; what required to be addressed now was 'the problem of general moral education – or, indeed, of education for life as a *citizen*, living in the *public sphere* of civil society' (I. Taylor, 1989: 107).

A more pragmatic, policy-orientated contribution was forwarded by environmental psychologists Canter, Comber and Uzzell (1989). Displaying a marked symmetry with the Government's position on the symbiosis of violence and football, Canter *et al.* (1989: 136–7) averred that previous research findings on hooliganism 'help to exonerate the clubs and point a finger at some other agency'. The psychologists then proceeded to dispense a set of proposals for change *within* the game to combat hooliganism, such as increasing fan representation within clubs (see Clarke, 1978; I. Taylor, 1971a and b); sanitizing conditions for 'spectators'; upgrading the safety and control skills of the groundstaff; repackaging the game for more effective mediation to the public; and emphasizing the historical links between club and community, through football *qua* heritage industry. Yet the post-Hillsborough British debates on fan disorder were more satisfactorily anticipated by analyses of the practices and demeanours of the 'problem supporters' themselves. The cultural studies field produced fresh approaches by Redhead (1986) and Frith (1988), which identified critical social commentaries in the 'casual' style, in terms of regional rivalries and the disavowal of unemployment culture respectively. The sociological field, meanwhile, republished the ethnographic *Hooligans Abroad* (Williams *et al.*, 1989).

Post-Hillsborough, April 1989: say no more or more of the same?

The post-Hillsborough period of May 1989 to the time of writing displays a steady withering of governmental 'law-and-order' resolve on football hooliganism. Refuting Ian Taylor's (1989: 92) observation of 'a suspension of the aggravation and enmity that has characterized football rivalry', there appeared to be no immediate abatement in its manifestation, with 220 arrests in one weekend of matches a single month after the tragedy (*Hansard*, 16 May 1989). Opposition to the passage of the Football Spectators Bill through the Commons oscillated around the lack of 'participatory democracy' in the constitution of the proposed Football Membership Authority for everyday supporters, as well as on the sheer impracticality of admitting thousands of fans to stadia at computerized checkpoints within a matter of minutes (*Hansard*, 30 October 1989). The publication of the Taylor Report in January 1990 effectively aborted the membership scheme, even suggesting that in the short term it might induce more hooliganism outside grounds (P. Taylor, 1990: 73; *Hansard*, 29 January 1990). The *quid pro quo* for this enlightenment was the statutory provision for all-seater stadia to be introduced at all English First and Second Division, and Scottish Premier League grounds by August 1994; and to all other English and Scottish league grounds by August 1999 (see I. Taylor, 1991a). This latter section of a flagship policy was modified by June 1992, in light of the crippling costs of enforced modernization about to be incurred by poorly attended clubs (see Duke, 1994). A third measure, dealing with barring certain types of offensive and violent behaviour inside grounds, was recommended by Taylor and enacted as the Football Offences Act of April 1991. By mid-October of that year, it had netted 73 offenders (*Hansard*, 17 October 1991).[13]

Subsequently, the issue appears to have been pushed into the parliamentary recesses, a disappearance as much due to its political exhaustion as to the costs of legislation predicted by Downs (1972) and Houlihan (1991). It resurfaced *via* the Bournemouth v. Leeds United riot in May 1990, with 104 arrests and £40,000 damage to property. No new legislation was planned to combat this violence, save for ensuring the football authorities' future compliance with police requests to reschedule 'high risk' fixtures. One month later, at the 1990 World Cup Finals in Italy, over 200 fans were arrested following fan disorder, but reports of holidaymakers being among the deportees isolated the Minister for Sport's instinctive perorations on England's 'effluent tendency' abroad (*Hansard*, 26 June 1990). Accordingly, parliamentary discussion of English fan violence abroad has since become an infrequent and routinized political topic. Twenty-two fans were reported arrested following disorder in Turkey (*Hansard*, 19 June 1991); early in 1992, ministers fielded questions on police and Government liaison with Swedish counterparts in prospect of the 1992 European Championships in Sweden. The disorder there involving English fans in June 1992 elicited no Opposition attacks on Government negligence or over-zealous law enforcement. Both the newly created Minister for National Heritage, David Mellor, and the new Prime Minister, John Major, deamplified the incidents, pointing to the involvement of a 'small minority' of fans (*Hansard*, 15 June 1992; 16 June 1992). Indeed, the political bone of contention reworked an established theme, the confusion of 'British' with 'English' fan disorder: a sensitive matter for Scottish parliamentarians, whose constituents' behaviour in Sweden was extraordinarily gregarious (Finn, this volume; Giulianotti, 1993b, 1994b).

The most significant development in the last few years has been the endeavour of some English Opposition MPs to deconstruct the earlier binary of 'English hooligan' and friendly others. This has involved a questioning of the latter's peaceability, and Scottish club supporters have not been unaffected. Frustration at the proposed imposition of the membership scheme on England and Wales (the Scottish Office successfully resisted it) spilled over into an Opposition challenge on its statistical basis from backbencher Robert Wareing.

> During the last football season there were 33 arrests associated with matches at Liverpool, 24 arrests at Everton and 38 at Manchester United. At Hampden Park, Glasgow, there were 152 arrests and at Ibrox Park, the home of Glasgow Rangers, there were 407 arrests. Yet it is the supporters of English clubs . . . who are to be penalised by the identity card scheme. Will the Prime Minister tell us where the sense is in that?
>
> (*Hansard*, 4 April 1989)

Subsequent debates on the Football Spectators Bill and the Bournemouth violence elicited further Opposition contrasts between swingeing Government reactions and the presence of football violence overseas. While listing fan disorder in Holland and Greece in detail, Robert Wareing further maintained:

> The argument that England is unique or has the worst problem

is wrong. . . . We tend to take all the stick, as we did for the Heysel stadium incident. Italians were involved in that incident, but not one Italian – some of them were flaunting Fascist banners – has faced the same consequences as Liverpool supporters.

(*Hansard,* 17 July 1989)

Tom Pendry and Denis Howell later combined to point out that fan disorder had occurred in five European countries on the same weekend as that in Bournemouth, and that this should be drawn to UEFA's attention (*Hansard,* 8 May 1990). The process of popular revision has been greatly assisted by the faithful reportage of European fan disorder, at club and international level, by the full spectrum of the British press – most notably that involving Dutch and German fans at Italia '90 and Euro '92 in Sweden.

The 'new realism' was confirmed in the Home Affairs Committee (1990, 1991) investigations of football hooliganism. In a throwback to the corporatism of the 1960s, evidence from twenty-one agencies operating in the football field was compiled (HAC, 1990). In the report's supporter-friendly conclusion, the committee backed the new Football Licensing Authority as a potential 'honest broker' in the game, a role which would be cemented if a supporters' representative were appointed to its directory. It also maintained that although football hooliganism was neither new nor exclusive to Britain, it was not an essential feature of the sport either. The report asserted that for too long, non-hooligan supporters had borne the brunt of a 'them' and 'us' mentality. Rather disingenuously, the report's parliamentary authors ignored the prior political function of this outlook, to chastise the national football authorities and, to a lesser extent, the police:

> The national football authorities owe it to these people [the supporters] to ensure that they can regard themselves as partners in the game, not as fodder for exploitation by those who cream off soccer's rich pickings. . . . Supporters also expect more from the police: to be treated with dignity whether they are at home or away, in Aberdeen or Arsenal, and not criminalised simply by their association with the game.

(HAC, 1991: xxxviii)

Since Hillsborough (or to a far lesser extent, Heysel) academics writing on football have been classified into two camps, of 'continuity' and 'change' on football hooliganism. The 'change' lobby is comprised most prominently of Ian Taylor (see Dunning, this volume) and Steve Redhead (1991a and b; see Giulianotti, this volume). In the wake of Hillsborough, Taylor (who had been reared on football at the ground) sought to reclaim some of his earlier works' socialist praxis on soccer violence and social fragmentation. The disaster had thrown into stark and painful relief football's lost contact with its followers and its own *raison d'être*, as an emblem of locality and community. By 1991, a transformation was monitored in the new 'carnival' persona of English club supporters (I. Taylor, 1991b), as though they were catching up with the essentially performative aspects of non-hooligan fans following Scotland, or the club *ultras* on the continent (Bromberger *et al.*, 1993a and b; Dal Lago and De Biasi, this volume; Giulianotti, 1991). For Redhead (1991a), the new fan peaceability contained an internal dynamic – the ecstasy of 'rave' culture.

What this type of discourse underplays is the shared culture of violence in European football. There is no subcultural statute which proscribes a taste for disorder if one is already involved in the culture of 'display'. The early 1990s have been marked by a strengthening of the display–disorder nexus among Italian, Spanish and Portugese *ultras*. During the 1992–3 season alone, fighting between fans of Italy's Brescia and Atalanta (of Bergamo) went on until 11 p.m., hospitalizing 70.[14] The two clubs had their grounds closed by the Italian football authorities for one and two matches respectively. At a 1993 Portugal–Scotland World Cup qualifier, local Benfica and Sporting Lisbon fans ignored the presence of 3,000 Scots to resume inter-club feuding, repeating the disorder of the same fixture twelve years earlier (McDevitt, 1994). Similarly, at the Poland–England fixture in Chorzow, one Polish fan was stabbed to death by a compatriot, during disorder involving rivals from Szczecin and Krakow. In France, Marseilles fans faced smoke-bomb and missile attacks from visiting Paris St Germain fans, when clinching the domestic championship. The French champions were earlier fined by UEFA for fan disorder against Bruges fans, who had themselves been fined for violence involving Rangers supporters. Both Italian and German domestic soccer have taken steps to curb indigenous club subcultures of racist violence (Benson, 1993). Then there were the 'offs' involving German, Swedish, English and Dutch fans at the 1992 European Championship Finals (Giulianotti, 1993b).

In Britain, the relevance of continuing research into football hooliganism has been sustained by writers as diverse as Leicester's figurationalists (Murphy *et al.*, 1990; Dunning *et al.*, 1991) and ethnographers (Williams, 1991a; Williams and Taylor, 1993); anthropologists (Armstrong and Harris, 1991); criminologists (Hobbs and Robins, 1991); those working within contemporary cultural studies and post-modern theory (Giulianotti, 1993a and b; Redhead, 1993a); public administration and communications theorists (Houlihan, 1991: 174–200; Waddington, 1992: 117–39); and left ethnographers (Robins, 1990). Meanwhile, writers on fan behaviour and disorder, from Austria, Germany, Italy, Denmark, Holland, England and Scotland, were widely drawn upon in a Council of Europe Report after the 1990 World Cup Finals (Williams, 1991b). A 1991 *Sociological Review* issue devoted to football confirmed the international academic interest in fan disorder, anticipated by a pan-European collection in Italian (Roversi, 1990), and enhanced by conferences on soccer culture staged in Florence (1990) and Aberdeen (1992).

From this purview of the 'football hooliganism' genealogy, I will limit myself to four observations. Firstly, as an example of policy formulation and exhaustion, Downs's (1972) tripartite model appears excessively reductive and qualitatively unevaluative. In England particularly, 'football hooliganism' has been discovered and rediscovered politically on several occasions. The actual content of proposed 'solutions' to its manifestations, be they low-key and corporatist (the late 1960s) or concertedly draconian (the late 1980s), serve to define the nature of political interest in the phenomenon, a matter which Downs's technicist model finds essentially peripheral. Secondly, and more specifically, there are indications in the 1980s of conflicting political party records in policies on fan disorder, precipitated as much by policy legacy and the two-part system, as by direct changes in the incidence or seriousness of football hooliganism *per se*. Conservative endeavours to deamplify the phenomenon in the 1986–9 period brought forth as evidence the *rise* in arrests and ejections from grounds in one season; the English club membership scheme moved from a non-panacea to the flagship policy for eradicating hooliganism – after international fan disorder in Germany! Alternatively, the Labour Opposition both affirmed the seriousness of football hooliganism and the emotive language in which it was discussed up until the late 1980s, but discontinued this brinkmanship when the Government's disciplinary rhetoric on the game attained its legislative consequence, on all-seater stadia and the membership scheme. Third, a continuing cross-fertilization of political and academic discourses on fan disorder has been prevalent. Academics assisted in speculating on and defining 'football hooliganism' in the late 1960s and early 1970s; reflected political concern with 'problem' clubs in the 1970s through ethnography; were engaged to provide more comprehensive approaches to the phenomenon in the 1980s, through seminal research, consultation and commentary; and have been required to confront and reassert/deny the *raison d'être* of their researches in the post-Hillsborough political climate of deamplification. Fourth, and finally, it is clear that political policies on football hooliganism have harboured a growing regard to its international significance. National differentials in fan identity (England v. Scotland: violent v. friendly) have been defined by a hooligan referent; English preconcern with fan disorder has been generally at its acutest when manifested abroad. However, the post-1990 deamplificatory narrative is at its most perspicuous, not when quibbling over arrest figures or the effects of existing legislation at home, but when applying a *de*differentiation of national fan identities, and highlighting the incidence of fan disorder elsewhere. Yet thus far, apart from a few brief discussions, there has been little endeavour by British academics to engage fully an international dimension on football fan disorder, and to highlight the variety of academic perspectives which may be offered on the subject. It is the intention of this collection to redress in some way such an imbalance.

NOTES

1 I outline some of the key tenets of these perspectives later. For further explications of the Marxist, anthropological and figurational viewpoints, see the chapters by Archetti and Romero, Dal Lago and De Biasi, Dunning, and van der Brug.

2 This statement is more than counterbalanced by the substantial volume of print expended by other sections of the media and the *literati* on football fan behaviour, paying particular reference to hooliganism. See, for example, the books by Buford (1991) and Hornby (1992) and the litany of reviews; the continuing production of tele-

vision documentaries on the subject e.g. *Critical Eye* (Channel 4, 1993); and fictional films about fan violence in Britain (*The Firm*) and abroad (*Proc?* from Czechoslovakia, *Ultra* from Italy).

3 For a critical discussion of Marxist depictions of youth subcultures see Redhead (1990) and Giulianotti (1993a).

4 For example, and *contra* Taylor's postwar thesis, Murray (1984) and Finn (1991, 1993) provide extensive evidence that Scottish football hooliganism's lineage traces back to the sectarian rivalry of Glasgow's Rangers (Protestant) and Celtic (Catholic). The animosity became particularly virulent between the wars.

5 R. Taylor (1992: 158–63) notes that the concern with fan vandalism on trains extends back to the 1950s. However, public alarm with organized groups of travelling supporters stretched back to the Scottish 'Brake Clubs' used by Rangers and Celtic supporters for away matches in the early twentieth century (Murray, 1984). The fact that travelling supporters had, therefore, always elicited a degree of public concern goes some way to refuting Margaret Thatcher's view that 'violence is caused partly because there is now more money and far more mobility than there was in the past, and that enables people to move between one soccer club to another much more quickly' (*Hansard*, 3 June 1985).

6 In its purest sense, ethology is the study of animal behaviour which is inherent (non-learned). Its application to human behaviour begins with the assumption that the most fundamental dynamic in interaction (e.g. aggression) is a 'natural' feature of the male individual's genetic structure, and therefore an historically continuous phenomenon. Marsh *et al.* (1978) qualified this position through an 'ethogenic' account of football hooliganism, which sought to apply some 'symbolic interactionist' findings in deviancy research, to explain variations in social action and learned behaviour on the terraces. Two key concepts in their analysis are the 'career structure' in football subcultures, socializing young fans into different types of behaviour at distinctive stages in their life on the terraces; and the 'deviancy amplification spiral', instigated by hyperbolic media and political reportage, which sees the essentially 'ordered disorder' on the terraces framed and popularised as 'violent' and 'dangerous' – with a direct and negative consequence on how the soccer subculture came to regard itself and hence behaved.

7 For a robust defence of the Leicester research, and the propriety of Elias's 'figurational' or 'process-sociological' approach in explaining fan disorder, see Dunning (this volume). Critical studies of the Leicester position are to be found in Archetti and Romero (this volume) and Dal Lago and De Biasi (this volume).

8 For an assessment of the role of this legislation in producing a new fan self-knowledge in Scotland, see Giulianotti (this volume).

9 Giulianotti (1991, 1993b) and Finn (this volume) provide commentaries on the transformed image of Scottish supporters abroad.

10 In fact, it is instructive to note that, along with monetarist economic policy, the Thatcher approach to football ground safety originated

during the Labour administration of 1974–9. Until the mid–70s, there was a regular spate of parliamentary questions on ground improvement and safety from both sides of the House of Commons. With the further delegation of responsibility for ground safety to local authorities in the 1975 Safety of Sports Grounds Act, the issue dwindled in political interest relative to football hooliganism; indeed, I can identify no written answers to parliamentary questions on this matter from January 1980 to January 1984.

11 This measure was later covered in the Sporting Events (Control of Alcohol, etc.) Act 1985. Scottish MPs and the Scottish Office successfully fought any extension of Government legislation on hooliganism, arising from the Taylor Report, to north of the border.

12 A FIFA ban on English club competition at a global level was lifted before the end of the year.

13 The legislation sought to counteract obscene and racist language; throwing missiles; and running on to the pitch without due cause.

14 My sincere thanks to Guiseppe Sardo for information on this disorder, and weekly reports on troubles involving Italian fans, which brevity alone denies further reportage here.

REFERENCES

Archetti, E. P. (1985) 'Fútbol, violencia y afirmación masculina', *Debates* (Buenos Aires), 3.

Armstrong, G. and R. Harris (1991) 'Football Hooligans: theory and evidence', *Sociological Review*, 39, 3: 427–58.

Benson, R. (1993) 'Football v Racism', *The Face*, March.

Bromberger, C. and others (1993a) 'Fireworks and the Ass', in S. Redhead (ed.) (1993b).

Bromberger, C. with A. Hayot and J.-M. Mariottini (1993b) 'Allez l'O.M., Forza Juve', in S. Redhead (ed.) (1993b).

Brug, H. H. van der (1986) *Voetbalvandalisme*, Haarlem: De Vrieseborch.

Buford, B. (1991) *Among the Thugs*, London: Secker & Warburg.

Canter, D., M. Comber and D. Uzzell (1989) *Football in its Place*, London: Routledge.

Clarke, J. (1978) 'Football and Working Class Fans: tradition and change', in R. Ingham (ed.) (1978).

Cohen, P. (1972) 'Subcultural Conflict and Working Class Community', *Working Papers in Cultural Studies 2*, Birmingham: CCCS.

Cohen, P. and D. Robins (1978) *Knuckle Sandwich*, Harmondsworth: Penguin.

Cohen, S. (1980) *Folk Devils and Moral Panics*, second edition, Oxford: Blackwell.

Council of Europe (1985) *European Convention on Spectator Violence and Misbehaviour at Sports Events and in Particular at Football Matches*, Strasburg, 19 August, London: HMSO.

Downs, A. (1972) 'Up and Down with Ecology – the "Issue Attention Cycle" ', *Public Interest*, 28.

Duke, V. (1994) 'The Drive to Modernization and the Supermarket Imperative', in R. Giulianotti and J. Williams (eds) *Football, Identity and Modernity*, Aldershot: Avebury.

Dunning, E., P. Murphy and I. Waddington (1991) 'Anthropological versus Sociological Approaches to the Study of Football Hooliganism: some critical notes', *Sociological Review*, 39, 3: 459–78.

Dunning, E., P. Murphy, and J. Williams (1988) *The Roots of Football Hooliganism*, London: Routledge.

Dunning, E., P. Murphy, J. Williams and J. Maguire (1984) 'Football Hooliganism before the First World War', *International Review for the Sociology of Sport*, 19.

Elias, N. and E. Dunning (1986) *Quest for Excitement*, Oxford: Blackwell.

Evans, A. (1986) 'Freedom of Trade under the Common Law and European Community Law: the case of the football bans', *Law Quarterly Review*, 102.

Finn, G. P. T. (1991) 'Racism, Religion and Social Prejudice: Irish Catholic clubs, soccer and Scottish society – I. The historical roots of prejudice', *The International Journal of the History of Sport*, 8, 1.

—— (1993) 'Faith, Hope and Bigotry: case-studies of anti-Catholic prejudice in Scottish soccer and society', in G. Jarvie and G. Walker (eds) *Ninety Minute Patriots: Scottish sport in the making of a nation*, Leicester: Leicester University Press.

Frith, S. (1988) 'Art Ideology and Pop Practice', in C. Nelson and L. Grossberg (eds) *Marxism and the Interpretation of Culture*, London: Macmillan.

Giulianotti, R. (1991) 'Scotland's Tartan Army in Italy: the case for the carnivalesque', *Sociological Review*, 39.

—— (1993a) 'Soccer Casuals as Cultural Intermediaries: the politics of Scottish style', in S. Redhead (ed.) (1993b).

—— (1993b) 'A Model of the Carnivalesque? Scottish football fans at the 1992 European Championship finals in Sweden and beyond', *Working Papers in Popular Cultural Studies No.6*, Manchester Institute for Popular Culture.

—— (1994) 'Scoring Away from Home: a statistical survey of Scotland football fans at international matches in Romania and Sweden', *International Review for the Sociology of Sport*, forthcoming.

Guttman, A. (1986) *Sport Spectators*, New York: Columbia University Press.

Hall, S. (1978) 'The Treatment of Football Hooliganism in the Press', in R. Ingham (ed.) (1978).

Hall, S., J. Clarke, C. Critcher, T. Jefferson and B. Roberts (1978) *Policing the Crisis*, London: Macmillan.

Hall, S. and T. Jefferson (eds) (1976) *Resistance Through Rituals*, London: Hutchinson.

Hansard (House of Commons Parliamentary Debates), various dates.

Hargreaves, J. (1986) *Sport, Power and Culture*, Cambridge: Polity.

Harrington, J. A. (1968) *Soccer Hooliganism*, Bristol: John Wright.

Hills, G. and R. Benson (1993) 'Casuals', *The Face*, August.

Hobbs, D. and D. Robins (1991) 'The Boy Done Good: football violence, changes and continuities', *Sociological Review*, 39.

Home Affairs Committee (HAC) (1990) *Policing Football Hooliganism: memoranda of evidence*, London: HMSO.
—— (1991) *Policing Football Hooliganism: second report*, London: HMSO.
Horak, R. (1991) 'Things Change: trends in Austrian football hooliganism from 1977–1990', *Sociological Review*, 39.
Hornby, N., (1992) *Fever Pitch*, London: Gollancz.
Houlihan, B. (1991) *The Government and Politics of Sport*, London: Routledge.
Igbinovia, P. (1985) 'Soccer Hooliganism in Black Africa', in *International Journal of Offender Therapy and Comparative Criminology*, 29.
Ingham, R. (ed.) (1978) *Football Hooliganism: the wider context*, London: Inter-Action Imprint.
Jones, N. (1986) 'Hooligans: the forgotten side', *New Society*, 29 August.
Lang, Sir J. (1969) *Report of the Working Party on Crowd Behaviour at Football Matches*, London: HMSO.
Lever, J. (1969) 'Soccer: opium of the Brazilian people', *Transaction*, 7.
Levine, P. and P. Vinten-Johansen (1981) 'The Historical Perspective: violence and sport', *Arena Review*, 5.
Lewis, J. M. (1982) 'Crowd Control at English Football Matches', *Sociological Focus*, 15.
—— (1989) 'A Value-Added Analysis of the Heysel Stadium Soccer Riot', *Current Psychology*, 8.
Lewis, J. M. and J. M. Veneman (1987) 'Crisis Resolution: the Bradford fire and English society', *Sociological Focus*, 20, 2.
Limbergen, C. van and C. Colaers (1989) 'The Societal and Psycho-Sociological Background of Football Hooliganism', *Current Psychology*, 8.
McDevitt, R. (1994) *Long Nights and Red Lights: the memoirs of a Scottish football supporter*, (forthcoming).
Marsh, P., E. Rosser and R. Harre (1978) *The Rules of Disorder*, London: Routledge and Kegan Paul.
Morris, D. (1981) *The Soccer Tribe*, Cape, London.
Murphy, P., J. Williams and E. Dunning (1990) *Football on Trial*, London: Routledge.
Murray, W. (1984) *The Old Firm: sectarianism, sport and society in Scotland*, Edinburgh: John Donald.
Pearson, G. (1983) *Hooligan: a history of respectable fears*, London: Macmillan.
Pearton, R. (1986) 'Violence in Sport and the Special Case of Soccer Hooliganism in the United Kingdom', in C.R. Rees and A.W. Miracle (eds) *Sport and Social Theory*, Champaign, Illinois: Human Kinetics Publishers.
Popplewell, O., Lord Justice (Chairman) (1986) *Inquiry into the Crowd Safety and Control at Sports Grounds*, London: HMSO.
Pratt, J. and M. Salter (1984) 'Football hooliganism', *Leisure Studies*, 3.
Redhead, S. (1986) *Sing When You're Winning*, London: Pluto.
—— (1990) *The End-of-the-Century Party*, Manchester: Manchester University Press.
—— (1991a) *Football with Attitude*, Manchester: Wordsmith.

—— (1991b) 'An Era of the End, or the End of an Era: football and youth culture in Britain', in Williams and Wagg (eds) 1991.

—— (1993a) 'Always Look on the Bright Side of Life', in S. Redhead (ed.) (1993b).

—— (ed.) (1993b) *The Passion and the Fashion*, Aldershot: Avebury.

Redhead, S. and E. McLaughlin (1985) 'Soccer's Style Wars', *New Society*, 16 August.

Robins, D. (1990) *Sport as Prevention*, Oxford: Centre for Criminological Research.

Roversi, A. (ed.) (1990) *Calcio e Violenza in Europa*, Bologna: Il Mulino.

—— (1992) *Calcio, Tifo e Violenza*, Bologna: Il Mulino.

Shipman, M. (1988) 'Terrorist or Resistance Fighter? The case of the football hooligan', *The Limitations of Social Research*, Third Edition, London: Longman.

Taylor, I. (1969) 'Hooligans: soccer's resistance movement', *New Society*, 7 August.

—— (1971a) 'Soccer Consciousness and Soccer Hooliganism', in S. Cohen (ed.) *Images of Deviance*, Harmondsworth: Penguin.

—— (1971b) ' "Football Mad" – a speculative sociology of soccer hooliganism', in E. Dunning (ed.) *The Sociology of Sport*, London: Cass.

—— (1982a) 'On the Sports-Violence Question: soccer hooliganism revisited', in J. Hargreaves (ed.) *Sport, Culture and Ideology*, London: Routledge.

—— (1982b) 'Class, Violence and Sport: the case of soccer hooliganism in Britain', in H. Cantelon and R. Gruneau (eds) *Sport, Culture and the State*, Toronto: University of Toronto Press.

—— (1987) 'Putting the Boot into a Working Class Sport: British soccer after Bradford and Brussels', *Sociology of Sport Journal*, 4.

—— (1989) 'Hillsborough: 15 April 1989. Some personal contemplations', *New Left Review*, 177.

—— (1991a) 'English Football in the 1990s: taking Hillsborough seriously?', in Williams and Wagg (eds) (1991).

—— (1991b) 'From aggravation to celebration', *Independent on Sunday*, 21 April.

Taylor, P., Lord Justice (Chairman) (1990) *Inquiry into the Hillsborough Stadium Disaster: Final Report*, London: HMSO.

Taylor, R. (1992) *Football and its Fans*, Leicester: Leicester University Press.

Trivizas, E. (1980) 'Offences and Offenders in Football Crowd Disorders', *British Journal of Criminology*, 20.

Waddington, D. (1992) *Contemporary Issues in Public Disorder*, London: Routledge.

Williams, J. (1986) 'White Riots: the English football fan abroad', in A. Tomlinson and G. Whannel (eds) *Off the Ball*, London: Pluto.

—— (1991a) 'Having an Away Day: English football spectators and the hooligan debate', in Williams and Wagg (eds) (1991).

—— (1991b) 'Football Spectators and Italia "90" ', Council of Europe.

Williams, J., E. Dunning and P. Murphy (1984) (1989; 2nd edn) *Hooligans Abroad*, London: Routledge.

Williams, J. and R. Taylor (1993) 'Boys Keep Swinging' (unpublished paper).

Williams, J. and S. Wagg (eds) (1991) *British Football and Social Change*, Leicester, University of Leicester Press.

Chapter 3

Death and violence in Argentinian football

Eduardo P. Archetti and Amílcar G. Romero

The problem of violence by football fans continues to be an issue that merits reflection and study in European countries. This is due not only to the social, economic and cultural significance of football but also to the special meaning of violence and violent acts among youth in the ritual context of the game. Violence is found nowhere in the rules of football, nor does it have a place within the normal course of a game. Thus, we might expect that officials, fans, the police, political authorities and journalists will perceive and define acts of violence as abnormal, an interruption or the unexpected result of a game with dramatic significance, and will further conclude that winning or losing, no matter how important, should not give way to gratuitous manifestations of violence. This implies that the violence by fans introduces an element of disorder and discontinuity in what is by definition a public event designed to demonstrate the benefits of peaceful competition, numerical equality, respect for the rules of good conduct, clear penalties for infractions by players, team loyalty, respect for the adversary, group discipline, individual creativity, and victory as the prize reserved for the best players. Winning a football game should have nothing to do with the deliberate use of physical force with intent to injure, wound or destroy the adversary. In fact, success should be associated with individual mastery of technique and the tactical ability of the team. Physical force is an important element in the social universe of football, but it is associated with physical stamina, the ability to push the body to its limits.

Logically, violence among militant fans is a double threat. On the one hand, it threatens the values underlying all sporting events, according to which winners and losers accept, in the necessary spirit of 'fair play', the outcome of the event. Football, it must always be remembered, should work, ultimately, to cement brotherhood among the players who are temporary opponents in the context of a game. Individual respect and resignation in accepting the fact that the opposing team played better that day or were luckier are elements that should supersede loyalty to a team. But, militant fans are *a priori* unable to convert disappointment brought on by the defeat of their team into praise for the opposing team and respect for its fans. Instead, physical force intended to injure, wound or destroy the adversary is the central element in acts of violence perpetrated by militant fans. It is clear that those who engage in these acts reveal the underside of the game with their demonstrations of the tensions that exist between order and disorder, between peaceful play and manifest conflict, between 'civilized' behaviour and violence. Militant fans, acting collectively, and thus creating an image of a high degree of social organization, represent the limits of the acceptable, the normal, the legitimate, when they use physical force in order to achieve social ends. If individual violence is now difficult for European societies to tolerate, then organized collective violence and carefully planned actions, are unacceptable. This type of violence comes to be defined as a threat not only to the social order but also the legitimacy of the State and its legal institutions.

The study of violence among militant fans in England has focused not only on determining its origins in society but also on explaining why those involved behave as they do. In the first part of this article, we will briefly summarize some of the latest explanations for violence among football fans and the debates surrounding these explanations. This will enable us not only to characterize the type of analysis, and the intellectual and moral concerns, of British social scientists, but also to identify those areas on which they have evidently opted to remain silent. These areas of 'silence' will be used to legitimate our analysis of violent acts in which the outcome is the death of individuals of a certain age, individuals with names, families, friends, professions. Riches (1986b: 11–15) has convincingly argued on the power of violence to achieve social objectives. This ability resides in the efficacy of violence, both in instrumental terms to effect the transformation of a social context, and in symbolic terms to dramatize the significance of specific ideas and values. An act of violence that ends with the death of the victim or of one or several of the participants is, in principle, an efficacious act. At the same time, death, whether violent or not, forces society to come to terms with the fact that the deceased is not simply a biological entity but a social being whose disappearance tends to be seen as a sacrilege committed against the social order (Hertz, 1907). The coming together of violence and death obliges societies to deal with a series of dilemmas that must be resolved: the passage of time and the inevitability of death; the transfer of the body and the soul from one social order to another; and the image of life as a good with inherent limits (Bloch and Parry, 1982; Metcalf and Huntington, 1991).

Our main hypothesis is that these cases of extreme violence provide an opportunity to reflect on processes of social representation that go beyond the limits of football. In other words, in Argentina, as in England and those European countries where it is considered a national sport, football not only reflects social and cultural processes but is a part of those very processes. In this sense, football is an arena in which social actors symbolize and reproduce by means of their social practices the values dominant in a given period. At the same time, the wider context within which we have chosen to situate our analysis enables us to present the moral issues and cultural problems thus circumscribed. In regard to Argentina specifically, the case-study approach allows a discussion of the existence of the following: blind police repression; the presence of organized and violent minorities; the death of innocent victims; the importance of identifying guilty parties; the existence of powerful interests which impede the judicial process; and the intimate relationship between violence and the world of legitimate power.[1]

THE ENGLISH DEBATE ON FOOTBALL HOOLIGANISM

The recent academic debate on football hooliganism in England has involved disagreements over theoretical perspectives as well as on the quality of the data gathered and the validity of different methodological approaches. The disagreements reflect in many ways the existence of different research traditions in sociology and anthropology. Given that the sociological approach is in principle more nomothetic, its practitioners will try to find regularities and repetitions and will attempt to quantify information in order to test a general theory which explains football hooliganism. In addition, they will be inclined to classify acts of violence and violent behaviour within an 'external' frame of reference. For their part, anthropologists will be less concerned with providing a general model of explanation given that there are few ethnographies that describe the fans of different clubs, and at the same time produce consistent observations of actors, contexts and values. Moreover, anthropologists will rely on 'native' models rather than accepted legal definitions to explain and understand legitimate and illegitimate violence. We provide a brief summary of this debate below.

In a very early work, Taylor (1971a and b) emphasized the fact that subcultures composed of unemployed and downwardly mobile young working-class fans were being adversely affected by football's transformation into a middle-class, international game. These original fans, for whom the game was a serious matter, felt that they were being pushed aside by this process, that they no longer constituted a key element in the club. They resented increasing efforts to make the game appealing to a middle-class audience. In addition, they felt that players were being attracted by the jet-set lifestyle, becoming more middle-class in their orientation, and thus cutting their ties with working-class culture. Football hooliganism, Taylor asserts, must be seen as an answer, as a kind of protest and resistance movement, by working-class fans to regain control of the game. In his more recent works Taylor (1982a and b) has partly modified his main thesis. He maintains that the English working class has gone through a rapid process of economic and social differentiation. In this process the labour aristocracy has allied with the New Right represented by Mrs Thatcher, and voted for Conservative party candidates, while unemployed youth have become more isolated. In this context, the reaction of some members of the marginalized sectors is football hooliganism. In other words, rapid economic and political change in capitalist society provokes differentiation and a violent response from marginal social groups. As a consequence of this social situation, the discourse of order and repression gains force and legitimacy as the State takes advantage of fears of hooliganism. Taylor (1987) calls for a kind of moral education, lacking in the economic instrumentalism of Thatcherite social policy.

Taylor's thesis has been criticized on several grounds. Some have maintained that the arguments advanced by Taylor can be seen as a structural-functionalist perspective that uses simple causal explanations while assuming what it should set out to prove (Armstrong and Harris 1991: 429). Hobbs and Robins (1991: 554), for example, see Taylor's later contributions as a simplistic argument that blames hooliganism on the machinations of the capitalist State. These critics stress the fact that Taylor's macro-theory lacks supporting evidence and research.

The Leicester sociologists sympathize with Taylor's attempt to explain the genesis of football hooliganism in sociological terms, that is, in terms of a particular set of social relations that condition the specific experiences of working-class youth (Dunning et al., 1988: 29). However, they are critical of Taylor's romanticized view of the past, particularly of the past of the working class. The violence in question, they argue, is not a recent phenomenon related to rapid changes in the social composition of the working class. Therefore, they maintain, Taylor does not approach hooliganism as a phenomenon deeply rooted in the historical experience of the working class; instead, his interpretation of the history of football hooliganism is an arbitrary one not supported by the evidence. Dunning and his associates stress the fact that football hooliganism is nothing new. They demonstrate that violence in football games has always existed. Discontinuity is related to concrete changes in the type of violence and the sociological profile of militant fans. In the past, before the 1960s and 1970s, violence was directed at players on the opposing team and at referees. The modern forms of violence engaged in by young fans focus on fights between fans of opposing teams. As a result of this type of violence at matches, football's older fans, and also the 'respectable' ones, tend to stay away.

Dunning and his associates find the explanation for this persistent sociological fact in the subculture of the working class which reproduces in young males a predisposition to public displays of aggression. They identify hardcore hooligans as the 'rowdy' working-class male youth group (Dunning et al. 1986: 173–4; 1988: 210–12). Their model is related to Suttles' research on the formation of gangs in the city of Chicago (Suttles, 1968). Following Suttles' American model they emphasize that a dominant feature in working-class communities in England is the existence of 'ordered segmentation' based on highly segregated gender and age-groups, strongly identified with a given territory. Other social mechanisms reinforce this trend: the comparative freedom of working-class children and adolescents, the fact that much of their early socialization takes place in the streets, and the tendency towards gender segregation and male dominance in families and communities. Given these mechanisms, those sectors of working-class youth identified as 'rowdy' will be encouraged to fight and engage in other types of aggressive behaviour. Hence, fighting, as well as the general use of physical force for achieving control and dominance, will be seen as both appropriate and desirable. This cultural model is put in a historical perspective derived from Norbert Elias's theory of the 'civilizing process' which emphasises the gradual but uneven incorporation of the working class into that process with rowdier groups, who tend to be attracted to football matches, not fully incorporated into it (Dunning *et al.*, 1988: 233–6).

Some researchers argue that the assertion that British football hooligans are the rowdier male members of the lower working class is not borne out by empirical evidence (Hobbs and Robins, 1991: 557). Armstrong and Harris (1991) also propose the view that the Leicester sociologists are jumping to false conclusions based on insufficient empirical evidence. They conclude that though this particular sociological approach is interesting in principle, it is weakened, like the Taylor thesis, by the inadequacy of supporting data (Armstrong and Harris, 1991: 431).

Dunning and his associates have provided aggregate empirical evidence of spectator misconduct and disorderliness in football games. Most of their historical information has been gathered from English Football Association records and newspaper accounts. The original typology includes verbal misconduct and disorder, pitch invasions, encroachments and demonstrations, and physical violence and assault, including throwing objects, assault and attempted assault, all of these taking place at a match and involving players, match officials and other fans (Dunning *et al.*, 1988: 51). In the 1960s there were more acts of violence registered, and these included fights with the police, more riots before and after matches, vandalism involving public property, and especially, fights with fans of the opposing team. In this period, European matches gave British fans an opportunity to prove themselves in confrontations with foreign supporters and police. Those who studied this phenomenon distinguished between 'instrumental' violence designed to achieve a social goal, and 'expressive' violence or violent behaviour as an end in itself

(Dunning *et al.*, 1988: 236). They emphasize that hooliganism is a mixture of instrumentality and expressivity; the affective experience in different kinds of confrontations is crucial, as is the instrumental nature of the violence. The fight must occur in the right place and at the right time (Dunning *et al.*, 1988: 237). However, Dunning fails to present a single account from the hooligans themselves nor does he provide a detailed study of a single case of violence. The massive crowd disturbances of 1985, which culminated in the Heysel tragedy, are mentioned but are neither detailed ethnographically nor analysed. The research presented is marked by a reliance on the normative historical model and by a kind of 'social distance' which permits easy generalizations. We never hear enough the voices of the hooligans themselves; in most cases they are transformed into statistical facts. Lack of extended field research, including the absence of systematic comparative information devoted to clubs and specific groups of fans, is a clear shortcoming inherent in this kind of approach.[2]

The methodological weaknesses described constitute, in principle, a recommendation for the anthropological approach.[3] Social anthropologists Armstrong and Harris (1991) have strongly criticized the lack of empirical evidence in sociological interpretations of football hooliganism. Their paper is based on Armstrong's ethnographic findings after two years of fieldwork among the Blades, a group of Sheffield United fans. On the basis of Armstrong's observations, the authors assert that the hooligans were not particularly violent people, that there was amongst them no core of violent men from deprived working-class subgroups, and that much of the hostility directed against them was based on fears fanned by the police and the media (Armstrong and Harris, 1991: 432). However, they recognized that football-related violence was real and endemic. This apparent paradox must be explained. Violence occurs as a result of, and in most cases is related to, the way ordinary working-class men enjoy the game of confrontation and transform symbolic opposition into concrete physical encounters (Armstrong and Harris, 1991: 434). Moreover, Armstrong found that the Blades are not well organized, nor are their activities directed by formal leaders: in his words, they are 'acephalous'.

Armstrong and Harris argue that symbolic humiliation of rivals is the primary goal of the 'hard-core fan'. They write:

We would argue, however, that any preference that most of the core Blades had for the excitement of fighting was kept within strict bounds. It is primarily a game that aims to humiliate rivals and oblige them to recognize the challengers' superiority; to achieve this aim, however, there has to be a willingness to turn the game into a bloodsport, like foxhunting. . . .

(Armstrong and Harris, 1991: 447–8)

They recognize that to understand violence and violent behaviour, a proper analysis of the nature of very complex motivations is needed. They acknowledge the reality of violence and the use of physical force in confrontations with other fans. However, it seems that the desire for symbolic rewards in the absence of real violence is also of vital significance (ibid.: 448). Thus, symbolic domination is as important as exercising power through the systematic use of physical violence. They conclude by pointing out that fans are recruited not on the basis of how well they can fight, but primarily because they are enjoyable to be with, providing uncritical, free and easy association with mates who are simply 'fellow fans' (ibid.: 455). They end the paper with no clear theory of the causes of football hooliganism. Nevertheless, the ethnographic findings of Armstrong are an important step in determining what issues need to be researched in the future. The general historical models of many sociologists must be reinforced by systematic comparative analysis of the behaviour of groups of fans supporting different clubs and football traditions.

The description by Hobbs and Robins (1991) of hard-core hooligans complements the picture given by Armstrong and Harris. For many fans, willingness to fight and love of fighting, is a key motive for joining the most militant groups; fighting is described as a 'euphoric hyped up sensation' (Hobbs and Robins, 1991: 568–9). Football arenas thus provide an ideal environment for the implementation of a variety of violent strategies. These strategies are set in motion in a context dominated by media and television.

It [the match] becomes the perfect medium for asserting neighborhood, regional or national identity. Given these unique dramaturgical possibilities, the continued insularity of many traditional working class communities, and the isolation of most modern counterparts, football hooliganism can be seen as sensible, even sensually compelling.

(ibid.)

It is important for the hard-core group of fans to 'go mental', in other words to ignore any restrictions on combat and all rules of engagement. In this way to take part in violent acts is a clear celebration of a commitment to violence beyond any reason comprehensible to others. Here, as we might imagine, lies a mechanism of domination and control because, as the authors correctly point out, 'the absence of reasons induces reason in others' (ibid.: 570). Once a group of violent fans has been characterized as 'essentially mad' it is clear that a complex mechanism of social panic has been put into motion.

Hobbs and Robins concentrate their description on several legendary hooligans. They are fully involved football crazies, committed to the club and prepared to die for the sport. They get a perverse sense of dignity and pride from their activities (ibid.: 573). Consequently, they will fight for things like honour, reputation and above all pride (ibid.). Some of them will become local personalities, and some will become known on a national level. They conclude the article by pointing out the need for detailed ethnographies: 'not just of hooligans but of the communities that provide football's deviants, players, coaches, administrators, indeed the entire range of individuals who are touched by the game' (ibid.: 577).

This short summary of the debate surrounding football-related violence illustrates some of the shortcomings inherent in the collection of evidence and the construction of theories. The polemic has been accentuated by the way sociologists and anthropologists define their research methodologies. Dissimilar research strategies imply variations in the kind of questions and answers and, above all, in the way cultural and social processes are conceived. However, some common gaps and omissions in research are evident when we try to conceptualize hooliganism and football violence cross-culturally. From the point of view of Argentinian football, it seems that the main gap is related to the analysis of different violent acts or incidents among fans that bring about death. Because of this omission, a boundary can be established between hooliganism and criminal behaviour resulting in homicide. As we have seen, hooligans can be very aggressive and violent, and may even enjoy physical confrontations, but they are never depicted as 'criminals'. In other words, when they fight with other fans or with the police, their purpose is not to kill. Thus, when death does occur, as it has in the stadium incidents

mentioned by various authors, it is taken as an unintended consequence. Let us explore this.

In the analysis of the Leicester sociologists, the debate is largely
focused on aggression and aggressive behaviour and its relation
to masculinity; there is less emphasis on 'violence' as such.
Aggression is conceptualized as a tendency generated within a
given type of male living in a cultural and social context that
favours its concrete manifestation. Fighting, invading the pitch,
vandalizing trains, and assaulting and sacking supermarkets are
some typical acts intimately related to what is generally described
as football hooliganism. A hooligan is not by definition a criminal.
His acts, possibly and eventually defined as criminal by legal
authorities and public opinion, are seen as a cultural and social
product. The aggressive masculinity of the 'rough' working class
is ordered segmentally into friendly and hostile gangs. Therefore,
the 'hooligan' tends to view his behaviour, at least initially, as
acceptable.

In the anthropological perspective chosen by Armstrong and
Harris, the emphasis is on identifying different types of hooliganism. They operate with a clear boundary between real and symbolic violence: the first, we assume, is intended to inflict physical
harm on another person while the second is the threat of this
harm. Real violence is not the primary objective of hooligans.
Therefore, hooligans have a potential for violence but only of a
type, the so-called low level, a type also characteristic of other
dispossessed groups in society.

If we accept the rather restricted view of violence proposed by
Riches, and if we reduce the scope of analysis to matters of
'contested physical harm' to humans, much of the behaviour
of hooligans does not fall within the realm of violence (Riches,
1991: 292–3). Obviously, the destruction of material objects or
the deployment of some form of symbolic violence is not violence
at all. This restricted definition renders cross-cultural studies
impossible. If a systematic consideration of violent behaviour
aimed at producing contested physical harm is omitted from the
debate, we are reduced to a discussion of aggression and aggressive behaviour.

We agree that one form of extreme violence is the use of
physical force or of any other kind of force to bring about the
death of another person. We assume that key moral, emotional,
political and social issues are clearly involved when individuals,

families and representatives of the State are confronted by contested and untimely death. Moreover, the way we understand, describe and accept violence takes on a new, dramatic meaning when it leads to death in the context of a popular sport such as football. We believe that careful consideration of how societies conceptualize and tolerate different kinds of deaths associated with football is a central topic for a limited, systematic study of the cultural representation and social acceptance of violence. Hobbs and Robins (1991: 553) write that:

> Since 1974, when a 16-year-old Bolton Wanderers fan was stabbed to death during a half-time encounter with visiting Liverpool supporters in the tea room behind the club's main stand, there has been a steady stream of deaths directly related to football, which we conservatively estimate as averaging six a year.

This implies, in the period 1974–90, an extremely high number of deaths: approximately 96.[4]

It is interesting from a sociological point of view that analysis of these cases has not been at the heart of the debate in England. To try to explain this silence, or omission, in the debate on hooliganism is not the purpose of this paper. However, the analysis of some Argentinian cases must be seen as an attempt to provide an illustration, and perhaps a preliminary test, of our main assumption: that football does not simply reflect society or culture but is part of a general process of the way society models some of its central existential, moral and political issues.

VIOLENCE ON THE FOOTBALL FIELDS IN ARGENTINA

As was the case in England, up to the 1950s, disorders and inappropriate incidents on Argentina's football fields were associated, for the most part, with aggression directed at the referee or players from the opposing team. Fans also commonly entered the playing field. Nevertheless, physical confrontation between rival fans, especially those that commonly occur between neighbours or long-standing rivals, have traditionally become the basis for legends describing feats perpetrated by Argentinian fans. At the beginning, ritualized fist-fights were very common: the fans knew the place and the time for this type of duel. Moreover, a new form of aggression developed: surprise attacks to steal emblems or banners that become the spoils of war. It then became a point of honour for their rightful owners to achieve their recovery. Over time, this type of confrontation generated a system of rivalry among clubs and fans that became difficult to change. In Argentina, there are different types of conflicting relations among supporters. The most traditional one is in cities with two competing professional clubs playing in the first division: Racing Club and Independiente in Avellaneda; Newells Old Boys and Rosario Central in Rosario; and Gimnasia y Esgrima and Estudiantesde la Plata in La Plata are exemplary cases. In the city of Buenos Aires, where there is a plethora of professional clubs, the conflicts are diverse. Clubs located in the same neighbourhood can become mortal enemies, like the historical rivalry between Huracán and San Lorenzo de Almagro. The same can be said in the case of clubs situated in adjacent neighbourhoods, like Atlanta and Chacarita Juniors. However, the paradigmatic opposition in Argentinian football is exemplified *par excellence* by the enmity between Boca Juniors and River Plate, the only clubs with supporters across the country as a whole, even in the most remote villages. Located in opposite quarters of the city of Buenos Aires the clubs represent in the popular imagination contrasting social classes, styles of playing and historical achievements.

Acts of violence associated with football in Argentina have led to confrontations between distinct social actors, the fans and the police, each with a different role to play. The fans are part of civil society while the police represent the State, the judicial system, and, in abstract terms, a number of general values including neutrality and social morality. The police, therefore, represent legitimate authority and the long arm of the law in public places where events, rituals and games should unfold in an orderly fashion. By their very presence, and also by their ability to intervene, the police guarantee that a football game will unfold in just that way. In this respect, the police have a monopoly on the use of public force. This situation calls into question the relation between consent, on the part of both citizens and political and judicial authorities, and any violence on the part of the police. Consent regarding the use of violence by the police is based not only on its reasonable use but on the ability to correctly identify potentially unlawful or disorderly behaviour that should be curbed or stopped through police activity. However, it is entirely possible that the use of physical force, aided by arms of some kind, may be perceived as exclusively destined to harm, wound, injure, or, in some cases, kill other persons, and not as an act intended to stop unlawful behaviour that is taking place or may take place. In the course of examining various cases in terms of police intervention, as well as the participation of fans in acts of violence, we will see that there exists a relationship between the violence in question and acts of 'contested physical harm'. The same is true for situations involving only the participation of fans, and no police activity. What is important to point out is that the incidents analysed here have been carefully selected to facilitate an effective deconstruction of the violence in question.

We have chosen cases that we consider to be paradigmatic of the violence causing death that occurs at Argentinian football matches. One type of violence exclusively engages the militant fans of opposing clubs. In the other type the police confront the fans and play the active role of using violence against diffuse acts of public disorder or aggressive behaviour which can degenerate into explicit riots. We will not attempt to describe the history of violence in the stadiums, nor will we explain the changes that have occurred over time or carry out a complete analysis of all cases of violence. However, we feel that some general statistical information is necessary in order to draw a picture of the historical extent of this violence. From 1958 until July 1992, fifty-five acts of violence causing death were registered in football matches in Argentina. The number of victims is very high: 118, and the majority of them young people. Seventy-one deaths (60 per cent of the cases) can easily be classified as resulting from confrontations between the police and the fans, while forty-seven deaths (40 per cent) were caused by inter-fan conflicts. The judiciary was involved in, and investigated, all cases, but in only twelve cases were the perpetrators of the crimes found and sentenced. Up to 1992, four policemen had been found guilty of using violence and killing four spectators. Twelve civilians were jailed for similar offences. It is easy to conclude that the majority of deaths are still unpunished and that acceptance of the use of violence by police is easily understood and justified by the judiciary.[5]

The detailed presentation of individual cases brings to the fore the role of police and fans, in a context marked by ambivalence to the legitimacy of violence perpetrated by members of both groups. This type of analysis has not been attempted in England;

the emphasis has been on understanding hooligans and hooliganism as marginal deviance cases in an ordered society where the
police have high prestige and legitimacy. Argentinian society is
less ordered and the police are highly controversial due to a
terrible record of violence and arbitrary repression. Active participation of the police in cases of violence enables an analysis of
how they are perceived: as effective representatives of political
and judicial authority, as representatives of civil society, or as
another type of actor representing the limits of what, in human
and moral terms, is acceptable (Parkin, 1986: 210). The same
ambivalence is apparent as regards the fans and their responses
in confrontations with the police and one another. Thus, an
analysis of violence in football is one way to approach broader
themes related to the complex relation between morality and
violence. This is lacking in England; and we hope that our
extended cases will be understood as an attempt to fill this gap
in the sociological literature dealing with violence in football.

1958 – THE FIRST DEATH: INNOCENCE, VICTIMS AND POLICE BRUTALITY

The 1955 coup and the fall of Peron opened a highly unstable
period in the history of Argentina, one marked not only by the
declaration of *peronismo*'s illegality, but also by an increase in
violence perpetrated by members of the police and the military.
Early deaths related to football are a clear example of this
phenomenon. The first of these occurred in 1958 when Alberto
Mario Linker, a Boca Juniors fan, died. In the political mythology
of Argentina, 1958 is the 'year of the betrayal'. After President
Frondizi, who ran on a nationalist and progressive platform, was
elected with the aid of Peron's supporters, he opened the country
to massive investment by foreign capitalists and reformed laws
governing university education, thus permitting the establishment
of private and religious institutions. As a result, 1958 was a year of
student protests, conflict, struggle, and physical violence among
members of different student factions. Consequently, 1958 was
also a year of heightened police repression. We must keep in
mind that Argentina's police have never been noted for their
delicate treatment of suspects nor for their concern with the
rights of minorities. Both are indispensable requirements if
the police are to maintain the 'neutral' image associated with

state representatives whose job is to afford effective protection to citizens.

Linker, the Boca Juniors fan, had just turned 18, and five days before Sunday, 19 October 1958, he had received his official identification documents testifying to the fact that he was now an adult enjoying all the rights of full citizenship. That Saturday, he had thought about going the following day to watch Boca Juniors play San Lorenzo de Almagro, a game that promised to be a classic as both clubs were among the top five teams in domestic competition. Boca Juniors were to play on Sunday at nine in the morning at Huracáns' ground because their own ground had been closed, following incidents several Sundays earlier between police and fans. Linker rose too late so he listened to the game on the radio. Boca Juniors earned a respectable draw, 2–2, after what was deemed a boring game. Afterwards, Linker lunched with his parents, celebrating Mother's Day and his father's recovery from a long illness as a result of which recovery he would be able to return to work. He had just gone to bed for a nap when a neighbour invited him to the game between Vélez Sarsfield and River Plate at Liniers, the former's ground. As his neighbour liked to sit in the box seats, Linker assumed he would be alone for much of the afternoon, so he took his portable radio with him.

Half an hour before the game began, there was the usual friction between rival fans outside the stadium and at the entrance. There was fighting. Then someone started to throw stones. The police arrived. Some fans fled. There was the usual pushing and shoving and the police used their billy clubs liberally. The air was especially tense. Linker, a fan of Boca Juniors, decided to watch the game with River Plate fans. It may have been fascination with the enemy or simply an act of solidarity with those with whom he shared a state of rivalry. His friends later stated that Linker was not an intolerant, fanatical supporter of his team, but a peaceful fellow. He himself had been fond of pointing out that he was an 'easy-going kind of guy'.

The game between Vélez Sarsfield and River Plate was nothing special. Vélez won, 2–1, and well into the second half the goalkeeper began to slow the pace of the game down. When the ball went out of bounds, he sauntered over to it, clearly taking his time about kicking it back into play. He was at the goal post behind which the River Plate fans were stationed. At first they shouted insults at him. Then, each time he got near the fence, they spat at him. Finally, because he kept doing all he could to slow things down, they started throwing stones at him until, forty minutes into the game, he fell to the ground, his face covered in blood. The referee found a penknife at his side; the weapon had hit him in the face. At the time the rules prohibited substitutions and also prohibited a team from remaining on the pitch if one of its players was sent to the bench due to injuries not directly caused by play. The referee decided to suspend the game; as a result, Vélez won the two points.

The response was instantaneous. First the lower part of the stands, where the civilized River Plate fans were seated, went up in flames. Firemen were able to douse the blaze quickly. At the same time, the fans in the 'bleachers' became more aggressive and threatened to move on to the pitch. Within minutes they did exactly that, clearly intending to injure the local players and the referee who was still on the field. In view of events, the police officer in charge of the force ordered his men to fire a teargas canister at the fans on the pitch and into the stands, where most fans had remained. The police refused. In the face of their refusal, the official grabbed a teargas launcher from one of his men and shot a canister into the stands. When the stampede was over and the cloud of gas dispersed, a single individual remained where he had fallen, with a portable radio in a leather case at his side.

There was a tremendous outcry. The River Plate fans left the stadium and attacked police cars, fire trucks, and private vehicles parked in the area. Mounted police, who seldom approached the stadium, descended on the crowd; they even rode into a local pizza place with their horses and arrested all the customers. Six police officers were injured and more than 100 persons were arrested. That night a large demonstration of River Plate fans paraded from the congressional building down the Avenida de Mayo, protesting against the police. Stopping at a newspaper stand, they shouted 'Kil-lers, kil-lers,' the traditional chant favoured by demonstrators against police brutality. At the same time, rumours of various deaths caused by the football incident spread throughout Buenos Aires.

Linker was dead on arrival at Hospital Salaberry. Doctors there said that death was caused by perforation of the skull which left the encephalic tissue exposed. Then, without pausing and before the reporters could even ask, they said that the wound was due to the impact caused by a teargas canister fired from a distance of ten metres. They asked that reporters hold their story until the victim's mother could be located. The father, already in the hospital waiting room, had been told that his son was in a serious condition; the doctors had decided to wait for the mother's arrival to break the bad news to both parents simultaneously. Alberto Mario was, after all, their only child.

On Sunday night and in the days that followed, the federal police attempted to deny the implications of Linker's death. At first they said that there had been an avalanche of people descending the stairs and that the victim's skull was fractured when he hit his head against the cement bleachers. Then, later that night, an official release recognized that Linker had died as a result of 'causes that are still being determined'. The following day, Monday, the chief of police called a press conference to reiterate the announcement of the previous night, and to assure reporters that the police had done no more than was called for in view of the aggressive behaviour and violence perpetrated by the fans of River Plate. The forensic medical report described a wound approximately six centimetres in length and noted that it had been produced by an object of the same approximate size.

In its Monday edition *La Razón*, a Buenos Aires daily, published the account of a fan who said that he had witnessed the incident. He confirmed not only that the police official fired the first teargas canister, but said he continued firing canisters into the crowd, thus preventing people from getting close to the victim to help him. On Tuesday, 21 October, the same newspaper published the following:

> It is evident that the victim's wounds were the result of a teargas canister. It is also evident that the the police are responsible; on this point there is no discussion. This does not justify the disorderly behaviour of the angry fans. This kind of incident, resulting from uncontrolled passions stimulated by a variety of immediate circumstances, is common everywhere. . . . The police will never be able to control even the most minor of incidents if, at a football game, they are stationed by the pitch rather than in the stands. They can view the game better by the pitch but they cannot fulfil their obligation to prevent unfortunate incidents, thus ensuring that events take their

proper course and that the public is provided with due safe-guards. The clubs, key participants in sporting events, also have a responsibility to keep an eye on those fans known to cause trouble, both locals and visitors, whose location in the stands is the same, Sunday after Sunday.

The Penalty Board of the Football Association of Argentina relo-cated four games to be played at the River Plate stadium. The following Sunday, River Plate was at its stadium at the appointed time, ready for play. The stadium was empty. At the same time, Huracán, the team scheduled to face River Plate, was at the stadium of Ferro Carril Oeste where the match was supposed to be played, together with a referee and two line officials. After waiting for River Plate for fifteen minutes, the members of Hura-cán were declared the winners. River Plate's violation of the penalty imposed was not punished, and the remaining three-game ban was lifted.

Sunday, 26 October, became a date to be remembered in the history of professional football in Argentina: no police official was present at any of the games played that day. Tensions were so high that the police, fearing attacks by fans, decided to stay away from football grounds. That first death, in a sport that Argentinians identified with so intimately, was unacceptable. The fact that the victim was innocent of any wrongdoing was some-thing neither the press nor the public was willing to forget. Linker represented the true fan, somebody who would go to a football game even if his team was not playing, who would sit with the 'enemy' at a game. His tolerance was met by the intoler-ance of the police. Sunday 26 October was, for many, proof that the very presence of the police served to provoke their longstand-ing rivals: the fans. On that day, with not a single police officer at a single game, not a single incident occurred at any of the Buenos Aires grounds.

Certain groups in Argentinian society were still able, at that time, to react with indignation to police methods. Linker's death was a clear demonstration of the atmosphere of violence pervad-ing the games: acts that produced physical harm, in this case, irreparable harm, went unpunished. The police refused to accept that an officer had intentionally done something to physically harm an innocent bystander. Instead, they insisted that the cause had been the offensive and aggressive behaviour of the River

Plate fans. The fans of River Plate called the act murder. Linker's parents said nothing and did not request that the judicial system identify the guilty party. The identity of the police official, who in the face of his men's refusal, decided to throw the deadly canister himself, was never made public, nor was information ever issued as to what became of him. The judicial system of Argentina never came to any decision regarding the case. Official foot-dragging coincided with a growing belief that the limits which the authorities were not to exceed might have been extended to include, perhaps, the death of innocent bystanders. According to a line of reasoning based on Christian resignation, the suffering of innocents is the price that must be paid for the activities of sinners. Linker's death came to be a reminder of the existence of the arbitrary, of that which is in effect beyond control, in the final analysis, of fate and certain external conditions not easily changed nor affected in any way. Police power took on the aura of omnipotence and, at the same time, lost all legitimacy both in moral and social terms.

1967: THE DEATH OF AN INNOCENT BYSTANDER AND THE VIOLENCE OF FANS

Police violence continued to be a fact in the stadia of Argentina. On 6 November 1960, at a game between Boca Juniors and Independiente, the police once again used force. Boca Juniors players were clearly in charge that day: they created a number of opportunities for scoring, but they were unlucky, and there was, above all, a penalty ignored by the referee. As often happens under these circumstances, Independiente managed a goal, accompanied by mocking remarks from their team's fans towards Boca's players and fans. The latter reacted by throwing at their rivals anything they could lay their hands on and attempting to invade the pitch. The police reacted with a massive display of force: from a safe distance, they shot both teargas canisters and live ammunition into the stands where the terrified fans desperately sought refuge. The outcome was dramatic: dozens of spectators with wounds of every description.

The years during which the Frondizi administration ruled were marked by a gradual loss of popularity and legitimacy. On 29 March 1962 Frondizi was removed from office by the armed forces; he was subsequently arrested and sent to a prison on an island on Rio de la Plata. The economic crisis deepened and, in a single day in April, the dollar gained 55 per cent over the peso. The army divided between the 'blues', determined to defend the constitutional order, and the 'reds', in favour of replacing the vice-president with a military official. In April there was an armed confrontation between the two factions. This was followed by further conflict up to September. The crisis ended with the triumph of the 'blues' and, thus, a call for new elections which were scheduled for July of 1963. The *peronista* party continued to be proscribed.

The new government was characterized by a calm, co-operative, democratic style and, as a consequence, was thought to be slow and inefficient by the public. For several months in 1964, serious conflicts with factory workers occurred. The police were immediately called in and, as well as cases of wounding, there were a number of deaths among the workers. 1965 was also a year marked by social conflicts. While all of this was going on, the Argentina all-star football team prepared to play in the World Cup final scheduled for 1966 in England. Finally, on 28 June 1966, President Illia was removed from office by the military. One image would remain engraved forever in the history of contemporary Argentina: the president leaving the executive building and being abandoned in the street by his escorts, the famous Infantry Guard of the Federal Police, who had used tear-gas to disperse his defenders. And thus, the nation found itself in a period of crisis.

After the famous match against England in which the members of Argentina's all-star team caused an uproar in the football world, military president General Onganía provided them with a heroes' welcome. Months later, the military took over the nation's universities, thereby marking the beginning of the massive exodus of scientists and intellectuals. In 1967 the so-called 'great revolution' took place in the football championship in Argentina. Until then, the championship had been dominated by clubs from Buenos Aires and its industrial belt, including La Plata, Rosario and Santa Fé. But beginning in that year, teams from larger inland cities – Córdoba, Mendoza and Tucumán – were eligible to participate in what was to become the 'national championship'. The former 'national championship' was now called the 'metropolitan championship' (an allusion to the metropolis of Buenos Aires which had previously dominated professional football in

Argentina). Professional football was now played throughout the nation.

On Sunday, 9 April 1967, Huracán played Racing. Racing were champions, with a single loss and a string of thirty-nine victories. Before the game there were clashes between rival fans. Leaders of the Huracán supporters brought along trophies from other wars: pennants and caps with the Racing insignia that had been 'expropriated'. When the fans were in the stadium, one of the leaders of Racing's supporters organized a commando operation. At great risk, he infiltrated the section where the Huracán fans were seated and managed to appropriate an umbrella painted with the red and white colours of the opposing team. Huracán fans immediately chased after the responsible party but were unable to grab him. The Racing fans had carefully planned the getaway, as well as a reception for the Huracán fans who were in hot pursuit. Two Huracán fans were brutally beaten. The majority of Huracán fans, who were at the other end of the stands, decided that this would not happen again, and prepared to protect their territory at any cost.

Fifteen minutes before the main game began, a group of three Racing fans innocently entered the stands already occupied by Huracán fans. An industrialist, an honest citizen and a football fan, had brought his 14-year-old son and 16-year-old nephew to the game, along with a friend, Héctor Souto, 15 years of age. Héctor Souto was in his third year at a technical high school, and was the cousin of the wife of Roberto Perfumo, who was a centre back for Racing. The factory owner's son had brought with him a package of confetti, traditionally thrown as the favoured team came on to the field. As they entered the stands, the teenagers heard the ear-splitting chants of the Racing fans. They joined in enthusiastically. The Huracán fans, prepared to defend their territory no matter what, took the youths' chants as a provocation that called for retaliation.

A Huracán fan grabbed the package of confetti from the industrialist's son who reacted by kicking the fan. This sign of resistance was not taken kindly by a group of thirty Huracán fans who were instantly on him. Héctor Souto, in a move that was almost instinctive, came to the defence of his friend. The fans were immediately on top of him. Souto was, literally, massacred. Fifteen years after his death, his friend remembered:

He was on the ground, they were all over me too, when I
looked to where Héctor had fallen, and I remember clearly
the guy in the maroon shirt jumping up and down on him.
He was hanging onto the fence. . . . It was just a glimpse I got.
They were kicking me all over. I remember that maroon shirt,
Hector on the ground and the guy over him. I thought, he's
jumping on him.

(Romero, 1984: 18)

Some hot-dog vendors tried to intervene but were dissuaded by
some of the more irate fans. Their attempt did help one of
Souto's friends to escape unhurt. The only clear intervention
came from one of the Huracáns' owners who, irate and indig-
nant, came down the stands to rebuke the leader of the fans,
shouting 'Murderer, murderer' at him (ibid.: 30). The rest of the
fans merely observed the attack and a few timid protests were
heard.

At 1.50 p.m., ten minutes before the match was to begin, Souto
was taken to the stadium infirmary, already dead. The doctor
who saw him later said that the body showed no signs of violence
and that death was probably the result of internal injuries or a
heart attack. The president of Racing was told about the incident
by the industrialist who had also said that Souto was the cousin
of the star player, Roberto Perfumo. The president went down
to the infirmary to plead that the player not be told about the
death of his relative. Roberto Perfumo was told after the match
that a cousin of his had died in the stadium. Many years later,
he would remember the death of his cousin:

They told me after the game . . . that something had happened
to my cousin. My cousin? Which one? I didn't have cousins who
even went to football games, much less cousins who looked for
trouble at the games. I changed and went to the police
station. . . . A police officer told me: 'Everything's burst
inside.'. . . They told me that a bunch of them came at him.
That the kid had come in with a Racing pennant, that some
guys from the Huracán section had come at him and that they
got confused, they told me. . . . It didn't seem like a big thing
to me. I didn't know the kid was a football fan and later they
told me that he went to see the game because I was playing.
That really shook me.

(Romero, 1984: 12)

Perfumo continued commenting on the violence that would increase in succeeding years and be endemic by 1984:

> The problem is that the player sees a lot of violence, constantly. Football is, in and of itself, a violent game. It's violent in the way the trainer acts, the referee, the other players, the game, the competition . . . the fans go crazy because the conditions are ripe for it, the possibilities for craziness are there. . . . The crazy fans are there just like the green Falcons are there, the Triple A, and all the rest. It's all the same thing.
>
> (ibid.)

As Perfumo sees it, fan violence at football games is a reflection of the political and social violence that devastated Argentina, beginning in 1966.

Souto was an innocent victim, his death gratuitous, and for many it would be seen as an act of 'class vengeance'. Souto was an adolescent from the middle class, a good student, tall, good-looking, dressed well on the day he died. He had a 'good boy' reputation. His death was the end of football as 'pure party' in the mythology of Argentina. Souto was the victim of his own innocence which led him to join the chants for Racing while among Huracán fans. The tradition of clashes and confrontations was not the cause of death. The tradition, according to which fans moved from one stand to another at half-time, a tradition that symbolized the peaceful coexistence of the fans, would disappear completely from the stadia of Argentina. After the death of Souto, it became dangerous to make the mistake Souto made; similar incursions into enemy territory could be punished with death.

Souto was buried at midday on Tuesday, 11 April, 1967. By eight o'clock that morning, residents of his neighbourhood were outside, waiting for the funeral procession to pass, and merchants had decided to lower their metal doors in a sign of mourning. Students, teachers, and the director of the primary school he attended formed a guard of honour. His friends from the neighbourhood and his classmates from the Otto Krause Technical School joined the mourners. The casket was carried by pallbearers to the cemetery. Along the way, people spontaneously threw flowers. It was, perhaps, one of the final manifestations of affection and consternation in the face of irrational violence, senseless death, and the transformation taking place in what used to be the 'fiesta' of football in Buenos Aires. Living in Argentina would become increasingly difficult in the years to come and the stadia would become sites at which violence was not an exception.

Souto's attackers, thirteen in all, were identified and punished. Of these, only four were adults older than 18 years of age and thus held responsible for their actions. After a long trial, on 18 August 1970 the 'man in the maroon shirt' was sentenced to three years and four months in prison. Because many of those arrested were minors, they were not sentenced to prison. Their backgrounds were diametrically opposed to Souto's. Most were labourers and apprentices whose passion in life was football.

1976: FOOTBALL, POLITICAL VIOLENCE AND POLICE REPRESSION

The arbitrary nature of Argentinian politics, a phenomenon that began with the 1966 military coup, gave way to a variety of responses. In May 1968, students rebelled in many cities throughout the country, a rebellion that coincided with student activities in Paris. On 15 May a university student was shot by police in the city of Corrientes. Two days later, in a demonstration protesting the death of this student, another was killed in Rosario. On 29 May Córdoba was virtually taken over by protesting students. The violence of 1969, the following year, lasted for a week and resulted in a dozen deaths. Beginning in 1969, but especially though 1970, the cycle of violence increased with the appearance of guerrilla groups with ties to *peronismo*, the Montoneros, as well as the People's Revolutionary Army, a leftist group with a Trotskyite philosophy. General Onganía was deposed in June 1970, an event that marked the beginning of a period of negotiations intended to restore democracy in Argentina. Guerrilla activity increased in 1972, as did police repression. Elections were scheduled for 1973, but the military did not allow Perón to be his party's candidate for the presidency. After the *peronistas* won the elections, the president-elect announced that he would resign and call new elections. In September of that year, Perón won 62 per cent of the vote.

Perón's followers were divided, and repression against the Montoneros, the left of the *peronista* party, was increasingly intense. It would become especially violent from 1974. The guerrillas became bolder with every passing day, and the number of violent actions increased. The People's Revolutionary Army (PRA) carried out assaults on military installations in 1974. The Montoneros went underground, and paramilitary groups, especially the infamous Argentina Anticommunist Action Group, supported by factions in the Peronist Government, increased their activities. The city of Buenos Aires and the rest of the country was pervaded by a climate of insecurity and violence. In 1975, the army launched a massive counter-offensive against the PRA guerrilla group in Tucuman. Death threats were received daily by intellectuals, artists and scientists suspected of leftist leanings. Many were forced to leave the country. On 23 December the PRA attacked a military barracks in the province of Buenos Aires. The attack failed and dozens of guerrillas were killed. More than 500 people died in 1974 and 1975. On 24 March 1976, the military overthrew the government elected in 1973. Repression by the armed forces and the police intensified. Their goal was to make the guerrilla groups 'disappear' and bring peace to the country for the 1978 World Cup Finals. There was very little time left.

The metropolitan championship began in February 1976. On Sunday, 16 May, Estudiantes and Huracán played in La Plata. Huracán was undefeated, with players like Houseman and Ardiles, who would be part of the all-star team for the 1978 World Cup, along with other veterans with long histories of international experience, including Brindisi and Carrascosa. In 1985, the son of Gregorio Noya recalled the decision to sit with his father in numbered seats because there were rumours of violence between rival fans who would be in the stands. The police were obsessed by the presence of members of the Montoneros who were expected to use the games to gain support for their cause. It was said that the Huracán fan club was infiltrated by Montonero militants. The only evidence for this was the fact that in 1973, the year Huracán won their first championship with César Luis Menotti as coach, when team members took the traditional lap of honour, Motonero banners appeared. The police also believed that the fans of San Lorenzo de Almagro, Huracán's most intense rivals, also included leftist extremists. Though neither of these suppositions has ever been proven, what is true is that the Montoneros had chosen the game between the Estudiantes and Huracán to protest at the massive repression which the armed forces and the police had unleashed since the March coup. Moments before the game began, a banner was hung from a post at the head of the stands occupied by Huracán fans. The police, after much effort, managed to take the banner down, but only after the game was well into the first half. The success of their efforts brought a protest from the crowd. This protest was not, necessarily, a demonstration of support for the guerrilla cause. Any police action in a football stadium in Argentina is unanimously condemned.

Noya's son doesn't remember the Montonero banner. Nor do other witnesses. Nevertheless, it is reasonable to believe, given the number of witnesses who have testified to having seen it, that the Montoneros did hang a banner and that, in addition, they released balloons filled with helium which also bore the name of the movement. At half-time there was, according to the official version, an exchange of gunfire, the result of aggression from guerrillas and fans towards the police. The result was the death of Gregorio Oscar Noya, just as he took his seat after returning from the toilets. He was struck in the back by a bullet that punctured his lung. According to the police version, the guerrillas attacked the police and one of their bullets hit the spectator. But what the official version does not explain was why Noya was mortally wounded before there was any reason for police intervention. Gregorio Oscar Noya's son was 16 at the time and he remembers exactly what happened during the twenty-two hours between the time his father was wounded and his death. His version is straightforward: the police came into the stadium from the street, and to frighten the spectators, they began to fire into the air. One of these bullets hit his father (Romero, 1986: 74). That was, without a doubt, the exchange of gunfire mentioned in the official report and in the first newspaper articles on the subject.

The death of Gregorio Oscar Noya, 38 years of age, a public auctioneer and Huracán fan, passed without comment. The country was firmly enmeshed in the reign of violence and the destruction of the guerrillas regardless of the cost. On Tuesday, 18 May 1976, Noya was buried with only his most immediate relatives attending, along with a few friends and acquaintances. Noya was not Souto, 1976 was not 1967. The 'accidental' deaths caused by the intervention of the 'forces of order', or by attacks from 'illegal organizations', no longer caused the same moral indignation as they had in 1967. The Noya family did not take legal action against the police immediately. In 1985 Noya's son remembered:

> When something like that happens, the last thing you're interested in are law suits and the problems they cause. You want to let it go, you don't want hassles. Later we realized that we were wrong. It was incredible: there were people who got our phone number somehow and began to call us. They said they would talk about what they knew: they were all from La Plata. When dad fell, we all hit the ground and looked between the boards from where the shots came and we saw it was the police. I even began to yell a lot of things at them, I was crazy like, and they grabbed me and told me to keep quiet: 'Stop it, kid, be cool, you don't know what could happen to you.'
>
> (Romero, 1986: 75)

They finally decided to get the advice of a lawyer and take the case to court. The trial would, as its objective, prove that the police, and not members of an extremist group, killed Noya. After years the court closed the case without any formal accusation of attack by the police on the day that Noya died.

1983: ORGANIZED FAN VIOLENCE

Relations between the fans of Quilmes and Boca Juniors were never very good. Friction began in 1978 when Quilmes won the metropolitan championship, and Boca lost the title by only one point. To this must be added the fact that Boca fans felt insulted at being replaced by militant Quilmes fans when the latter were selected to go with Argentina's all-star team to the World Cup in Spain in 1982. At the same time, it must be remembered that it was Quilmes fans who composed one of the most humiliating verses about Boca fans:

> You need two things
> To be a Boca fan:
> A shack in a shantytown
> And a Chamamé longplay.

This refers clearly to the characteristics of the stereotypical Boca fan: he is from Paraguay rather than Argentina (so he likes the chamamé), and he lives in a slum.

On 26 September 1982 Boca Juniors played in Quilmes. The

local police carefully frisked the Boca fans for arms. The game was played by the rules in every sense and ended in a draw, 1–1. On leaving, however, the Boca fans destroyed everything in their path in the area surrounding the stadium, breaking windows and damaging the yards of nearby homes. The police were on the scene immediately, forcing the fans to leave the city of Quilmes. Police repression was accompanied by the appearance of four Ford Falcons (the cars used by the paramilitary groups in Argentina during the time the military ruled); the individuals inside the cars threatened the fans with firearms and a number of shots were fired, resulting in a race, on foot, to get away that probably broke some world records.

The well-known Negro Thompson, leader of the Quilmes fans, received a number of anonymous messages suggesting that it would be better if he didn't show up at Boca's ground on 5 January 1983, the day Quilmes was scheduled for the return match, following Boca's September visit to Quilmes. Negro Thompson didn't go to the stadium that day, but he did go to the nearest police station to announce, like a good leader, the number of vehicles that were on their way from Quilmes, the number of fans, and, above all, to insist that they were not looking for a fight with the fans of Boca Juniors. That day, the Quilmes fans were on a peace mission. Negro Thompson and the Quilmes fans had no way of knowing what the real intentions of the Boca fans were.

The police decided to keep the fans apart in the streets surrounding the stadium to avoid a clash and the accompanying incidents. The same manoeuvre was planned for the game's end when the fans would be leaving. About fifteen minutes before the end of the game, Boca fans resorted to the commonest of ruses: they left the 'lightweights' in the stands, sounding their drums and waving their pennants. Meanwhile, the 'heavies', the good warriors, left carefully, staying inside the barricade put up by the police. They patiently circled the stadium and penetrated enemy territory. They approached the train and there they remained, waiting for the Quilmes fans. When they appeared, they were attacked without mercy with any blunt weapon the Boca fans could get their hands on. At the sight of their attackers, Quilmes fans attempted to flee along the railroad tracks. Soon after he started running, Raúl Calixto, 17 years old and an asthma sufferer, began to have difficulty breathing, but he knew that if he stopped he was a dead man. He tried to run as fast as he could until he came to some ditches filled with high weeds. There he hid, thinking that he would thus be safe from the Boca fans. There, alone and without a friend in sight, he had an asthma attack. Hours later he was found dead.

While Calixto was dying in the ditch, a second group of Boca Juniors fans was waiting for the Quilmes fans who were running to get away from the first group. Then a red car, a Torino, appeared carrying the cream of the Quilmes fan club. Witnesses say they saw Negro Thompson in that car, and that he said 'Hang on, Quilmes'. A number of shots were fired from the Torino into the group of Boca fans. Paraguayan Raúl Servín Martínez, 18 years old, was killed by a bullet which perforated his thorax. The wall of an antique shop bore the marks of other bullets that missed their mark.

Negro Thompson, the leader of the Quilmes fans and a personality, went to the police on Thursday 6 January to find that a warrant for his arrest had been issued. He was placed in preventive detention, accused of participation in the murder of Servín Martínez, and there he remained until 21 December 1984, a period of almost two years. Another Quilmes fan was arrested at the same time and accused of firing the shots that killed the victim. Since 1978 when Quilmes won the championship, Negro Thompson had been a well-known personality in Quilmes and in the world of football in Buenos Aires. He was widely known by football coaches and by the members of the Argentinian Football Association, and his name occurred occasionally in newspaper articles. He was the 'total fan', prepared to give his all for Quilmes. During the 1982 World Cup, he was in charge of organizing the trip for the Argentinian fans who were to go to Spain, a trip that was cancelled in the end because of the Falklands War. Negro Thompson maintained his innocence from the beginning to the end of the investigation into the murder, alleging that he had not even gone to the stadium on the day of the game. A campaign on behalf of the accused was immediately launched by the most committed 'beer fans' with open support from the local newspaper, El Sol.

The campaign was designed to leak different versions of the events to the local and Buenos Aires press. The first was that, in reality, the Federal Police were responsible for the killing of Servín Martínez, and that this was part of a plot to set Negro

Thompson up for arrest and trial for the crime. The other version, a variation of the first, transformed the victim into a militant member of the leftist Peronist Youth organization. According to this version, the police killed him the day before the game and then planted the body in the area surrounding the stadium. After the incidents on the day of the game, the police made it look like he was a victim of acts committed by Quilmes fans. Another version circulated in Quilmes. The real murderer, the story went, was a member of the inner circle of Quilmes fans; and he remained free and was walking about in broad daylight, with his hair dyed and his moustache shaved to avoid identification by the police.

Some time passed before Servín Martínez's murderer was eventually identified. The principal suspect first had been absolved of all guilt in December 1984. Negro Thompson, imprisoned for being the alleged instigator, had also been set free in December 1984. A massive barbecue was organized in his honour, attended by leaders of the club, defence lawyers, representatives of local businesses who supported the club and reporters from *El Sol*, the local newspaper which had taken on the defence of the accused throughout the time he was in prison. Speeches were made at the barbecue, accusing the police of acting in an arbitrary fashion, the courts of moving too slowly, and reporters working for the Buenos Aires press, whose attitude toward the accused was cruel. The president of the Argentinian Football Association was invited to the barbecue but he did not attend. He sent a letter instead, in which he expressed his solidarity for the difficult moments the accused had undergone and his satisfaction that, at last, justice had established his innocence unequivocally (Romero, 1986: 135–6).

A year later, in December 1985, the principal suspect was sentenced to nine years in prison by the Appeals Chamber. At sentencing it was made clear that he was the sole individual involved. It was also stated that the death of Raúl Calixto required no further investigation, that it was due to simple chance given that the deceased had been asthmatic.

CONCLUSIONS

Our four cases can be seen as illustrating the different logics and processes of violence in Argentinian football. The first case belongs to the 'traditional' violent reaction of the militant fans protesting against enemy players, attacking them, thus creating a favourable atmosphere for the violent reaction of the police forces, with the ensuing rapid response of the police generating chaos and innocent victims suffering. In this context violent death is perceived as arbitrary and unjust, especially when the police, imagined to be neutral and balanced, react with such brutality. The justification of death becomes impossible. In the confrontation between fans and police what matters is to find out who is responsible and, in the last instance, who is more blind in the use of violent means for achieving goals. The police in the stadia, therefore, are perceived not as a neutral and shallow actors but as central and active participants. To resist and to attack the police force is thus seen as morally justified. The fans of River Plate interpret their own violent behaviour as legitimate, as a reaction against tricks and lack of fair play. According to this kind of thought it is easy to see that from their point of view the disorder in the game has been introduced by the enemy players themselves. The violent reaction of the police is defined as exaggerated and supportive of bad players and permissive referees. This explains the public reaction on the day of the incident and the massive pacific response of moral indignation two weeks later when all matches in the League were played without police presence. In addition, we must not forget that the death of Linker in 1958 was the first in the history of Argentinian football. It was exceptional, it was defined as absurd and it was impossible to accept as normal. The passion of grief shown by the fans was mixed with a sentiment of protest against the police. The individual tragedy was transformed into a social act of protest, an individual death acquired a symbolic political meaning.

The second case can also be seen as the death of an innocent, but on this occasion not due to police brutality. Sporadic physical confrontation between opposing groups of fans was a part of the folklore of Argentinian football. The confrontations were not dramatic; in 1967 fans changed ends at half-time (the idea was to support and protect their own goalkeeper). In most cases, these movements were done without conflict. The death of Souto introduced an unknown dimension: the use of blind and organized violence in expressing club loyalty and defending fans' male prestige. This time grief was shown by the public in a general protest against hooliganism. Football and its stadia began to be perceived as dangerous places. From then onward the militant fans qualitatively changed in the organization of their activities during matches. If the police were still the main enemy, the public suddenly discovered that the opposing groups could also kill.

The third case relates to the impact in the game of societal and political violence. The police came to define the fans as a political enemy. In this perspective the fans are transformed into political enemies under the assumption that guerrillas infiltrate the militant core of fans and use the stadium for making political propaganda. Stadiums were then converted into open political arenas. Consequently, since 1979 stadia have been used by fans for protesting against the military junta and many matches were and are still transformed into political happenings when fans loudly comment upon political events and judge governments and politicians.

We regard the fourth case as the most modern expression of organized violence and open confrontation between minority groups of fans. Many of these groups are evolving into kinds of elite military regiments dominated by the formation of small well-trained commando groups with a material infrastructure which includes weapons and cars. Operations are planned. It seems a task for professionals. The main leaders are well known and some of them are public figures with good relations in the world of football and politics. The Huracán supporters who killed Souto were real amateurs compared with the groups emerging in Argentinian society during the terrible years of military dictatorship and repression. In this new context the violence is very selective and usually only engages the core of violent fans. They know very well what they are doing. However, physical violence and killing is executed in exceptional circumstances. Symbolic dominance and control is still the main strategy used by militant fans (see Archetti, 1992). The description of English hooligans given by Hobbs and Robins (1991) is very near to the ideology and state of mind represented by El Negro Thompson, a football fanatic, committed to the club and prepared to die and to kill for the sport.

Our cases are undoubtedly very selective. The main aim has been to show that football does not simply reflect society or culture but is part of a general process of the way society models some of its central existential, moral and political issues. We have shown that in Argentinian society the killing of innocents is morally condemned and that this kind of death is perceived as a threat to the image of life as good; it is a sacrilege against the social order. If individuals accept that death is tragic and inevitable, to provoke it before time is more tragic, an explicit alteration of the passage of time. Linker, Souto and Noya's deaths are in this sense paradigmatic. The political content of these cases is related to blind brutality. This violence jeopardizes the legitimacy of the behaviour of the police forces. Our last case can be seen as an expression of the 'paramilitarization' of Argentinian society. The arbitrary brutality of these groups, tolerated by the State during the years of military dictatorship, has created a much more permissive public attitude towards them. It seems that Argentinians tolerate more the death of people engaged actively in acts of violence than the death of innocent victims.

Sociological and anthropological perspectives about British soccer hooliganism have been focused narrowly on the behaviour of football fans. The examination of the wider context, which includes the actors in the institutional world of sport, the reaction of the legal system through a careful consideration of trials and sentences, the conduct of the police in normal and violent situations, as well as the reactions of friends and relatives of victims and the theoretical debates which were presented earlier, have undoubtedly permitted a development and consolidation of a field of studies devoted to the understanding of 'deviant' behaviour of spectators in the social arena of football. This is a considerable achievement. However, a change of scope in the study of hooliganism, should make it possible to conceive the moral issues and cultural dilemmas of death and violence in football as general sociological problems. How English society copes with death and violence seems to us a more relevant subject of study than to continue in the type of research which aims at a better understanding of the logic of a fan's behaviour. A better contextualization of English hooliganism and different outcomes of acts of violence should enable a comparative analysis of the way English society conceives and tolerates death in football. This change in focus implies a movement from the analysis of culture of football fans to the general field of cultural analysis. Football is then transformed into an arena in which social actors symbolize, reproduce or contest by means of their social practices the social values dominant in a given period. Consequently, football, and sport in general, become a central dimension in the analysis of social and cultural processes.

NOTES

We owe a special debt of thanks to Richard Giulianotti, University of Aberdeen, for his comments on earlier drafts of this paper and for his help on improving our English. Norman Bonney, University of Aberdeen, read the penultimate draft and made valuable comments.

1 The research into all the cases has been carried out by Amílcar G. Romero over a long period of time (see Romero, 1984, 1985 and 1986). He is still systematically working on the incidence of violence in Argentinian football. The statistical information presented later in the chapter derives from his extremely up-to-date data bank.
2 Qualitative fieldwork has been carried out but without the kind of systematic endeavour which characterizes the anthropological approach (see Murphy *et al.*, 1990: 129–66; Williams *et al.*, 1989).
3 The exception being the pioneering anthropological work by Marsh and associates (1978).
4 Murphy, Williams and Dunning (1990: 19) draw attention to spectator tragedies in Europe since 1945: 300 deaths, most of them occurred at football and involved British, usually English fans. They write:

some of these fatalities have resulted from hooliganism combined with inadequate and unsafe spectator facilities. . . . But most of them have been the product of large crowds being herded into aged and out-dated facilities which are palpably ill-equipped to deal with occasions of emergency, misjudgements in the management of crowds or spectator panic.

It is interesting to note that when they mention other deaths they relate to players who died as a consequence of injuries received while playing football (Murphy *et al.*, 1990: 34, 109).
5 According to our information, before 1958 only two violent confrontations causing death occurred in Argentinian professional football. In 1938, in a first division match between Lanus and Boca Juniors, the police attacked Boca Juniors supporters killing two of them. In 1944 at River Plate stadium the police charged San Lorenzo de Almagro fans. Spectators tried to escape but the doors were closed. Seven were killed. It is said that in 1916 in an international match opposing Argentine against Uruguay one spectator was killed.

REFERENCES

Archetti, E.P. (1992) 'Argentinian Football: a ritual of violence?', *The International Journal of the History of Sport*, 9, 2: 209–35.

Armstrong, G. and R. Harris (1991) 'Football Hooligans: theory and evidence', *Sociological Review*, 39, 3 : 427–58.

Bloch, M. and J. Parry (eds) (1982) *Death and the Regeneration of Life*. Cambridge: Cambridge University Press.

Dunning, E., P. Murphy and J. Williams (1986) ' "Casuals, Terrace Crews and Fighting Firms": towards a sociological explanation of football hooligan behaviour' in D. Riches (ed.) (1986a).

——, —— and —— (1988) *The Roots of Football Hooliganism: An Historical and Sociological Study*, London: Routledge.

Dunning, E., P. Murphy and I. Waddington (1991) 'Anthropological Versus Sociological Approaches in the Study of Soccer Hooliganism: some critical notes', *The Sociological Review*, 39: 459–79.

Hertz, R. (1907) 'Contribution à une étude sur la représéntation collective de la mort', *Année Sociologique*, 10: 48–137.

Hobbs, D. and D. Robins (1991) ' "The Boy Done Good": football violence, changes and discontinuities, *Sociological Review*, 39: 551–80.

Marsh, P., E. Rosser and R. Harré (1978) *The Rules of Disorder*, London: Routledge.

Metcalf, P. and R. Huntington (1991) *Celebrations of Death: the anthropology of mortuary ritual*, Cambridge: Cambridge University Press.

Murphy, P., J. Williams and E. Dunning (1990) *Football on Trial: spectator violence and development in the football world*, London: Routledge.

Parkin, D. (1986) 'Violence and Will', in D. Riches (ed.) (1986a).

Redhead, S. (1991) 'Reflections on Discourses on Football Hooliganism', *The Sociological Review* 39: 480–6.

Riches, D. (ed.) (1986a) *The Anthropology of Violence*, Oxford: Blackwell.

—— (ed.) (1986b) 'The Phenomenon of Violence', in D. Riches (ed.) (1986a).

—— (1991) 'Aggression, War, Violence: space-time and paradigm', *Man*, 26, 2: 281–98.

Romero, A.G. (1984) 'De april de 1967: el asesinato de Hector Souto. Muerte en la cancha', *Todo es historia* 29: 8–44.

—— (1985) *Deporte, violencia y política*, Buenos Aires: Centro Editor de America Latina.

—— (1986) *Muerte en la cancha (1958–1985)*, Buenos Aires: Editorial Nueva America.

Suttles, G. (1968) *The Social Order of the Slum: ethnicity and territory in the inner city*, Chicago: University of Chicago Press.

Taylor, I. (1971a) 'Football Mad: a speculative sociology of football hooliganism' in E. Dunning (ed.) *The Sociology of Sport: a collection of readings*, London: Frank Cass.

—— (1971b) 'Soccer Consciousness and Soccer Hooliganism' in S. Cohen (ed.) *Images of Deviance*, Harmondsworth: Penguin.

—— (1982a) 'On the Sports Violence Question: soccer hooliganism revisited', in J. Hargreaves (ed.) *Sport, Culture and Ideology*, London: Routledge and Kegan Paul.

—— (1982b) 'Class, Violence and Sport: the case of soccer hooliganism in Britain', in H. Cantelon and R. Gruneau (eds) *Sport, Culture and the Modern State*, Toronto: University of Toronto Press.

—— (1987) 'Putting the Boot into a Working Class Sport: British soccer after Bradford and Brussels', *Sociology of Sport Journal*, 4.

Williams, J., E. Dunning and P. Murphy (1989) *Hooligans Abroad*, second edition, London: Routledge.

Chapter 4

Italian football fans
Culture and organization

Alessandro Dal Lago and Rocco De Biasi

FOOTBALL CULTURE IN ITALY

Madrid, July 1982. When the Italian football team won the World Cup in Spain, the whole country was in a football fever. Thousands of respectable citizens drove through the cities with national flags and sang the national anthem. President Pertini and Prime Minister Spadolini flew to Spain in the presidential airplane, attended the final match, and came back to Italy playing cards with famous football players such as Dino Zoff and Paolo Rossi. The awful events of the 1970s, terrorism and the murder of Aldo Moro, seemed to be overcome and forgotten. The country was apparently unified by the new symbol of football or, as we say in Italy, *dal pallone*.

Milan, June 1990. At the beginning of the World Cup Finals ('Italia 90'), Argentina met Cameroon. In Milan's San Siro Stadium, following the pre-match display by cheerleaders, nearly 70,000 spectators were ready to watch a football star such as Maradona against unknown African players. On the terraces a few Cameroon supporters (less than a hundred), in traditional African dress, cheered their heroes against several hundred Argentinian fans. At the ends of the stadium, the audience was divided into supporters of the two Milan teams (AC Milan and Inter FC), and when the match started the Italian public was neutral. But, as Cameroon skilfully managed to withstand the stronger South American team, the stadium became more and more pro-Cameroon. Among the Italian spectators, traditional hatred for Maradona (captain of the Napoli side from Naples) combined with a typical sympathy for the weaker team. When Cameroon scored, all of the stadium (except, of course, the terraces occupied by the Argentinian fans) was rejoicing. At the end of the match, thousands of Italians began to applaud the Cameroon team and the Cameroon supporters. After the match, Italians ran down the streets greeting every black they met with chants such as 'Ca-me-roon, Ca-me-roon', or 'Maradona fuck you', and so on. Perhaps some of these new Cameroon supporters were the very same fans who had previously daubed anti-black-graffiti and slogans on walls around the stadium (some of the Inter *ultras* are known to be skinheads and racists) (Dal Lago, 1990).

When Argentina met Brazil in Turin, two weeks later, the Turin fans (of Juventus FC and Torino) behaved in the same way. They booed the Argentinian national anthem and supported Brazil; television viewers throughout the world watched Maradona trembling with anger at the Italians. The outcome of this struggle between northern football fans and Maradona was not what most would expect, though understood by Italians. Napoli supporters abandoned the Italian national team and became supporters of Argentina. For Napoli *tifosi* the identification with their team (and with its captain Maradona) was stronger than their national sentiments (Bromberger, 1990).

How to explain these different attitudes of Italians with regard to the national team? In the first case, Madrid 1982, a new sense of national pride was aroused by the performances of the national team. Moreover, Italians were playing in a foreign country and the traditional city and regional loyalties and antagonisms were set apart for a while. But when Italy itself became the theatre for the World Cup Finals, the conflicts between supporters (particularly between northern and southern football fans) reappeared; the tournament was re-interpreted within a parochial and municipal framework. And we can present another example of this tendency. Fears of trouble between Italian and English supporters notwithstanding, during the 1990 World Cup Finals Italian *ultra* groups did not overcome mutual hostilities to join together to fight the common 'enemy'. In several interviews some *ultras* (well known as right-wing oriented) told us that they respected and admired English football fans and that they would not fight them. This attitude is confirmed by a recent survey on the national sentiments of northern football club members. More than 90 per cent stated that they were not interested in the

Italian national team and that they never attended a match of
the *azzurri*, in Italy or abroad (Dal Lago and Moscati, 1992: 76).

In other words, Italian football culture is local and municipal.
This does not mean that some important teams – such as AC
Milan, Juventus, Inter and Napoli – are not supported in regions
and cities other than their natural homes. But this culture can be
explained as a form of extended municipalism. For a supporter,
whether or not he lives in the city of the team, the team colours
are the most important symbol of his football faith, dominating
any other symbol or cultural meaning such as nation, class or
political party. What we are suggesting is that in Italy the realm
of football is quite independent from class stratification, political
conflicts or religious values. We do not yet have complete socio-
demographic data to build a picture of the social stratification of
supporters; nevertheless, it is evident that in Italy football culture
does not represent only one social class, but involves each social
group. A survey of a sample of official football club members
from Lombardy (500 supporters of AC Milan, Inter and Atalanta,
with 88.8 per cent males and 11.2 per cent females) shows the
following occupational distribution:

Table 4.1 Socio-economic status of northern Italy football fans

Economic activity	Number	%
Employed	379	75.8
Unemployed	12	2.4
Students	65	13.0
Working students	14	2.8
Retired	25	5.0
Housewives	5	1.0
Total	500	100.0

Source: Dal Lago and Moscati, 1992: 38.

The social composition of supporters of course varies according
to the region or city. According to some sociologists, the presence
of young members of the working class is stronger among small-
town football fans, for example Bologna (Roversi, 1990). In cities
such as Naples, where the unemployment rate is close to 20 per
cent, unemployed workers are likely to support the local team.
But in Italy football cannot be regarded as the typical sport of
the working class – football fever occurs in every social *milieu*.
Tycoons such as Agnelli or Berlusconi, political leaders such as

Andreotti or Craxi, are well known as football fans, and no negative label is attached to this form of public commitment. In other words, the football world in Italy has to be regarded as a cross-class culture.

Table 4.2 Social class membership of northern Italy football fans

Employment status	Number	%
Professionals	35	7.0
Teachers	5	1.0
Entrepreneurs and managers	11	2.2
Shopkeepers	47	9.4
Craftsmen	38	7.6
Industrial workers	144	28.4
Employees	130	26.0
Other occupations	10	2.0
Unemployed	82	16.4
Total	500	100.0

Source: Dal Lago and Moscati, 1992: 38.

If *tifo* (football fanaticism) does not depend on social class or religious values (in Italy there are no religious conflicts), why are thousands of fans driven to support a team of another city? And, moreover, why do football fans in cities such as Turin, Milan, Genoa or Rome divide themselves in groups supporting one of the two home teams? In the first two decades of the twentieth century, the beginning of football culture in Italy, these urban rivalries represented strong social and cultural differences. For example, AC Milan, founded by English sportsmen, was traditionally supported by the upper and working-class strata. Conversely, the second Milan team, Internazionale FC, was founded by professionals and supported by the middle class. In Rome, Roma was supported by city centre inhabitants (unskilled workers and craftsmen), while Lazio was backed by people living in the suburbs. Accordingly, Roma supporters are reputed leftists and Lazio supporters are known as right-wing oriented. Today, however, the social roots of these football fans are far more varied and complex. According to our survey on northern football fans, no relevant difference can be identified, in terms of social stratification or educational level. Milan and Inter fans appear to be differentiated in the same way.

We believe that the vicissitudes of *tifo* are related to diffuse social phenomena such as street corner socialization, family influence and perhaps to aesthetic values typical of football as a sport and, so to speak, popular art (the style of playing and so on). In other words, football culture in Italy is an autonomous realm, not dependent on external factors, but able to influence and direct the social behaviour of ordinary people.

Table 4.3   Social class and club membership of AC Milan and FC Internazionale

Social class	Inter FC %	AC Milan %
Professionals	11.0	10.3
Entrepreneurs and managers	3.9	1.7
Shopkeepers	9.1	16.0
Craftsmen	9.1	5.7
Industrial workers	34.4	22.3
Employees	30.5	39.4
Other occupations	2.0	4.6
	n = 154	n = 175
Total	100.0	100.0

Source: Dal Lago and Moscati, 1992: 38.

We are aware of the fact that the picture we are drawing of Italian football is quite different from the analysis of football and popular sports of famous scholars such as Norbert Elias and Eric Dunning (1986). Perhaps today football is an important prism through which we can look towards *different* societies. In our opinion, however, the main difference between English and Italian football cultures does not lie in the social class distribution of the supporters, but in the presence or absence of a strongly structured form of association. Italian football culture is not only local and independent of social stratification, but is also firmly organized. Football in Italy is a national fever and, above all, for millions of citizens, workers, students and professionals, a structured way of life.

FOOTBALL ASSOCIATIONS

The supporters' associations have, as a social phenomenon, greater importance in Italy than in England. Supporters' clubs involve structured activities and several forms of socialization for many individuals, even outside the ground, in ordinary everyday life. All this needs the mobilization not only of material resources, but also of symbolic resources, because of the meaning of the social activities surrounding football in Italian society (De Biasi, 1993).

In Italy there are two kinds of supporters' associations: the official supporters' clubs and the *ultras*. The basic characteristic of the official supporters' clubs is their recognition by the favoured football club. Usually, all the supporters clubs linked to the same team are related to a 'Co-ordination Centre', which is a member of the FISSC, the Italian Federation of Supporters of Football Teams, founded in 1970. Non-club-based national associations of supporters, such as the FSA in England, do not exist in Italy. Particularly in the case of the leading Serie A clubs (First Division), the supporters club can be situated in towns far from the location of the favourite team. In this case, another federation co-ordinates the clubs dispersed throughout the country. For instance the AIMC, the Italian Association of the Supporters Clubs of AC Milan founded in 1967, comprises 1,340 clubs, 11 of which are located abroad.

The role of this kind of federation of supporters clubs is very important, in order to organize travel for away matches, particularly abroad. For example, for the 1989 European Cup Final in Barcelona, the Italian Association of the Supporters' Clubs of AC Milan, was able to assemble 450 coaches, one ship and 25 flights, for 26,000 supporters. The other Milanese team, Internazionale FC, has a Co-ordination Centre which consists of 800 Supporters' Clubs, with a total of 90,000 members. The activity of a supporters' club is not limited to organizing support on match-day. Such clubs have their premises in a pub or elsewhere, at which they usually organize social occasions, not necessarily related to football itself. Nevertheless, the most important thing for members of supporters' clubs is having the chance of obtaining a ticket for special occasions which are officially 'sold out'.

Official football clubs represent the respectable side of Italian *tifo*. In a sense, they are derived from the tradition of local associations, religious or political, deeply rooted in Italian culture. But we would suggest that their growth is connected to the decline of political commitment and the crisis of traditional mass parties (cf. Cavalli and de Lillo, 1989). The clubs provide football fans not only with tickets, organized travel and the opportunity to be recognized by the football club, but also with several forms of social expression. Organized fans can influence, through official interventions or demonstrations inside the stadium, the policies of the club. They organize meetings and parties with the players. But above all they find in their participation in club activities the opportunity to create social relations. On the other hand, football fan organizations represent a strong financial and 'political' resource for football clubs. For TV and media tycoons such as Berlusconi, or industrial magnates such as Agnelli (or even political leaders like Andreotti), football clubs are an important background resource. They provide financial support (AC Milan has 70,000 season ticket holders); social consent (it is well known that Fiat workers are traditionally Juventus fans, managed by Fiat); and indirect political support (the Christian Democrat leader Andreotti was for many years the secret eminence of Roma FC). In sum, official football clubs represent, in the sporting realm, the general trend towards a politics of exchange, widely prevalent in Italian society.[1]

ULTRA GROUPS

From the very beginning, Italian *ultra* groups (wrongly considered the equivalent of English hooligans) reflected a more heterogeneous youth movement than that which populated British terraces. According to several sociologists, when English hooliganism was at its peak, the fans on the terraces were linked by a common social class or lifestyle, and also by shared youth subcultures (Dunning *et al.*, 1988; Taylor, 1985). In Italy, the *ultra* style of support has never been dominated by any particular social stratum or any specific youth style. The unifying element for the youth of Italian *curvas* (stadium ends) has always been support itself, and not social consumption, or class status, or political belief, or musical fashion, etc. Thus, it is crucial to investigate the peculiar autonomy of *ultra* rituals within the stadium (Dal Lago, 1990: chapter 2).

If a member of an official football club can be said to be a citizen of the football world, an *ultra* has to be considered as a militant. This does not mean that every *ultra* is fully involved in all group activities. Many young people who usually attend the match in the *curva*, do not have any commitment to the *ultra* club in their everyday life. For them, *ultras* are more or less a reference group, the *ultra* club also providing a structure of services. These young spectators are supporters who go into the *curva* on Sunday – with the ticket they have obtained at a special price through membership of the *Brigate Rossonere* or the *Fossa dei Leoni*, in the case of AC Milan – and they find a scenario and a choreography already prepared by a few committed *ultras*.

In the environment of the stadium the cultural task of the *ultras* is to conduct a spectacular display associated with the footballing spectacle, by a lively and persistent choreography of collective support, with big banners and flags, firework displays, choruses and chants which, sometimes, involve everybody in the stadium. The following is a definition of the *ultra* group by a member of AC Milan's *Brigate Rossonere*.

> As an *ultra* I identify myself with a particular way of life. We are different from ordinary supporters because of our enthusiasm and excitement. This means, obviously, rejoicing and suffering much more acutely than everybody else. So, being *ultra* means exaggerating feelings, from a lot of points of view.[2]

Although *ultras* have been able to create a specific form of support, which changed the image and style of *tifo* in Italy, some of their attitudes and behaviour are often compared to those of English hooligans. Some Italian sociologists, for instance, speak of 'assimilation and imitation of the forms of the British hooligan style of support and aggression' (Roversi, 1992). Nevertheless, it seems to us that violence among Italian fans is manifested in forms different from that of British hooligans. This is especially evident if we take into account the organization of Italian *curva* fans, and the different attitudes and repressive tactics of the Italian police and *carabinieri*, a duality which is contextually very similar, from a formal point of view, to that which emerged during the political violence of the 1970s. An *ultra* group has to be regarded as a firmly structured form of association, in which some individuals may have a particular disposition towards aggression. But such associations base their own existence on the organization of a spectacular event: the choreography and the encouragement typical of the *curva*. It is a kind of youth association, which, strangely enough, Italian sociologists have neglected for a long time. But, despite this, for a lot of young people, participation in the rituals of the *curva* on Sunday, or the midweek commitment to the *ultras* group in the case of the *militanti*, is one of their most significant social experiences.

The *ultra* style of support is based upon visibility, and this is also relevant to the issue of hooliganism. If we consider that in England, several years ago, some hooligans even travelled incognito for an away match (by train and well-dressed), so that the police could not identify them, Italian *ultras*, on the contrary, clearly want to be conspicuous. The issue of visibility is very important from a sociological point of view. *Ultras* travel in large groups and often, when there is trouble, they adopt strategies very similar to the types of fight evident in political riots.

In order to understand the social dimension of Italian 'hooliganism', we have to take into account the relevance of Italian political protest and disorder during the 1970s. Political riots brought about an increased potency in the equipment and techniques of repression used by police and *carabinieri*. In turn, the intensification of police control inside and outside the stadia led the *ultras* to adopt a mode of military organization and a warlike attitude against the police. As a result, football hooliganism *qua* social problem has to be regarded as the legacy of such policing. The tactics police usually adopted against political extremists during the 1970s, they are now inclined to repeat against *ultras*. For example, at the match between Genoa and Liverpool on 4 March 1992, there were 1,200 policemen and *carabinieri* stationed in the city. How many police officers were in Liverpool two weeks later for the return fixture (Taylor, 1992)?

The legacy of political conflict also influenced the associations of young supporters located in the stadia *curvas*, but only from a formal point of view. We are not referring to the political symbols displayed on the banners. Such symbols and emblems, within the Goffmanesque 'frame' of the *curva*, assume another meaning, losing their original reference (Goffman, 1975). In the early years, *ultra* groups did not take any political commitment into the stadia. Nowadays, the firmly structured organizational dimension of some extremist political youth associations has been adopted, as shown by the following features: the presence of a *direttivo*, a sort of political bureau; the assembly-like or democratic style of decision-making in the *ultra* groups; the strong commitment of some members during the week (meetings, preparation of banners and choreography, distribution of leaflets); and even the use of flagpoles as weapons. All these are elements which were already present in political extremism. We do not mean that political riots have moved from the schools or the factories to the stadia. We want to emphasize that the political groups of extreme left or right have represented a form of association which tends to present itself again in new contexts, even after the crisis of political commitment among young people in Italy.

If we analyse the case of English society, the subcultures related to phenomena such as teddy boys, skinheads, punks and so on, assume a more important role than the political associations. And, in the more specific case of football fans, the informal character of some of these groups was reflected in the loose groups of terrace supporters, whether hooligans or not. In the early days of the Italian *ultra* culture, on the contrary, the issue of commitment (or 'militancy') involved the most active members of the *ultra* groups (Segre, 1979). In addition, the pattern of fighting among groups of rivals, or between *ultra* groups and police, mirrors, to some extent, the political violence linked to the extremism of left or right.

It is also true that in Italy there are modes of transgressive behaviour (vandalism, machismo, exhibitionism, etc.), typical of youth mobs rather than of political groups. Nevertheless, in the Italian case, those elements, typical of the British experience, are welded to other dimensions of group life, which, at least at the beginning, remind us of the political associations of the 1960s and 1970s.

In England, terrace rituals are based on a more limited number of songs and chants. A small group of supporters begins to sing, and often a larger number then join in. In the Italian *curva*, some *ultra* leaders do not see the match: the ones who lead the singing turn their backs to the ground. They have the task of prompting the songs, by use of a megaphone, at certain moments of the match. Usually, these conductors are members of the *direttivo* (the executive), members who define the policies to be adopted, choosing the supportive rituals of symbolic provocation of rival fans.

The *direttivo* is an institution that is typical of *ultra* organization. Its members each have specific tasks to perform: delivering tickets, organizing away travel, selling club memorabilia such as scarves, administering the budget, speaking or negotiating with the representatives of the football club or the police, co-ordinating choruses and chants, and so on. Amongst all these activities, it is difficult to find somebody responsible for editing fanzines. Fanzines are scarcely relevant within Italian football culture, in which other more important media hold the monopoly of communications, both written and spoken. These considerations apply also to the match-day programmes. They are not integral to match attendance in Italy. In the San Siro stadium, for instance, a match-day programme, *AC Milan Today* or *Internazionale Today*, is widely available and free, but supporters do not take it seriously, often throwing it away without reading it. It is generally considered to be an advertising leaflet. For example, Genoa supporters, in Liverpool, did not consider it important to buy a programme, as a match-day souvenir, which surprised the programme sellers.

In the context of Italian football culture, the publication of a fanzine is just one task, and not the main one, of an *ultra* group. It is less important than organizing trips to away games, or the campaign for membership cards, or the preparation of choreography, and so on. Among English supporters, this kind of collective organization is not present. Each fanzine is produced by single editors, or small groups of friends, who do not usually represent any association or club. It usually contains the proviso: 'Published articles and letters are the views of individual contributors and do not necessarily reflect the views of the editors.'

English terrace supporters are not organized like *ultras*. Instead, there are other types of association, such as the FSA, which represent the interests of fans (see for example the campaign about all-seater grounds), and which create an alternative culture, against the hooligan element, among football supporters. Alternatively, the *ultra* phenomenon shows a strong ambivalence, based on the coexistence of the spectacular and expressive elements with the hooligan disposition. Journalists and chairmen of clubs call *ultras* wonderful spectators, when everything is going well, such as a celebration, but they call them hooligans when there is trouble. But, in both cases, they are talking about the same people.

Today, even the football club cannot ignore the importance of the *ultras* and the influence they exert on the game. There are relationships between the football club and *ultras* groups, which necessarily lead to negotiation. We doubt that English hooligans in the past had this sort of relationship with the club. As one

member of *Brigate Rossonere* explains, 'AC Milan gives 100 tickets
to the *Fossa dei Leoni*, 100 to the *Brigate*, 60 to the *Commandos
Tigre* for home matches. For away games we are not given any at
all.' Nevertheless, AC Milan has a number of cheap tickets which
are sold to the *ultras* groups, who in turn sell them exclusively to
those who have a membership card. This issue is important for
a comparative analysis. For example, in England there have surely
been supporter protests against the club or the team, but we
doubt that there has ever been any real supporter strike such as
there have frequently been in Italy. Or try to imagine what a
protest against all-seater stadia would be like in Italy. Or imagine
translating into an English context what happened in Naples
when Maradona played there. As the French anthropologist
Bromberger (1990) wrote:

> The *Commando Ultra*, which is located in the centre of the B
> *curva* in the San Paolo stadium is closer to a firm than a
> more traditional brotherhood: managing its capital of 6,000
> followers, making preparations for professional banners, spon-
> soring its emblem, publishing a magazine, producing a weekly
> TV programme ('One Hour with the B *Curva*').

The organizational difference between Italian and English football cultures can be illustrated by an episode in which one of us
was involved. At Genoa airport, the day before the Genoa–Liverpool match, one of the leaders of the Genoa *ultra* group, *Fossa
dei Grifoni*, met the FSA representatives, Liz Crolley and Paul
Hyland. He asked one of us if they were the leading Kop *ultras*.
It was difficult to explain to him that an equivalent of the Italian
ultra group does not exist at Anfield. Moreover, when, a short
time before the game, the supporters of the *Fossa dei Grifoni*
displayed their choreography, the visitors from Liverpool were
greatly impressed. But the representatives of the Football Supporters Association, with whom one of us was attending the
match, were more surprised by the cost of the choreography:
more than £20,000 for the laser ray and the giant banner 'We
are Genoa', (written in English), which covered, for some
minutes, the whole main stand of the Luigi Ferraris stadium.

FOOTBALL WARS

The general frame or dominant metaphor of the Italian *ultra* culture is war. We can understand what happens in Italian stadia every Sunday by applying the political concept of 'opposition between friends and foes' to the realm of football (Schmitt, 1927). In Italy a general war, mainly symbolic and theatrical but sometimes real and bloody, is fought by organized groups of young football fans, the so-called *ultras*. It is a war in which temporary or permanent alliances (*gemellaggi,* from the Italian word *gemello* or 'twin') are formed, maintained or broken, a war lasting from the 1960s when the first *ultra* groups were created, and that will probably last as long as football remains the main interest for large strata of Italian teenagers and youngsters. About fifty teams in three main football divisions offer *ultras* the opportunity to create fan groups (from the Milan 'South End' with 20,000 members to small groups in towns such as Como or Caserta, with less than 100 members) (Dal Lago and Moscati, 1992).

After describing the peculiar organization of these groups, we present a short analysis of the ritual rules of this football war. Paradoxically, the war cannot be too violent and bloody. Like medieval warriors who shared a common code of chivalry, despite their loyalty to king, baron or feudal chief, Italian *ultras* share a common *ultra* culture. They sing the same songs and shout the same slogans, only changing some words, when necessary, to declare their identity and celebrate their team. For example, if the Milan end sings the official anthem 'Rossoneri siamo noi, ma chi cazzo siete voi' ('Red and black we are, and you are nothing'), the Juventus fans will invariably answer 'Bianconeri siamo noi, ma chi cazzo siete voi' ('Black and white we are, and you are nothing').

To share a common culture means for *ultras* to share a fighting culture. The fight is mainly symbolic from two points of view. First, during a football match, every group fights to impose its symbolic strength in terms of the beauty and impressiveness of the choreography (flags, choruses and songs) and in terms of displaying courage (to steal in front of all other fans the enemy's flags, scarves, or even hats is considered by the youngest *ultras* the noblest of group activities). Second, every group, before or after the match, regards the end, the stadium and the open spaces surrounding the stadium (including underground stations, railway stations and so on) as its exclusive territory to be defended against the enemy's raids (Bale, 1992). In the stadium the fight is limited to a symbolic duel because its purpose is to show to the 'enemies', spectators and even the TV audience which are the best and strongest groups. A Milan *ultra* told us, after the 1989 World Club Championship match between AC Milan and Medellin in Tokyo, attended by several hundred of his fellows: 'By now even the Japanese have learned to know and respect the *Fossa dei Leoni*' (one of the more important sections of the Milan South End).

Of course, when the war is fought outside the stadium there can be violence. In order to defeat the enemies on the field, *ultra* groups try to adopt urban guerrilla tactics (particularly setting ambushes near to stations and involving the police). But the violence is restricted to the throwing of stones and to sudden attacks. Usually every group is satisfied by the escape of the enemies from the sacred territory, and by a short resistance against the police. During several observations of these fights around the Milan stadium we noted that the attacks did not usually involve non-*ultra* (that is, 'normal') fans of the opposite team. According to the informal *ultra* code of honour, there is no glory in beating ordinary people. We noted also that the leaders not only tend to control and limit the length and the intensity of the fights but also, so to speak, to avoid extreme dangers for themselves and even for the enemy. As one of the leaders of the *Fossa dei Leoni* told us during an interview:

> During a fight with the 'Drughi' [Juventus *ultra* group] one of them came near to us [the leaders]. We did not attack him and we told him to run away as quickly as possible. If he should happen to be found among the others [ordinary members of the *fossa*] he would be severely wounded.

In this sense the *ultra* violence is mainly ritual. Young *ultras* learn to be brave before their peers (and of course before the girls), to show the group's strength, avoiding at the same time big trouble, to be reliable and accountable for important tasks in the group. And, moreover, they enjoy these ritual fights. They enjoy all this, not only because it is a sort of sport (their own match), but also because it demonstrates their attachment to the end group, their identity as *ultras*. But the fights are rituals from another and more important point of view. The whole group is expected to be involved in these fights, to attack and to defend its territory and to be attacked if invading the enemy's territory. In other words, every *ultra* knows when they are likely to 'win' and when to lose. But, and this is the most important of all considerations, every *ultra* group needs the participation of the enemy in order to continue the war. On this issue, the *ultra* groups co-operate to maintain their common culture – limiting the violence, feeding the romance with stories of victories and defeats, of heroism and cowardice, of joy and sadness. For example, a Milan song, adapted from a traditional communist song, says:

> Tifosi rossoneri, tifosi milanisti,
> teniamoci per mano, in questi giorni tristi.
> Di nuovo giu a Marassi, di nuovo al Comunale,
> tifosi rossoneri, finiamo all'ospedale.
> Sangue nei popolari
> Sangue giu nei distinti
> Ne abbiamo prese ma non siamo vinti.
> E' ora di rifarsi, e ora di lottare
> Per quel che abbiam subito, dobbiamo vendicare.
> Spariamo giu a Marassi, spariamo al Comunale,
> e adesso siete voi che andare all'ospedale.[3]

The need for enemies is particularly strong during matches. The opposing *curvas* try to invent new insults, new choruses. During the matches a choral dialogue is engaged in between the two. The stronger the answers, the stronger is the commitment to typical *ultra* activities: singing, booing, menacing or goading the enemy. If the number of the enemy is small, a chorus is extended to tease the *ultras* of the opposing end: 'Dove sono gli ultra?' ['Where are the *ultras*?']

In conclusion, we think that the phenomenon of football youth organization and culture in Italy must be seen in a larger perspective than that of football hooliganism and street violence. Unlike the English case, the machismo and masculinity typical among the young males of the lower classes are not sufficient to explain hooliganism. We have arrived at this conclusion not only because of the presence of several females among the most active *ultra* gangs,[4] but also, and more importantly, because of the richness of the *ultra* experience, in terms of socialization, group solidarity, folk culture and 'artistic' performances in the stadia. Obviously, this is only the starting point for a more comprehensive analysis of football fan cultures. Only through the convergence of efforts to make ethnographic comparative studies, on a European scale, can the differences between supporters' cultures be understood, without neglecting the fact that, as Bromberger (1990) remarks, 'There are few events which can be deemed to be "complete social phenomena", if this suggests – following Marcel Mauss rather than some of his commentators – phenomena which in some cases mobilise the totality of a society and its institutions.' At least in Italy, football is one of these phenomena.

NOTES

1 Some years ago the new left newspaper *Lotta continua* reported that the political influence of political leaders on Roma supporter clubs dated from the early 1970s. Conversely, *ultra* groups are independent of political parties.
2 From an AC Milan *ultra*'s unpublished autobiography.
3 The song translates as:

> Red and black comrades, Milan fans,
> let's stay hand in hand, in these gloomy days.
> Again at Marassi, again at Comunale,
> red and black comrades, we are led to the hospital.
> Blood on the terraces,
> blood on the stands
> We were taken but we are not defeated.
> It's the time of revenge, it's the time to fight
> for all we have suffered, we have to take our revenge.
> Let's shoot at Marassi, let's shoot at Comunale,
> and now you bastards have to die.

This illustrates the formal continuity between political groups of the 1970s and contemporary *ultra* groups. Here, the *ultras* are using political songs without any reference to the original meaning.
4 In some Second Division *ultra* groups, women are leaders or speakers for the group (for example in Bologna or Reggio Emilia). In bigger organizations, such as Milan South End, several women are currently assuming important roles in the group.

REFERENCES

Bale, J. (1992) 'Il pubblico come fonte di topofilia: il pubblico e lo stadio', in P. Lanfranchi (ed.) *Il calcio e il suo pubblico*, Napoli: Edizioni Scientifiche Italiane.
Bromberger, C. (1990) 'Ciuccio e fuochi d'artificio: indagine sul rapporto fra la squadra di calcio napoletana e la sua citta', *Micromega*, 4.

Cavalli, A. and A. de Lillo (1989) *Giovani anni 80: secondo rapporto Iard sulla condizione giovanile,* Bologna: Il Mulino.

Dal Lago, A. (1990) *Descrizione di una battaglia: i rituali del calcio,* Bologna: Il Mulino.

Dal Lago, A. and R. Moscati (1992) *Regalateci un sogno: miti e realta del tifo calcistico in Italia,* Milano: Bompiani.

De Biasi, R. (1993) 'Le culture del calcio: un'analisi comparativa dei rituali e delle forme del tifo calcistico in Italia e in Inghilterra', Ph.D. Dissertation in Sociology, University of Trento.

Dunning, E., P. Murphy and J. Williams (1988) *The Roots of Football Hooliganism: an historical and sociological study,* London: Routledge.

Elias, N. and E. Dunning (1986) *Quest for Excitement: sport and leisure in the civilising process,* Oxford: Basil Blackwell.

Goffman, E. (1975) *Frame Analysis: an essay on the organisation of experience,* Harmondsworth: Penguin.

Roversi, A. (1990) 'Calcio e violenza in Italia', in Roversi, A. (ed.) *Calcio e Violenza in Europa,* Bologna: Il Mulino.

—— (1992) *Calcio, Tifo e Violenza.* Bologna: Il Mulino.

Schmitt, C. (1927) 'Der Begriff des Politisschen', *Archiv fur Sozialwissenschaft und Sozialpolitik,* 1.

Segre, D. (1979) *Ragazzi di Stadio,* Milano: Mazzotta.

Taylor, I. (1985) 'Putting the Boot into a Working Class Sport: British soccer after Bradford and Brussels', *Sociology of Sport Journal,* 4.

Taylor, R. (1992) 'Pre-Match Liaison between Supporters in Europe: a report on the UEFA cup ties Liverpool v. Genoa 1992', Sir Norman Chester Centre for Football Research, University of Leicester.

Chapter 5

Football violence
A societal psychological perspective

Gerry P. T. Finn

INTRODUCTION

There is no one explanation for violent behaviour in general, or
at soccer matches in particular. Any human involvement in sport
is a complicated and complex social phenomenon, requiring not
only careful analysis but a recognition of the limitations inherent
in any one perspective. No single perspective can encapsulate the
whole of any social phenomenon. That is as true of so-called
football hooliganism[1] as of other human activities. Yet the debate
on the nature and extent of violence by football spectators has
taken on an increasingly adversarial complexion. The conflict
surrounding a *Sociological Review* special issue on this theme led
the editors to refuse to allow contributors to continue the debate.
The editorial verdict that they had not 'expect[ed] the pro-
ponents of different views ... to comprehend one another' is
damning.[2] Progress in understanding soccer violence demands
an acceptance of theoretical and methodological pluralism, which
this chapter will pursue by adopting a societal psychological perspective.[3]

Some confusions in the debate about hooliganism have arisen
because of insufficient clarity in the description and analysis of
what supporters do and what they perceive. The behaviour displayed by soccer fans can be perceived as threatening because
the actions are associated with the striking of aggressive poses.
In this sense the activities of many supporters can genuinely be
defined as being aggressive, but that is not the same as being
violent. Aggression and violence are different but difficult concepts: confusions in exploring spectator violence arise out of the
conceptual confusion of aggression and violence (Smith, 1983).

Numerous attempts have been made to distinguish between aggression and violence,[4] but most have some drawbacks. One of the best attempts at differentiating aggression from violence was made by Siann (1985: 12), who argued that a full understanding of aggression had to take into account the set of non-pejorative meanings within the wide range of uses covered by the term. 'Aggression involves the intention to hurt or to emerge superior to others.' An attempt to demonstrate superiority may only be non-pejorative aggression, but if there is an intention to hurt another, either physically or emotionally, then it is pejorative aggression. Pejorative aggression 'does not necessarily involve physical injury', but violence does. 'Violence involves great physical force or intensity.' Siann argues that the confusion between aggression and violence occurs because aggression is usually the motivation underlying violence.

Aggression and violence are therefore related, occupying different positions on the same continuum. Aggression is used non-pejoratively to describe aspects of a a range of different sports. Golfers can be described as aggressive for the manner in which in they tackle a golf-course or compete against an opponent. Participants in sports as varied as boxing, tennis or chess can have their style described as being aggressive. Participants can also be aggressive in the pejorative sense. That can even include chess if one opponent intends to demoralize the other. Sports can also be violent in practice. Combat sports such as boxing most obviously include a legitimized element of violence, as do association and rugby football. Tackling within the rules in both sports legitimizes the use of 'great physical force'.

SOCCER: AN AGGRESSIVE AND VIOLENT COMPLEX

Soccer is, in both the pejorative and non-pejorative sense, an intrinsically aggressive event which sanctions some violence in attempts to win, and retain, possession of the ball. As a result players prize physical hardness; they physically challenge one another for the ball. It can be no surprise that the sport is imbued with a culture of hard masculinity. All players are expected to be determined, brave, fearless and hard, the very qualities that Danny McGrain (McGrain with Keevins, 1987: 137), sixty-two times a Scottish internationalist, argues successful footballers need to possess:

the first thing they will require is the heart to go right to the very top, the willingness to be first to the ball and to be unafraid of going in where it might hurt to get it. The difference between being hard and being dirty has to be emphasised.

A very hard-tackling defender himself, McGrain was probably the most skilled full-back Scotland ever produced (Lamming, 1987). That he finds it necessary to emphasize that there is a difference between hard and dirty play indicates the difficulty in locating the dividing line. His own complaints about the illegal use of elbows or the head show that it is often crossed. To distinguish between hard and dirty play is equivalent to distinguishing aggression and legitimate violence from illegitimate violence. Footballers need to be aggressive and to employ legitimate violence to succeed, but when the line is crossed, illegitimate violence results.

Another complicating factor then arises. Players' own views of what is acceptable violence goes well beyond what the rules of the game deem legitimate. When Scotland's international goalkeeper Andy Goram (1990) spoke of the importance of being prepared to dominate other players, he mixed aggression and violence in his recipe for success. His reports of exchanges between players include pejorative aggression and physical violence. Verbal abuse was used by Goram and his opponents in attempts to intimidate. Many exchanges involved acts of physical violence. Goram explained that he soon learned after he had been 'knocked about a bit'. The assistant manager of his first club:

> encouraged me to get stuck in and stamp my authority in the box so that anyone coming in knew it was a battlefield. It's basic psychology. A player is less likely to come in on you with a boot or an elbow if he knows you're looking out to protect yourself.
>
> (Goram, 1990: 24)

Goram confessed to long-running personal battles with some players. His account of the experiences of his late father, also a goalkeeper, shows that these are not recent developments in the game. Goram senior believed football was much more physically violent when he played – a judgement supported by former Rangers and Partick Thistle goalkeeper, George Niven (*Herald*, 27 June 1992).

Some illegitimate violence is tolerated by players. A culturally sanctioned normative framework evolves, but the limits of tolerance vary. When teams from countries with very different codes of acceptability meet, the cultural collision can lead to outbreaks of violence disapproved of by either culture. When Uruguay played Scotland in the World Cup in Mexico in 1986, the Scotland squad experienced acts of increasingly violent intimidation. One of the more unusual was when a defender stuck his finger up the anus of a Scottish forward as both players manoeuvred for position at a corner kick. Perhaps the lack of mobility and competence demonstrated by some Scottish players in their defeat that night is now explained. Glove puppets are known for neither their independence of movement nor their football skills.

These brief allusions to the aggressive and violent dimensions of soccer reveal why players have to be 'hard' men. Soccer matches do offer a variety of challenges; players experience different types of fear before the match. That is why hard men who can lead by example are made captains. Leading captains such as Willie Miller, now the manager of Aberdeen, and Terry Butcher, captain of Ipswich, Glasgow Rangers and England, and ex-manager of Sunderland, were described in this way. Indeed, Butcher seems to have gone almost over the top in his pre-match aggression (Davies, 1990: chapter 3). Graeme Souness, later to be manager of Glasgow Rangers and Liverpool, was proud of his hard-man reputation as captain of Liverpool (Souness, 1987). Perhaps the best example of the importance of the strong, all-dominating captain is Roy Aitken, formerly of Celtic and Scotland, now player and assistant manager of Aberdeen. Aitken's fellow professionals in Scotland admired him as a captain and judged him to be fearless. Aitken was described by Goram as an 'ideal captain' and an inspirational figure. Scotland coach Andy Roxburgh and the other Scottish internationalists, often themselves club captains, like Maurice Malpas of Dundee United, agreed about Aitken's ability to make his own team-mates play. The standing of Aitken among his fellow professionals is hinted at by their frequent description of him as 'Big Roy'. One of Aitken's strengths was that he seemed able to disregard the opposition's attempts at intimidation, inspiring other players to do the same. Tommy Burns, manager of Kilmarnock, who previously played with Aitken for Celtic and Scotland, explains, 'You would look around the room before going out, and your eyes would focus on Roy. It made you feel safe, knowing that he was there with you' (*Scotland on Sunday*, 13 October 1991). Goram's report of the 1990 World Cup match against Sweden in Italy reveals that 'Big Roy' also knew very well how to make the opposition feel unsafe:

> it was the most emotional atmosphere in a dressing room since I had been in the squad. It was unbelievable how wound up we all were. We were shouting and screaming at each other how we were going to beat the other lot. When we lined up in the tunnel Glen Hysen was at the front looking cool as ever. He knew Gary Gillespie and some of the other Anglos. But the rest of their team looked like the nice boy next door. Not one of them looked a real hard nut. They were all pleasant chaps and none of them would put the fear of God into you.
>   I took a look along our line and you couldn't get a bigger contrast. Roy Aitken at the front, smeared with vaseline on his forehead looked as if he was about to climb in beside Mike Tyson. Jim Leighton behind him is not exactly noted for his good looks. Then there was Alex McLeish who would give himself a fright in the mirror. Big Roy had obviously been weighing all this up. He turned round to us and says, 'These guys are all shitting themselves. Look at them!' I took a look at the Swedes and their eyes were all glazed. Big Roy starts shouting, 'Let's get into these Swedish bastards.' The whole line of us joined in shouting and screaming at the Swedes. It was as though someone had let us out of our cages. I swear the Swedes bottled it there and then. I looked across at Thomas Ravelli, the Swedish keeper, and his eyes were just about popping out of his head.
>   The rest of us took our place on the bench still growling as the teams kicked off. Within a minute the ball came loose right in the middle of the park, and about ten tackles went in. Once the ball moved on . . . there were still blue shirts flying in. The attitude of the Scots that night summed up for me what the Scots are all about.
>
> (Goram, 1990: 106–7)

Scotland won that match. Goram prefaces his description of

events by describing the friendly exchanges between Scottish and Swedish fans (cf. Giulianotti, 1991). The juxtaposition with the behaviour of the Scottish players is ironical, whether intended or not. But the players displayed the aggression, in the pejorative sense, that is deemed necessary to win. They attempted to intimidate the Swedes from before the start of the match. The rhetoric of professional football is that domination and intimidation of the other team is necessary to achieve victory. The intent is aggressive in both pejorative and non-pejorative senses. Some violence is legitimated by the rules of the sport. Some illegitimate violence is allowed by the normative rules of the participants. The whole intoxicating brew can spill over into illegitimate violence that is generally unacceptable to all concerned, but which remains understandable within the framework of uncertainty that accompanies these often inadequately expressed boundary lines.

So it is very easy to stray across the narrow dividing lines between aggression, legitimate violence, tolerated illegitimate violence and illegitimate violence in soccer. The code of acceptability remains uncertain because it is implicit, not explicit, embedded within the cultural traditions of the sport: that is why on-the-field aggression and legitimate violence can, and often does, spill over into unacceptable, illegitimate violence between players from the same culture. The cultural variations ensure that meetings of teams from very different cultural traditions are even more prone to misunderstandings and can lead to even more serious on-field disturbances. But regardless of the identity of the participants, all matches, from the best behaved to the least disciplined, are aggressive events which incorporate varying levels of violence within them. To play soccer is to be involved in acts of aggression and violence.

SUPPORTERS AS PARTICIPANTS IN THE MATCH

The contrast between the actions of the Scottish players and Scottish fans shows that the relationship between on and off the field behaviour is complex. None the less, committed supporters are by their very presence participating in what is an act of aggression in both pejorative and non-pejorative terms. They wish to see their team demonstrate its superiority by defeating the other. A great victory can involve the humiliation of the opposing team. The nicest of fans will admit that there are opposing teams that they hate; supporters share with players the appreciation of hardness and the ambiguities between aggression and different types of on-field violence (Bull, 1992; Hornby, 1992; Titford with Dunphy, 1992; R. Turner, 1990). To support a team means supporting acts of violence and being vicariously involved in them. Supporting one team means opposing another team, whose own supporters identify just as closely with their own team's efforts. The contest between supporters is aggressive, in both senses of the term: sometimes that can be transformed into violence.

That is because there is also some ambiguity about what is acceptable behaviour between football supporters. Respectable supporters of teams criticize violent behaviour, but they often accept pejorative aggression and there are even elements of ambiguity in some discussions of violence (Bull, 1992; Canter *et al.*, 1989; Hornby, 1992; Titford with Dunphy, 1992; R. Turner, 1990). Even those who admit to some involvement in violence display some ambivalence about it: self-styled hooligans feel the need to claim that they follow some code which targets only those who are similarly disposed to become involved in violence, excluding the innocent, those supporters or mere passers-by who are not interested in fighting.[5] Therefore, in the absence of overt definitions, there is a range of potential social meanings of what it is to be a supporter, allowing considerable scope for difference and deviation.

So the support given by fans goes beyond the merely financial. Admission money is only the price to be paid to gain entry to the ground in order to support the team. Soccer supporters are seen to participate actively in both the team's triumphs and the club's catastrophes. Strange powers are attributed to soccer supporters. Simple observation does show that the sports crowd is not a passive audience, but the extent of any direct impact on the game is arguable. None the less, it is still commonly believed that supporters are able to influence events directly. Beliefs in the power of the crowd are expressed in various forms by players, managers, supporters and sportswriters. The validity of these beliefs is a different matter (Edwards and Potter, 1992), but an examination of the accounts offered by individuals in these various categories is indicative of the strength of the common beliefs about the importance of the relationships between team and support (McClure, 1991).

Supporters of one team can be believed to have an intimidating effect on the opposing team. This belief is common. Crowds are 'hostile'. Managers and players issue pleas for their own support to be vociferous. The supporters can, it is stated, unnerve the opposition. Speaking before the 1991 Skol Cup Final against Hibernian, Dunfermline manager, Jocky Scott commented that 'the winners are those who cope best with the tension' felt by players in important matches. In the context of identifying factors that had to be overcome in order to succeed, he emphasized that a large support for the opposing team was a significant factor when calculating the potential winner of a match. Playing against Hibernian in the forthcoming final was better than meeting teams with a larger support:

> the fact that neither Old Firm team is present makes it much easier. When you play Celtic or Rangers, you have to overcome other elements – like the big, hostile crowd – even before the match starts. This is a genuine 50–50 match and my players know they have a real chance. I know they do too.
>
> (*Observer*, 27 October 1991).

But it is believed that the supporters can also have a negative effect. Players state that if their own fans turn on them, then their form can slump dramatically (McCoist with Brankin, 1992; Titford with Dunphy, 1992). The late Jock Stein of Celtic and Scotland believed that teams could be influenced by their supporters' feelings. He worried that supporters hysterically demanding victory could lead the Scottish national team to play in an equally hysterical manner (Macpherson, 1991). Concern that the tension of the fans could be communicated to the players leads managers to involve supporters in their game plans. It is common for the home team's manager to plead for patience from the home support, especially in two-leg cup ties when the team at home is seeking to retrieve a deficit from the away leg. Visiting managers can enlist this variant of the supposed influence of fans to counter the belief in the supposed advantage of a home club's large support.

Thus, the range of beliefs about the influence of the crowd are very wide-ranging. The complexities of these beliefs, which include apparently diametrically opposed positions, are akin to more important forms of social thinking, which also contain their own ideological dilemmas (Billig *et al.*, 1988). Clearly it is pragmatically useful to be able to contradict beliefs about the direction of the influence of supporters on games when different occasions demand it. Yet what is most important about these beliefs is that they do agree that supporters have some effect, and are commonly held and often reported in the media as the views of soccer professionals. As a result, they provide the material basis for considering what it means to be a supporter, and what being a supporter does do for the team. They buttress the belief that the supporter can directly influence the outcome of a game, that the supporter is directly involved along with the players, and that the intensity and nature of his commitment is important. These beliefs describe the dominant assumptions about the role, influence and importance of the football fan for his team.

SCOTLAND, TEAM AND SUPPORT: THE ULTIMATE IN UNITY?

Perhaps the sometimes magical beliefs in the significant contribution supporters make to their team's efforts has reached its ultimate expression in the recent history of the relationship between the Scottish national team and its supporters. While captain Aitken was giving the lead to Scotland's players to intimidate their Swedish counterparts in the 1990 World Cup Finals, the fans were producing 'cataracts of sound' to prove themselves 'Scotland's most potent weapon'. National coach Andy Roxburgh said of their efforts that, 'It was really the most remarkable environment in which to play football and our supporters were truly magnificent.' The fans were pleased by Scotland's victory which Roxburgh judged to be important 'because the supporters are representatives of the nation' (Forsyth, 1990: 207). Although these views are intensely expressed, they are well within the normal continuum of opinions expressed on these matters. When Scotland played in the European Championship Finals in Sweden in 1992 the relationship reached its apogee.

Scotland had qualified for these finals for the first time. The Scottish supporters, popularly known as the 'Tartan Army', had a party in Sweden, in which they successfully involved Swedish locals and other national supporters in their social events. Hopes of a good Scottish football performance had been low; media expectations had been very low indeed. Yet, after playing with some style and flair, Scotland narrowly lost to Holland in their first game. Scottish fans gave considerable support during the match, remaining to sing and chant praise for the team after it. Despite playing very well against Germany, Scotland went down to a 2–0 defeat which did not reflect the balance of play. The Tartan Army continued singing and chanting for an hour after the game. Roxburgh and many of his players were moved to tears by this display of support, loyalty and affection. There were emotional scenes of reciprocal adulation. Twice the manager and the team left their dressing-room to go out on to the field and acknowledge the cheering Scottish fans who were unwilling to leave the ground.

At the post-match press conference Roxburgh confessed to the strength of his feelings. He said, 'People expect football folk to be macho and not to show emotion. We are supposed to take it on the chin. But on this occasion we couldn't restrain our emotions.' He promised to go out and beat the CIS (constituted by the old Soviet Union) 'for the fans' (*Daily Record*, 16 June 1992). The impact of the travelling Scottish supporters on the manager and players had been so strong that two days later the whole Scottish squad turned up unannounced at the main camp-site occupied by Scottish fans. In the next match Scotland achieved a 3–0 victory over the CIS. Captain Richard Gough proclaimed that, 'We did it for our wonderful fans. They deserved this for the wonderful backing they've given us.' At the end of the match Roxburgh took all the Scotland squad over to the supporters. To scenes of ecstatic exchanges between players and supporters, they applauded one another. The sense of unity was so strong that Roxburgh positioned the team in front of the fans for press photographers. Referring to the Scottish support he said: 'They're part of our team just as much as the players. I made sure the lads lined up in front of the fans for the biggest team picture in the world' (*Daily Record* and *Herald*, 19 June 1992).

When the players arrived back in Scotland they received a 'heroes' welcome' at the airport from other Scottish fans. Again this demonstration of popular support moved Roxburgh to tears. He reflected on the Scottish support. 'It's just incredible', he said. 'The support the fans have given us is phenomenal. They're a credit to their country, and to us.' Players expressed similar sentiments. Davie McPherson gave the players' view, 'With fans like this, it makes you feel you can do almost anything.' Goal-keeper Andy Goram added, 'The fans were great. Thursday night (the match against the CIS) was something special. I'll never forget the scenes after the game, or today's reception' (*Daily Record*, 20 June 92). It was reported that, 'The Scots – players AND supporters – were such a hit in Sweden, both could be in line for EUFA Fair Play Awards' (*Daily Record*, 20 June 1992, original emphasis).

Predictions of success in these awards were half-right. The team came second, but Scotland's supporters took first place. In Autumn 1992 Roxburgh sent an open letter along with the per-sonal tokens of the 'Fair Play' award forwarded to those Scottish supporters known to the Scottish Football Association. Headed '*To the Tartan Army (Swedish Campaign)*', Roxburgh praised the supporters for boosting Scottish tourism: the Scottish Tourist Board was 'inundated with enquiries' as a result of 'the excitement, colour, good humour and respect which the Tartan Army brought to Euro '92'. He spoke again of the unity of Scottish supporters and squad:

> As I have said on many occasions, the Scottish team and the supporters are a family. The players represent the support on the pitch, while the fans represent the team off the field. In Sweden both parts of the family performed with distinction. Nobody can question the contribution that Scotland, fans and players, made to the Championship.

Roxburgh concluded with, 'the Tartan Army of 1992 are winners in every sense of the word. You're simply the best.'

CLUBBING TOGETHER FOR A SOCIAL IDENTITY

The case of Scotland in Sweden is an intriguing example of the close identification that can be achieved between supporters and team. In an exploration of the importance of the local town for its people, Worpole (1992) argued that the sense of local identity is one of the strongest emotional ties left in secular life, being perhaps the most potent symbol of an 'imaginary community'. Many individuals express strong positive emotions towards 'their' own local community. Local football teams have for a long time represented and crystallized that sense of community (Holt, 1988; Weir, 1991), which has added to the emotional significance invested in the local football club. For some supporters, the football team has become the most substantial embodiment of the local community, with the affairs of the local club being seen as a crucial determinant of the vibrancy of the local community itself (Mason, 1990).

The heady rhetoric enveloping the activities of Scotland and its supporters showed how far the distinctions between team, support and the wider community itself can be blurred (Giulianotti, 1993). Other sources of a sense of shared identity mean that, even with less extreme, and less intense, rhetorics of unity, fans are still predisposed to identify very strongly with their team. The range of beliefs about the powerful influence of fans on the performance of players and their club, and so on the outcome of matches, make it no surprise that most fans see themselves to be a central part of the club. Nor should the intensity of the identification of supporters with their club come as any surprise either. Football fans not only identify very closely with the club they support, the club symbolically becomes part of their own identity. Roxburgh's family metaphor has been used by other managers. Bill Shankly, manager of Liverpool, declared that he wanted to 'build up a family of people who could hold their heads high and say: "We're Liverpool" ' (Forsyth, 1990: 80). So it is no mere coincidence that fans identify themselves and each other by using the club's name. The intensity of the identification is matched by its complexity. The club becomes part of supporters' social identities (Abrams and Hogg, 1990; Doise, 1986; cf. Hornby, 1992), which means that there is an emotional and cognitive identification with the club, another imaginary community, for fans see themselves as the real *supporters* of the club. They see themselves as providing finance by their gate-money and believe themselves to uphold the traditions of the club: fans are the self-perceived moral custodians of the club, albeit custodians who feel exploited and frustrated at their lack of access to most club decision-making (Bull, 1992; H. Davies, 1990; Hornby, 1992; Titford with Dunphy, 1992).

The belief that the club belongs to the fans appears a distortion of economic reality, but is more a statement of the intensity of feelings fans have for their team and an expression of their belief that they are genuinely part of it. The very intense identification of fans with a team is important in exploring some of the reasons for crowd violence. There is little surprise when players overstep the mark, when their actions spill over into violence. Nor despite some comments to the contrary is anyone really surprised when club officials similarly misbehave. Yet the identification of supporters with teams is, at least in their own eyes, even more intense – and the sport itself is an event historically replete with aggressive and violent social meanings, in which supporters participate. Perceptions of a form of unity between supporters and clubs have been explored in the accounts already analysed. The sources and range of these social meanings require an exploration of the historical relationship between supporters and clubs.[6] It is the culture of football that provides the range of meanings of what it is to be a supporter and of what supporters are meant to do.

CULTURE OF QUASI-VIOLENCE

Most supporters have been socialized into their understanding of the sport through much rougher versions of the game, analogous to the old 'folk football' (cf. Elias and Dunning, 1986). The lowest levels of football differ from the professional game in many important ways: they are barely organized; there is no referee; they can often seem more like sequential acts of physical assault in the proximity of a football than a game with a football. Most games of football played are scratch matches in which the participants settle events for themselves. These players are also on other occasions spectators. Aspirant and dud footballers alike, the potential player and the eventual spectator, all commence their socialization in what amounts to a sort of contemporary folk football; in what can be a school of very hard knocks indeed. One consequence is that there is a common culture into which both players and fans are socialized alike. So supporters become football supporters through a complex socialization process with different social influences acting upon them. There is social interaction with other supporters but there are also the effects of playing some football itself.

Reports of the actions of hooligans reveal that they sometimes still participate in very rough scratch matches indeed (Allan, 1989; Ward, 1989), but that is not distinctive. Most young supporters do themselves play the sport (Henry and Love, 1992; Milson and Swannell, 1976), with the vast majority doing so at lower and rougher levels. Aggression and violence are soon recognized to be central to soccer. The socialization of the football fan leads individuals to adopt a cultural framework that stresses different values from those normally proclaimed appropriate for everyday social life. Both players and supporters are socialized into a culture of quasi-violence: a culture that accepts aggression and violence as central to the game but accompanies this acceptance with all manner of inconsistencies, uncertainties, qualifications and disagreements. For this reason it is more accurately described as a culture of quasi-violence than as a culture of violence.

Players recognize that the sport is fundamentally aggressive; certain violent actions are legitimate with others falling into categories of uncertain acceptability, toleration or strong disapproval. The extent of truly illegitimate violence is variable. Violence describes acts that are legitimate, (like strong physical tackles) or tolerated (perhaps shoving or pushing when challenging for a loose ball), or understood, if disapproved of (such as retaliation in some circumstances) or totally unacceptable (such as an unprovoked assault). The lack of clarity and implied qualifications in the last two examples only emphasize the extent to which the moral code involved is ambiguous and ambivalent. Yet the process of socialization means that this moral complexity is also very well understood by supporters. Moreover, illegitimate actions by players for their club often meet with supporter approval; even supposedly unacceptable actions can give pleasure to the fans (Hornby, 1992). At the very least, most supporters tolerate some on-field player violence.

The culture of quasi-violence also structures the fans' own activities. Off the field it is expected that fans will display pejoratively aggressive behaviour to both the opposing team and its supporters: it is understood that this may lead to the odd clash with other supporters (Canter *et al.*, 1989). This potential risk is recognized but judged to be acceptable, although violent responses can often be deemed unacceptable. So off-field behaviour is also guided by an ambiguous and ambivalent moral code. The extent of real violence is again variable. And the seriousness of a violent offence can be mitigated by a variety of factors: the nature of the action taken, the length of its duration, the extent and form of what is perceived to have been provocation (if any), the age of the participants, are all characteristics which determine whether violence will be treated seriously or even laughed off as trivial. The cultural framework of quasi-violence leads to some acceptance of aggressive and violent off-field behaviour by supporters. Despite beliefs to the contrary, this is not a recent development.

The case for some off-field violence in the past is put by a very famous Scottish supporter. Major film star Sean Connery was socialized into the values of Scottish football through playing and watching the sport. His recollections of going to football matches as a young boy, presumably in the 1930s and 1940s, outline the traditional cultural values associated with Scottish football. Connery recalled:

> When I was a boy we were all lifted over the turnstiles to get into grounds because none of us had the money to pay, and anyway, the clubs knew it was a way of keeping up interest amongst the kids. And I must say I saw a few punch-ups but it was all internal – one fan fighting another fan from another club – which I think was quite healthy in its own way because it was nothing to do with switch blades or anything like that. It was usually just overheated argument.
>
> (Forsyth 1990: 114–15)

Of course, despite Connery's romantic recollections, many fights did not fit this description. Blades and bottles were used. And the mention of bottles hints at another aspect of the Scottish tradition: the long-term association of football with alcohol (Cosgrove, 1991). Despite the charm offensive of today's Scotland supporters abroad, Connery's comments represent the fan's view of the traditional sporting values historically associated with being a supporter in Scottish football. Connery has summarized the fans' equivalent of McGrain's moral message of the importance of being hard but not dirty.

The envelopment of Scottish football in this traditional culture of quasi-violence means that the potential for real violence is present in many participants. No one can really be surprised at an admitted indiscretion by televison football commentator, Archie Macpherson, a former headteacher, and an outspoken opponent of football violence. He remembers how his frustration at Scotland's performance grew as he broadcast his commentary on the match between Scotland and the USSR in the 1982 World Cup Finals in Spain. Requiring a win to go through to the next round of the tournament, Scotland gave away a very soft goal and could only manage a draw.

A Russian in front of me, and perhaps a journalist or someone with the official party, had been raising his arms and waving them about until he was blocking our view. Attempts at persuasion failed. *In my frustration with the match I eventually punched him hard in the back*, put my mike away from my mouth and bawled at him to bugger off.

(Macpherson, 1991: 163, emphasis added)

Aggression and an acceptance of violence are central to the sport and, therefore, at the core of the cultural framework surrounding soccer. Participants, players and supporters, expect and, in different ways, accept aggression and violence. Social meanings of how to participate in the sport are derived from this cultural framework. These social meanings reflect the broad traditions of the sport but accommodate specific variations in traditional behaviour to be found at different levels of participation and in different geographical locations. Although the culture of quasi-violence is not the same as violence itself, aggression and an aura of violence are essential elements in the cultural framework that determines the experience of being involved in football. That is why it is necessary to explore the nature of the subjective experience that football matches produce.

EXCITEMENT AND SOCCER: PEAK EXPERIENCES

Supporters can feel bored at matches but sometimes they have no doubt that they have had an experience of real emotional intensity. Football fans report experiencing special peaks of excitement (Bull, 1992; Hornby, 1992; Titwood with Dunphy, 1992; R. Turner, 1990) which are not unrelated to their perceived participation in the match. The intense identity with the club, that makes supporters feel that they are as important as the players, means that these feelings are very potent elements in the experiences of soccer supporters.

John Peel, Britain's leading progressive music disc jockey, has described his intensely emotional experiences watching football. When Kennedy scored Liverpool's winner against AS Roma in the 1984 European Champions Cup Final in Paris, Peel 'cried like a baby'. Peel is uncertain whether he loves football or music more, but admits that:

I suppose I can't think of any musical equivalent to the feeling I felt when Allan Kennedy scored in the Parc des Princes. I can't think of anything to match that musically. I actually thought, if I die now, I won't care, you know, nothing could ever be as good as this again. I always say, rather flippantly, but it's not a million miles from the truth, that football supplies many of the requirements that other people seek and find in religion, with the difference that you can actually see the truth of it being demonstrated on the pitch every Saturday afternoon, and that's enormously gratifying.

(*When Saturday Comes*, Sep./Oct. 1987)

Peel's report of the strength of his feelings may appear extravagant to the non-supporter, but the common recourse to metaphors of addiction or obsession (for example Hornby, 1992) to describe supporters' feelings towards their clubs says much about the power and intensity of their identification with a club. Nor is being addicted to or obsessed by a football club a class phenomenon. Some rich fans, such as Blackburn's Jack Walker and Wimbledon's Sam Hamman, have either purchased or bank-rolled the club they supported. A religious metaphor is used by Peel in an attempt to describe the deep emotions he experienced supporting his team. His full account presents some insights into his intense identification with the club and the emotions aroused in him.

Steve Cram made a very telling statement of the intensity of both club identification and excitement experienced by football supporters in an interview given before the 1992 FA Cup Final between Sunderland and Liverpool. Despite his great success as an athlete, Cram claims that his identity is as much that of a Sunderland supporter as an athlete. Although Cram has been world record holder for the mile, 1500 and 2000 metres, 1,500 metres champion at the World, European and Commonwealth Games, and Olympic silver medal winner at the same distance, he still claims that he would have exchanged all of this athletic success to have played for Sunderland. Even more significant is that Cram compared and evaluated his experiences of supporting Sunderland as usually being at least as exciting as running in a race. And he expected the experience of being a fan at the Cup Final would beat even the ultimate high offered by athletics. He explained: 'Athletics can provide the atmosphere you get at, say, a tight away match at Wimbledon. God knows, my heart will be pumping harder a week on Saturday than it was at the Olympics' (*Scotland on Sunday*, 26 April 1992).

The interviews with Peel and Cram reveal the sheer intensity of the emotions football fans experience through their involvement with a football club. Both of these accounts indicate clearly that soccer matches can provide peak experiences, not just for the players, but also for the fans. Cram and Peel obtain their peak experiences by supporting their teams. Peak or optimal experiences have been characterized as being autotelic: an individual's actions are explained by the experience being itself intrinsically motivating, which is characteristic of desired leisure activities (Csikszentmihalyi and Csikszentmihalyi, 1988b; Csikszentmihalyi and Larson, 1984). In studies of optimal or peak experiences individuals reported their subjective experience that the activity was rewarding in and of itself: they experienced 'flow'; they were at one with the action. Individuals reported intense enjoyment. Studies of creative work or prized leisure activities frequently found this heightened quality of subjective experience. Settings for the individualistic attainment of a 'flow' experience are primarily those that make creative demands. Peak experiences can also be gained from leisure activities which are essentially social and liminoid or liminal (V. Turner, 1974), but there are some elements generally common to all experiences of flow.

A general precondition is that there is a balance between participants' skills and the challenges set them. As flow experiences are intrinsically motivating, there must be a challenge but that must offer the real possibility of being met. Too big a gap between a challenge and the skills required to overcome it, leads to disillusionment and disinterest: too small a gap and boredom ensues. It is meeting the challenge that leads to enjoyment, but the challenge means that not all of the flow experience is pleasurable. A set of common features is characteristic of most flow experiences. There is a certain loss of self-consciousness: action and awareness become merged, with attention centred and concentration focused on the participation in the occasion itself. Becoming so absorbed in the occasion leads to a transcendence of the individual's sense of self. Self-absorption is rendered impossible: the self is so engaged with the action that it becomes (sub)merged with(in) the flow. Participants can experience feelings, perhaps illusions, of competence and control. Actions are directed towards unambiguous goals and the feedback on the results of the activities is immediate. Flow experiences are autotelic: the enjoyment comes from the involvement in the activity itself. Csikszentmihalyi (1988a: 34) explains that 'the goal is really just an excuse to make the experience possible'.

Flow experiences can arise from individually challenging situations or from certain social occasions. Liminal situations, for example ritually rich social occasions such as carnival, in which normal social roles are suspended, are especially likely to produce flow experiences. They also produce a very strong sense of *communitas* (Csikszentmihalyi, 1988a; V. Turner, 1974). Participants experience an especially strong and emotionally rewarding sense of closeness with those others present. Kapferer (1984) has stressed that spectators are not peripheral but actors central to the event itself. In a sense the sum of their parts makes the whole: the peak experience comes from participating in the social event and their participation ensures that it is a liminal social event.

Attendance at soccer matches offers a range of different potential roles from mere spectator through to fanatical supporter (see MacAloon, 1984). For participants in the event, soccer matches provide occasions that are liminal, produce a deep sense of *communitas*, and offer peak or flow experiences: they can become immersed in the flow. That is obviously true for players. It also describes the effect of soccer on those other participants, the supporters who strongly identify with the club (Bull, 1992; Hornby, 1992; R. Turner, 1990), who can recount tales similar to those of Cram and Peel and whose intense sense of social identity is still further deepened by the sense of community seared in them by the shared experience of the occasion.

Supporters do not just identify very closely with their clubs, their social identity incorporates their club affiliation. Social identities are very complex, multi-dimensional, hybrid phenomena (Boyle, 1992; Finn, 1991a and b, 1994a and b). The extent to which club affiliation plays a prominent part in any one individual's social identity will be variable. The triggering of that element as a salient feaure of an individual's social identity will vary across different social situations. For some only the social events around the football match will induce a sense of collectively sharing in that social identity: for others this social identity will be much more widespread. To be a football supporter requires an individual to recognize some shared identification not only with the club, but particularly with the other supporters. Flow experiences dramatically intensify the feeling of being part of a community based around the team. The result is that fans will in victory embrace strangers, their fellow club fans. Despair brings mixed results, but there can be commiseration with strangers. Flow experiences allow an open expression of shared, collective emotionality: an outpouring of joy or sadness, strengthening a common social identity.

Not all matches produce flow experiences though: some are reported to be boring and dispiriting events (Bull, 1992; Hornby, 1992; R. Turner, 1990). Yet most supporters return time and time again and do sometimes experience that sense of being lost in the match itself. Apparently at one with the mass of the crowd, supporters believe that their efforts are also at one with the team. The characteristics required for a flow experience are fulfilled vicariously. Unambiguous goals are sought by both players and fans: both receive the same immediate feedback. Scoring goals is more than just an excuse for the experience, but other aspects of the game can also produce flow experiences. It is the optimal experience that is sought by the soccer fan: it is this that supporters primarily recall. The experience of the highs allows the 'obsessed' supporter to accept the less welcome lows (Bull, 1992; Hornby, 1992; Titford and Dunphy, 1992; R. Turner, 1990). The football fan wishes to be excited by the match; to become lost in the action. The quasi-violent culture of the sport is important in creating that sense of excitement. However, that has to be distinguished from actual violence. The accounts of Cram and Peel show that peak experiences can result from the emotional tension induced by the sheer sense of involvement in the match; an involvement marked by the personal sense of commitment to a shared social identity with players and fellow supporters alike. However, the culture of quasi-violence can sometimes produce genuine on-field violence, and for the committed football fan that can be a very good thing; it can transform an otherwise boring match into an exciting and gripping social occasion. Violence offers supporters the potential for realizing a flow experience. Hornby discloses that on-field violence is an essential characteristic of a really enjoyable match:

> one has to conclude, regretfully and with a not inconsiderable degree of Corinthian sadness, that there is nothing like a

punch-up to enliven an otherwise dull game. The side-effects are invariably beneficent – the players and the crowd become more committed, the plot thickens, the pulse quickens – and as long as the match doesn't degenerate as a consequence into some kind of sour grudge-match, brawls strike me as being a pretty desirable feature, like a roof-terrace or a fireplace. If I were a sportswriter or a representative of the football authorities, then no doubt I would purse my lips, make disapproving noises, insist that the transgressors be brought to justice – argy-bargy, like soft drugs, would be no fun if it were officially sanctioned. Luckily, however, I have no such responsibility: I am a fan, with no duty to toe the moral line whatsoever.

(Hornby, 1992: 237)

Connery captured the Scottish fan's off-field moral code. Despite his denial of any moral line, Hornby presents an account of the fan's on-field moral code. Hornby may be English, but his words speak for most supporters in Scotland as well. Any apparent ambiguity about hard or dirty play or about the line between legitimate and illegitimate violence is readily resolved by Hornby. He is aware of the apparent contradiction in societal attitudes to violence. Yet there is no real ambivalence in his eventual conclusion. The only qualification is his concern that real violence does not then dominate the match-events.

Hornby's account again emphasizes that it is the culture of quasi-violence rather than violence *per se* that is important for football matches. Aggression and some violence are often essential if supporters are to attain the excitement necessary for a flow experience. Again there is a parallel between players and supporters. Professional players attest to the need to be sufficiently aggressive to lift themselves up to play the game. Prior to one important match, Gordon Strachan (Strachan with Gallagher, 1991) felt that Leeds United players were too complacent. He lied to Vinny Jones that he had heard two opposing players boast of their intentions to inflict physical injury on Jones. Jones, a hard and dirty player, was enraged when he heard this. His dressing-room aggression and on-field violence sufficiently motivated the rest of the Leeds team with the result that Leeds played very competitively and won.

Hornby's and Strachan's reports illustrate some parallels between supporting and playing and reveal again how violence and quasi-violence can shade into one another. For players or supporters of a team, aggression and violence are intrinsic to the sport, and quasi-violence is central to the excitement of the event. Violence need not be a result of excitement: it can itself be the cause of excitement, as Hornby admits on behalf of fans and Strachan demonstrates for players, by winding up Vinny Jones to get other Leeds players sufficiently aroused. But this also stresses the most important part. Violence is not an end in itself; nor even is quasi-violence, which is intrinsic to the game. To paraphrase Csikszentmihalyi, violence or quasi-violence 'is really just an excuse to make the experience possible'. They can make flow experiences possible, but peak experiences can result from other factors as well.

That is why, despite the parallels between playing and support-ing, despite the shared culture of quasi-violence with its range of common social meanings for soccer behaviour, and despite the social identification of supporters with their team, and common beliefs to the contrary notwithstanding, there need be no direct correspondence between behaviour on and off the pitch. Many factors mediate between the available cultural meanings that guide social actions and the actual behaviour of players and supporters alike. Just as players and supporters can behave in totally independent ways, so can the behaviour within these two groups vary widely on the same occasion. The culture of quasi-violence provides the broad framework from which social mean-ings of how to participate in the sport are derived. The historical evolution of the intensity of the identification between teams and supporters is important. Yet it is a serious error to adopt a crude determinism between actual violence and the culture of quasi-violence: these cultural meanings describe the context within which violence can occur, but it does not explain specific inci-dents of soccer-related violence, let alone explain those many highly charged occasions when no violence occurs.

For example, while Aitken was urging the Scottish team to adopt an antagonistic approach and 'get into the Swedish bas-tards' in the 1990 World Cup, the fans were creating a different atmosphere altogether. The culturally framed social meanings available to supporters are not incapable of innovative adaptation: it is the flow experience, rather than the route to achieving it that matters. Scotland's supporters have evolved social practices that Giulianotti (1991, 1993, 1994) has captured well in the description 'carnivalesque'. The extent of this change can be overstated. The voyage of Scotland supporters to matches, especially to Wembley to play England, has long had its liminal dimensions (see Cosgrove, 1991; Forsyth, 1990; Moorhouse, 1989). Fans have given these dimensions much greater emphasis: Scotland supporters now seek to create the potential for peak experiences by their own performance around the social event of the match itself. There is a deliberate attempt to create a good time and to include fans of other nations as well, thus creating a sense of *communitas* for all. Flow experiences are the result of this mobile and on-going mini-carnival.[7] The football match has become the centre around which the whole social occasion itself is organized, but no longer is the match itself necessarily the central event. Instead the supporters have taken a much greater role for themselves. It is the occasion itself that counts: they are important participants within it (Giulianotti, 1993).

The behaviour of these fans demonstrates how the culture of quasi-violence in which Scottish soccer is immersed does not necessarily lead directly into acts of real violence. The cultural framework has not been totally discarded by these supporters: they still attend to some of its cultural elements. Anti-English sentiment is very evident (Giulianotti, 1991, 1993). Vigorous support is still given to the team. Flow experiences are still attainable by this vicarious, if more traditional route. However, the creation of the carnivalesque, with the more direct, collective participation of supporters in their own social occasion, is much more likely to produce a flow experience and a heightened sense of *communitas* than attending to the game alone, as the boring experiences of more conventional supporters have shown (for example, Hornby, 1992). The carnivalesque is a positive adaptation of cultural traditions, leading to more common intensely enjoyable experiences for Scotland's fans. Yet this displacement of footballing success from its usual position of central importance has led media pundits to condemn the Scottish fans for the alleged crime of taking themselves, rather than football, too seriously. Accused of 'embracing failure', their actions were absurdly judged to be 'ludicrous and dangerous' (Herald, 11 September 1992). Unfortunately, some other Scottish fans, who have also adapted elements of the culture of Scottish football to ensure more regular flow experiences, do undertake some activities which deserve to be described as dangerous.

THE FLIGHT FROM FAN TO HOOLIGAN

The historically derived range of social meanings of what it means to be a supporter makes some violent responses likely. Socialization into any cultural milieu is individually differentiated by a multiplicity of potential factors. Some misunderstandings of, confusions over, even differences of opinion about, the role of real violence must be expected amongst those socialized into a culture of quasi-violence. The emphasis on aggression and various forms of violence added to the marked blurring of the distinction between players and supporters makes inevitable the considerable confusion over the dividing lines between the acceptable and unacceptable social practices of being a fan. Understanding this cultural complexity means that violence is more accepted by regular soccer supporters (Canter *et al.*, 1989).

An everyday analysis of the acceptability of instances of violence around football does depend on a complex, sophisticated, moral calculus, which is associated with types of violent incidents that can be seen to be linked in some sort of way to the sports event. Many hooligan outbursts can be explained *post facto* in terms of immediately precipitating factors: but many cannot. The presence of apparently identical objective factors can result in no disturbances at all. The importance of adopting a richer and fuller societal psychological approach is clear (Finn, 1992; Himmelweit, 1990; Jahoda, 1989). Objective factors are important but an examination of the subjective understandings of those involved is essential, and their subjective belief system, their activities and accompanying set of social meanings, need to be located within the appropriate societal and historical value-system.

That becomes even more necessary when attempting to gain an understanding of those about whom most puzzlement and alarm is expressed: the persistent perpetrators of problem behaviour, alleged by others and proudly proclaimed by themselves to be hooligans. One reason that hooliganism itself remains misunderstood is because it is usually judged to be so different from the behaviour of other fans, let alone humanity in general. Given the appalling racism, sexism and violence of many hooligans, and the fatal consequences of some of their most notorious endeavours, this is unsurprising. But such judgements are also unhelpful, often overstated and fail to advance any understanding of football hooliganism (Whannel, 1979). Much of the purpose of hooliganism is not dissimilar to the concerns of other supporters or of humanity at large. Hooligans also seek peak experiences, but the means they employ do differ from those usually understood to deliver pleasurably intense experiences. An analysis of interviews with some Scottish hooligans, supplemented by observational data, will explore these similarities (Finn, 1987, 1989).

In the early 1980s adolescent Scottish football hooliganism adopted a new style, which emphasized smart dress-sense. Ideally designer-label casual wear was worn, even when group members displayed their other most obvious characteristic, fighting. Inevitably these fighting fans became known as 'soccer casuals'. Two clubs, Glasgow Celtic and Heart of Midlothian in Edinburgh, made special efforts to stop casuals becoming established among the fans. Directors of both clubs were very vocal in their criticisms of these new hooligans and their supposedly neo-fascist politics. Both made it clear that the directors wished the club's supporters to have no association with these groups: Celtic fans certainly took this message to heart. The supposedly right-wing beliefs of the casuals were at odds with the radical and working-class imagery associated with Celtic (Finn, 1991a and b; 1994a, b and c; Murray, 1984; Walker, 1990). So some Celtic supporters administered rough justice to those casuals who went to Celtic Park. Casuals were not only verbally abused. Some casuals were given what is termed 'a good kicking'. Ironically, these acts of violence were believed by Celtic supporters to be justified to protect the club's good name. Presumably these fans believed hooliganism literally had to be stamped out. Whether Hearts supporters followed a similar campaign in support of the club's anti-casuals crusade is unclear, but both clubs had some early success. As a result, the evolution of casual groups was different at these clubs, but eventually it did occur (Finn, 1987, 1989).

Interviews with casuals who followed Rangers were revealing.[8] They explained their main function was 'fighting wi' other mobs'. They also claimed to follow a moral code which, like Connery's comments, legitimized some fighting in specific circumstances. For example, they only fought with other similar groups. Other fans were not threatened: there was no danger to others. When pressed that this was simply not true, it was admitted that unfortunate 'accidents' had taken place[9] and some attacks on supporters who were not casuals were also justified. However, the casuals asserted that their values were very much the same as those of the wider community (see Mungham and Pearson, 1975). They stressed their decency and manliness compared to the many perverts they believed could be found in society. They also firmly believed that many other football supporters deserved to be called hooligans as well. Furthermore, their statements revealed that their activities, especially those likely to result in a violent exchange with another group, allowed them to achieve peak experiences: these were 'flow experiences'. The strength of their feelings was also confirmed by observation of their state of excitement on match days.[10] These participants did not use flow as a metaphor for their feelings but the characteristics can be recognized in their self-reports.

When asked how it felt to be involved with the casuals in a fight, one prominent member of the Rangers casuals stated, 'Brilliant! Efter you dae another mob – even better.' That was the point of the experience. He was neither keen on being really hurt nor did he wish to inflict serious injury on others. A real confrontation, especially when followed by a successful outcome, led to almost indescribable feelings. Rangers casuals claimed to have been the first to overcome the Aberdeen casuals, who had been seen up until then to be Scotland's top fighting team. The jumbled up comments that constitute the extract below convey something of the recollected excitement and sense of togetherness invoked by one casual when he attempted to relate how he felt that day. (His comment on the leaderless structure of Rangers casuals should be noted by those who persist in the belief that football hooligans are highly and hierarchically organized.)

> See efter ye get the ither mob, ye've never seen aught. We don't huv a leader. We were the first mob ever tae dae Aberdeen, right? An' that wiz up at Dundas Street. It wiz like winnin' the pools. We jist – Ah wiz thrown in a butcher's shoap. Ah cracked ma heid that day. An' we went doon that street jumpin' up an' doon. It wiz like winnin' the pools or the cup-final. An' everyone's dancin' an' grabbin' each other by the arms.

These comments reveal a sense of *communitas* in a shared peak experience (cf. Williams, 1991). Flow experiences do bond individuals more closely together. Amongst the casuals, it is essential that group members do intensely identify with one another. Given the considerable uncertainty in the world of the casuals, some constancy is essential. Security for the casuals depends on the group. Other members need to be reliable: mutual trust is essential. One casual's response can determine whether another casual receives assistance, or a bad beating, or even worse. A very close sense of a social identity is necessarily forged in these circumstances: the result is an intense feeling of cohesion and camaraderie.

The self-reports of those who have written about their involvement in hooliganism place even greater stress on the significance of flow experiences. Jay Allan was a prominent figure among Aberdeen casuals. Although he overstates both his own leadership role and the organized nature of the Aberdeen casuals,[11] his comments on the importance of the feelings he experienced do have the ring of authenticity. Allan (1989: 76–7) recalls one fight in which Aberdeen were supposedly outnumbered:

> we went into the rail bar and you wouldn't believe the scene. Although most of us were cut, bruised, and sore, we were hand-shaking and hugging each other. We did our city proud; we did it for Aberdeen. You would have thought we had just won an Olympic gold medal for our country in a relay race.

In writing his account Allan is obviously well aware of the content of the usual discourses about danger and fighting. He knows that most people find his enjoyment of these activities odd. But what Allan reports is that fighting leads to a peak experience that can be equated with little else in most people's lives. It is the arousal that matters. Only skiing or high-board diving, which are classic sources of flow rather than means of obtaining pleasure, are at all comparable.

> Most people can't understand how it could possibly be fun to be punched, booted and butted and to have bottles and stones thrown at you but believe me, I've experienced it, and when your [*sic*] in the thick of the action even sex doesn't come close to the feeling of being hyped-up so much.
>
> (ibid.: 135)

Allan's account illustrates that fighting is really only the excuse for achieving a flow experience. It is not all pleasurable, but it is highly enjoyable. Physical pain to the self is of little consequence to an individual who is submerged in the intensity of the flow experience itself. As casuals get into the flow, they transcend the turbulent torrent around them by becoming at one with it.

Ward (1989) has also reported his own football-associated experiences of violence. Fear, or in this extract 'terror', is used in an attempt to identify the intensity of Ward's feelings, and the extent of the challenge he faced, when he was engaged in fighting: the account demonstrates that terror is not used as an accurate label for the totality of the emotions he felt:

> we were getting beaten to hell . . . it seems like hours when you are on the receiving end. When it is all over and you are safely on the train going home, then the sheer terror recedes; but while you are going through it the experience is indescribable, and no drug could possibly reproduce that same feeling.
>
> (Ward, 1989: 48).

Overcoming this sort of challenge requires a number of different skills. Individual hooligans have to overcome their own personal fears, to fight their own stomachs as one casual described it, before they can evaluate their own prowess at fighting itself. Nor is this all that is required: those social skills that allow them to retain their coherence as a group are essential. Although Ward refers to feeling terror, the experience itself remains so intensely and positively overwhelming that he is unable to find any adequate description of the totality of the feelings that result. Ward talks of the 'tremendous feelings of identity' and the 'incredibly strong sense of belonging' he feels at football matches. Even stronger bonds are formed amongst those who fight together. Like accounts offered by other hooligans, Ward's comments are strangely reminiscent of those made by more conventional followers of football (for example Hornby, 1992). To explain the attraction of the experience of fighting, Ward hints at an addiction metaphor very similar to that used by fans to explain their attraction to the experience of supporting their team: both positions point towards the importance of flow experiences as motivational factors in football-related activities. Ward (1989: 180–1) identifies the optimal experience that results from fighting:

> Politicians and people who haven't experienced the thrill of football do not understand what makes a hooligan tick, but if any one of those people who condemn people who fight at

football could experience the feeling then perhaps they could begin to understand.

It is said that the brain can create its own drug to beat any of the most powerful opiates. If the substance created within a football hooligan to give that feeling could be marketed, then it would be called an ecstasy pill.

FLOWING TO A NEW SOCIAL IDENTITY – AWAY FROM FOOTBALL (AND BOREDOM)

The similarities in the descriptions of subjective experience between hooligans and other football fans are telling, but one similarity between the casuals and the rest has very different consequences. All who go regularly to football matches admit that there are occasions when they have experienced boredom at football matches (for example Hornby, 1992). However, those Rangers casuals interviewed now found football to be so boring that they were no longer very interested in the match itself. Observation of casual groups at football games indeed showed that much of their time was spent identifying opposing casual groups and gesticulating aggressively in their direction or talking in groups among themselves: direct attention paid to the game itself was often minimal.[12] One casual even claimed that it was 'cause the fitba is borin' that he had become a casual. He found football to be so boring, that now he only met up with the casuals for pre-match battles in the town centre; when the rest continued on to the match, he returned home.

As football games could not be relied on to produce flow experiences, the casuals' own activities produced a much higher emotional return, much more often. The very prospect of action aroused them. The uncertainty around the casuals' day out meant that it was frequently possible to perceive some action to be a real prospect, even in objectively unlikely circumstances. Peak experiences at the match had been replaced by the search for optimal experiences only loosely connected to the match itself. Flow experiences shared with other casuals in these prolonged periods of uncertainty and comparatively short bursts of sustained aggression or actual violence forged a new social identity among participants. These adolescents now identified themselves primarily as casuals.

One interviewee had been one of the original Celtic casuals.

His story was that after having taken too many beatings from other Celtic supporters for this deviation from social acceptability he gave up going to Celtic matches. Then he bridged the inter-ethnic divide, and went on to become one of the most prominent of the Rangers casuals. Although he remained somewhat critical of the Rangers club and its supporters, for him being a casual was much more important than the historical antagonisms between Protestant Scots and Catholic Irish-Scots and between the two Glasgow clubs most associated with these communities (Finn, 1991a and b, 1994a, b and c; Moorhouse, 1984; Murray, 1984).

His action in joining the Rangers casuals was, however, made much easier by their relatively loose identification with Rangers. At one point Rangers had to play a series of matches against clubs that the casuals considered posed little challenge – at least off the park. Rangers casuals judged that these clubs were unlikely to bring much support, let alone any significant number of casuals, when they visited Glasgow to meet Rangers. The clubs due to be visited by Rangers were also similarly dismissed as being unworthy of serious consideration by Rangers casuals. An apparently insoluble problem had a very easy solution. Some of these 'Rangers' casuals attached themselves to Partick Thistle, another Glasgow team, for around a month.[13] The temporarily ex-Rangers casuals found an additional benefit to accompanying a team in a lower Scottish division: often the policing was much less rigorous. That made some action much more likely. Over subsequent seasons casuals linked to Rangers adopted this alternative identity if they judged that the action around Rangers matches was likely to be disappointing.

The culture of quasi-violence encapsulates social meanings that allow for aggression and some violence. Traditionally soccer has emphasized strong identities among its fan groups. Football is meant to be exciting. That is what attracted the casuals in the first place; these football hooligans can not be classified as football's outsiders (cf. Dunning et al., 1988; Murphy et al., 1990). Football matches, though, are an uncertain source of flow experiences. Activities undertaken by the casuals are a more reliable source of peak experiences. There is a parallel here with Scotland supporters in pursuit of the carnivalesque. Scotland supporters have also evolved an approach to supporting their team that no longer prioritizes the game or its outcome. The casuals have evolved an approach that renders the team, the football game and its result practically irrelevant. For the casuals there is another game in town: their own match against the opposition. Rather than experience flow through some vicarious relationship with a soccer team and its efforts, the casuals make their own sport. The requirements for a flow experience are fulfilled. They may even gain 'macro-flow' experiences: they face situations in which they perceive both the challenges and required skills to be high (Csikszentmihalyi, 1982; Csikszentmihalyi and LeFevre, 1989). *Their* objectives are relatively unambiguous. Feedback on the effects of casual actions is immediately clear. Strong feelings of *communitas* are aroused in social episodes with a liminoid quality, thus ensuring the development of a very powerful shared social identity as a casual. So strong is this particular facet of these adolescents' social identities that it tends to dominate the total complex of their individual social identities: they are casuals above everything else.

Adolescents experiment with a variety of potential social identities. Much adolescent activity is specifically directed towards identity work (Beloff, 1986) and the soccer casuals have the same needs as other adolescents; the casual identity itself provides a certain cachet. Few other adolescent identities attract such media attention or lead to such close police scrutiny: this attention can also add to the flow experience.[14] The highly sought after flow experiences are important during adolescence and are most commonly found in leisure activities, often associated with sports (Csikszentmihalyi and Larson, 1984). Although many activities of the casuals are socially deviant, their subcultural *milieu* is derived from the wider culture of quasi-violence of Scottish football. Their activities not only make some sense within this framework, but they share some values with other Scottish football fans. The purpose of their actions is little different from that of the rest of humanity: they seek peak experiences. The search takes place within the social context of football, and in a deviant form, but their aim differs little from those seeking flow experiences as spectators at all sorts of dramatic events, ranging from large-scale sports events through theatre to grand opera. The casuals and other groups of football hooligans at sport can even provide considerable excitement, sometimes flow, for other supporters. The American writer Bill Buford (1992: 88), a participant observer of English football hooligans, details a series of assaults on the populace of Turin and describes how the hooligans, and he himself, felt during the experience:

'It's going off, it's going off.' Everyone around . . . was excited. It was an excitement that verged on being something greater, an emotion more transcendent – joy at the very least, but more like ecstasy. There was an intense energy about it; it was impossible not to feel some of the thrill.

As the violence grew, so did the build-up of excitement, and Buford was worried by its effect on him. He continued running with the group. He says, 'I felt weightless. I felt nothing would happen to me. I felt anything might happen to me' (ibid.: 92). Buford experienced a flow experience of sorts as a result of his attempt to be a participant observer. Football hooligans may use deviant means to obtain their peak experiences, but there is nothing abnormal about that experience itself. Buford demonstrates that even the supposedly abnormal hooligan flow experience can touch the emotions of a much wider section of the population than many would like, or will allow themselves, to believe.[15]

NOTES

1 Definitions of hooliganism are imprecise; the description has often been applied to activities that were disapproved of rather than threatening. See, for example, Ingham *et al.* (1978) and Melnick (1986). For self-styled hooligans the description is now used a mark of esteem: its use is now appropriate when describing these groups and their actions.

2 See *Sociological Review*, 1991, 39, no. 3. The editorial comments were made in *Sociological Review*, 1992, 40: 435–6. The analysis presented in this chapter essentially diverges from previous explanations, though there are some points of possible convergence. Limited space, perhaps fortunately, rules out yet another contribution to what has become an overheated exchange with a tendency to play the man rather than his ideas.

3 A societal psychological perspective has been outlined by Finn (1992) and Himmelweit (1990). This chapter will heed the advice offered by Jahoda (1989) on the characteristics of a truly social approach to psychology.

4 For example, see the contributions in the *International Social Science Journal*, 1992, 44, no. 132, *Thinking about Violence*.

5 The common hooligan claim to observe a 'moral code' is briefly explored below.

6 Limits on space have meant that this analysis, based on the history of violence around small clubs has been omitted. Historical and contemporary evidence from these levels of football has also been removed from the subsequent section, thus weakening the account of the culture of quasi-violence. I intend to present fuller treatments of these issues elsewhere.

7 English fans have shown some signs of similar ventures but claims by Redhead (1990, 1991) that hooligan behaviour in England is now out of fashion have sadly proved to be over-optimistic. Nor, despite some boastful claims, is it out of fashion in Scottish *club* football either.

8 The responses reported here were obtained in individual tape-recorded interviews, followed by a tape-recorded group session, with a small group of five casuals from the east end of Glasgow. Observation confirmed that two of these casuals were prominent in the wider grouping of Rangers casuals. Both had made a couple of court appearances because of their casual activities. A number of informal ad hoc interviews were carried out with members of various casual groupings throughout the 1980s. Observation of casuals and other football supporters also took place throughout this period.

9 A woman had been badly injured by a misdirected bottle in one of Glasgow's city centre shopping precincts three days before these interviews. One casual denied that an event like this would even happen, before verifying that the incident had taken place. Each casual stated that they did not like to endanger the general public. Other incidents were also recounted. Some genuine concern appeared to be expressed. But the overall feeling was that this was simply fate and quite outwith their control. If another group of casuals was present then that left them with no option other than to attempt to fight them: 'it couldnae be helped' if passers-by became trapped in the middle of it all.

10 On match days the level of arousal was evident. At the end of one match Rangers casuals were very excited as they tried to organize themselves and locate the casuals who followed the opposition. Finally some contact was made and a chase ensued. At the end of the exchange my two main informants reappeared at the head of the Rangers casuals in an extremely excited state. Both were very flushed and highly agitated, with wide staring eyes, as they continued to look around for some opponents with whom to fight. I was relieved that my earlier presence and lengthy conversation with one of these casuals during the match had been explained away to the others by his referring to me as his big brother.

11 I am indebted to Richard Giulianotti for this personal communication, which confirmed my own observations of the structure of the Aberdeen casuals in 1983–5.

12 This is very clear on match days. When not attending to the whereabouts of opposing casuals, a lot of time was simply given over to socializing with one another. At the match referred to earlier, someone produced photographs of a number of them 'marching' in the

streets of Ayr as Partick Thistle casuals. A lot of time was taken up looking at these photographs and finding the other casuals who featured in them, so that they could be shown them as well. The rest of the time was largely given over to small talk.

13 The appearance of the photographs led to the casuals discussing their reasons for becoming Thistle casuals. Observations of the composition of the Thistle casuals, supplemented by informal interviews, showed that this option remained a possible one for Rangers casuals throughout the rest of the 1980s.

14 Attempts to out-manoeuvre the police, plus verbally abusive exchanges with them, seemed to be another, secondary, source of flow experiences for the casuals. The close attention of the police was certainly seen as a source of some status. Some other supporters seemed to bestow some status on the casuals by apparently approving of their activities.

15 The evidence presented here conflicts with most explanations put forward to explain football hooliganism. Space precludes a detailed critique. The Leicester argument is that football hooliganism is produced by an allegiance to 'rough' working-class male culture. The class aspect is circular and thus not open to disconfirmation. The gender association can be shown to be overstated. After serious attacks on St Johnstone fans at Stirling railway station, three casuals were charged with 'mobbing and rioting, stabbing David Barnett and assaulting five other St Johnstone fans' (*Daily Record*, 30 November 1988). As well as being found guilty of this charge, all three were also found guilty of possessing offensive weapons. The dominant figure, who abused the judge when he passed sentence, was sent to prison, leading to the headline 'Jail for soccer riot *girl*' (emphasis added).

ACKNOWLEDGEMENTS

I am very grateful for the facilities, assistance and many kindnesses granted to me by Professor Alan McGregor, Training and Unemployment Research Unit, University of Glasgow, during my sabbatical period there. Dr Andy McArthur of the same unit provided invaluable information on the views and activities of the Tartan Army. Richard Giulianotti deserves special thanks for managing to reduce a chapter three times too long to a manageable size, while still retaining much of its argument.

REFERENCES

Abrams, D. and M. Hogg (1990) (eds) *Social Identity Theory: constructive and critical advances*, Hemel Hempstead: Harvester Wheatsheaf.

Allan, J. (1989) *Bloody Casuals: diary of a football hooligan*, Glasgow: Famedram.

Beloff, H. (1986) (ed.) *Getting into Life*, London: Methuen.

Billig, M., S. Condor, D. Edwards, M. Gane, D. Middleton, and A. Radley (1988) *Ideological Dilemmas: a social psychology of everyday thinking*, London: Sage.

Boyle, R. (1992) 'We are Celtic Supporters', paper presented to the International Conference, 'Soccer, Culture and Identity', University of Aberdeen, April.

Buford, B. (1992) *Among the Thugs*, London: Mandarin.

Bull, D. (1992) *We'll Support You Evermore: keeping faith in football*, London: Duckworth.

Canter, D., M. Comber and D. L. Uzzell (1989) *Football in its Place: an environmental psychology of football grounds*, London: Routledge.

Cosgrove, S. (1991) *Hampden Babylon: sex and scandal in Scottish football*, Edinburgh: Canongate Press.

Csikszentmihalyi, M. (1982) 'Towards a Psychology of Optimal Experience', in L. Wheeler (ed.) *Review of Personality and Social Psychology, vol. 2*, Beverly Hills, CA: Sage.

—— (1988a) 'The Flow Experience', in Csikszentmihalyi and Csikszentmihalyi (eds) (1988b).

Csikszentmihalyi, M. and I. S. Csikszentmihalyi (eds) (1988b) *Optimal Experience: psychological studies of flow in consciousness*, Cambridge: Cambridge University Press.

Csikszentmihalyi, M. and R. Larson (1984) *Being Adolescent: conflict and growth in the teenage years*, New York: Basic Books.

Csikszentmihalyi, M. and J. LeFevre (1989) 'Optimal Experience in Work and Leisure', *Journal of Personality and Social Psychology*, 56: 815–22.

Davies, H. (1990) *My Life in Football*, Edinburgh: Mainstream.

Davies, P. (1991) *All Played Out: the full story of Italia '90*, London: Mandarin.

Doise, W. (1986) *Levels of Explanation in Social Psychology*, Cambridge/ Paris: Cambridge University Press/Maison des Sciences de l'Homme.

Dunning, E., P. Murphy and J. Williams (1988) *The Roots of Football Hooliganism*, London: Routledge.

Edwards, D. and J. Potter (1992) *Discursive Psychology*. London: Sage.

Elias, N. and E. Dunning (eds) (1986) *Quest for Excitement: sport and leisure in the civilizing process*, Oxford: Basil Blackwell.

Finn, G. P. T. (1987) 'Casual Talk and Casual Observation: the phenomenon of the "soccer casuals" ', invited paper to the Annual Scientific Meeting of the Scottish Branch of the British Psychological Society, Glasgow, February.

—— (1989) ' "Tae be there an' that": the creation of social realities and social identities among the football "casuals" ', paper to the Annual Conference of the Scottish Branch of the British Psychological Society, 'The Psychology of Adolescence and Youth', Glasgow, September.

—— (1991a) 'Racism, Religion and Social Prejudice: Irish Catholic clubs, soccer and Scottish society. I – The historical roots of prejudice', *International Journal of the History of Sport*, 8 (1): 70–93.

—— (1991b) 'Racism, Religion and Social Prejudice: Irish Catholic clubs, soccer and Scottish society. II – Social identities and conspiracy theories', *International Journal of the History of Sport*, 8 (3): 370–97.

—— (1992) 'Societal Psychology: some approaches', invited address to the Annual Conference of the Scottish Branch of the British Psychological Society, Perth, October.

—— (1994a) 'Racism, Religion and Social Prejudice: Irish Catholic clubs, soccer and Scottish society. III – Rangers and conspiracy theories', *International Journal of the History of Sport*, in press.

—— (1994b) 'Sporting Symbols, Sporting Identities: soccer and intergroup conflict in Scotland and Northern Ireland', in I. S. Wood (ed.) *Scotland and Ulster*, Edinburgh: Mercat Press.

—— (1994c) 'Faith, Hope and Bigotry: case-studies in anti-Catholic prejudice in Scottish soccer and society', in G. Jarvie and G. Walker (eds) *Ninety-Minute Patriots? Scottish sport in the making of the nation*, Leicester: Leicester University Press.

Forsyth, R. (1990) *The Only Game: the Scots and world football*, Edinburgh: Mainstream.

Giulianotti, R. (1991) 'Scotland's Tartan Army in Italy: the case for the carnivalesque', *Sociological Review*, 39: 503–27.

—— (1993) 'A Model of the Carnivalesque? Scottish football fans at the 1992 European Championship Finals in Sweden', *Working Papers in Popular Cultural Studies No. 6*, Manchester Institute for Popular Culture.

—— (1994) 'Scoring Away from Home: a statistical study of Scotland football fans at international matches in Romania and Sweden', *International Review for the Sociology of Sport*, 4.

Goram, A. (1990) *Scotland's for Me*, Edinburgh: John Donald.

Henry, L. and J. Love, (1992) 'Youth and Sport: findings from a national survey', paper to the International Conference, 'Soccer, Culture and Identity', University of Aberdeen, April.

Himmelweit, H. (1990) 'Societal Psychology: implications and scope', in H. Himmelweit and G. Gaskell (eds) *Societal Psychology*, London: Sage.

Holt, R. (1988) 'Football and the Urban Way of Life', in J. A. Mangan (ed.) *Pleasure, Profit, Proselytism: British culture and sport at home and abroad*, London: Cass.

Hornby, N. (1992) *Fever Pitch: a fan's life*, London: Victor Gollancz.

Ingham, R., S. Hall, J. Clarke, and P. Marsh (1978) *Football Hooliganism: the wider context*, London: Inter-Action.

Jahoda, M. (1989) 'Why a Non-reductionist Social Psychology is Almost too Difficult to be Tackled but too Fascinating to be Left Alone', *British Journal of Social Psychology*, 28: 71–8.

Kapferer, B. (1984) 'The Ritual Process and the Problem of Reflexivity in Sinahalese Demon Exorcisms' in J.J. MacAloon (ed.) (1984b).

Lamming, D. (1987) *A Scottish Internationalists' Who's Who, 1872–1986*, Beverley, North Humberside: Hutton Press.

MacAloon, J. J. (1984a) 'Olympic Games and the Theory of Spectacle in Modern Societies' in J. J. McAloon (ed.) (1984b).

—— (ed.) (1984b) *Rite, Drama, Festival, Spectacle: rehearsals toward a theory of cultural performance*, Philadelphia: Institute for the Study of Human Issues.

McClure, J. (1991) *Explanations, Accounts and Illusions: a critical analysis*, Cambridge/Paris: Cambridge University Press/Editions de la Maison des Sciences de l'Homme.

McCoist, A. with C. Brankin (1992) *Ally McCoist: my story*, Edinburgh: Mainstream.

McGrain, D. with H. Keevins (1987) *Danny McGrain: In sunshine or in shadow*, Edinburgh: John Donald.

Macpherson, A. (1991) *Action Replays*, London: Chapmans.

Mason, T. (1990) 'Stanley Matthews', in R. Holt (ed.) *Sport and the Working Class in Britain*, Manchester: Manchester University Press.

Melnick, M. J. (1986) 'The Mythology of Football Hooliganism: a closer look at the British experience', *International Review for the Sociology of Sport*, 21: 1–19.

Milson, F. and R. Swannell (1976) *Football Hooliganism and Vandalism*, Birmingham: Westhill College of Education.

Moorhouse, H. F. (1984) 'Professional Football and Working Class Culture: English theories and Scottish evidence', *Sociological Review*, 32.

—— (1989) ' "We're off to Wembley": the history of a Scottish event and the sociology of football hooliganism', in D. McCrone and S. Kendrick (eds) *The Making of Scotland: nation, culture, change*, Edinburgh: Edinburgh University Press.

Mungham, G. and G. Pearson (1975) *British Working Class Youth Culture*, London: Routledge and Kegan Paul.

Murphy, P., J. Williams and E. Dunning (1990) *Football on Trial: spectator violence and development in the football world*, London: Routledge.

Murray, B. (1984) *The Old Firm: sectarianism, sport and society in Scotland*, Edinburgh: John Donald.

Redhead, S. (1990) *The End-of-the-Century Party: youth and pop towards 2000*, Manchester: Manchester University Press.

—— (1991) *Football with Attitude*, Manchester: Wordsmith.

Siann, G. (1985) *Accounting for Aggression: perspectives on aggression and violence*, Boston: Allen and Unwin.

Smith, M. D. (1983) *Violence and Sport*, Toronto: Butterworths.

Souness, G. (1987) *No Half Measures*, London: Grafton.

Strachan, G. with K. Gallagher (1991) *Strachan Style: a life in football*, Edinburgh: Mainstream.

Titford, R. with E. Dunphy (1992) *More than a Job? The player's and fan's perspectives*, Upavon, Wiltshire: Further Thoughts Publishing.

Turner, R. (1990) *In Your Blood: football culture in the late 1980s and early 1990s*, London: Working Press.

Turner, V. (1974) 'Liminal to Liminoid in Play, Flow, and Ritual: an essay in comparative symbology', *Rice University Studies*, 60: 53–92.

Walker, G. (1990) ' "There's Not a Team Like the Glasgow Rangers": football and religious identity in Scotland', in G. Walker and T. Gallagher (eds) *Sermons and Battle Hymns: Protestant popular culture in modern Scotland*, Edinburgh: Edinburgh University Press.

Ward, C. (1989) *Steaming in: journal of a football fan*, London: Simon and Schuster.

Weir, J. (1991) *A History of Cowlairs, 1876–1896*, Glasgow: SNLR.

Whannel, G. (1979) Football, Crowd Behaviour and the Press, *Media, Culture and Society*, 1: 327–42.

Williams, J. (1991) 'Having an Away Day', in Williams and Wagg (eds) (1991).

Williams, J. and S. Wagg (eds) (1991) *British Football and Social Change: getting into Europe*, Leicester: Leicester University Press.

Worpole, K. (1992) *Towns for People*, Milton Keynes: Open University Press.

Chapter 6

The social roots of football hooliganism
A reply to the critics of the 'Leicester School'

Eric Dunning

INTRODUCTION

The subject of this chapter is the social roots of football hooliganism, especially football hooligan violence. What I shall attempt is
to shed light on this issue by means of a reply to the critics of
what Richard Giulianotti (1989: 13), Alan Clarke (1992: 201) and
others have rather misleadingly called the 'Leicester school'. I
say 'rather misleadingly' because, by and large, I agree with Steve
Redhead (1991: 480) when he recently wrote of what he called
'the illusory theoretical unity of the work produced by the Leicester "school" ', going on to refer to the divisions among us 'over
the status of the dynamic provided by the theorization of the
"civilizing process" in the work of Norbert Elias'. I am not sure
that the theoretical unity of our *work* is an 'illusion' but Steve
Redhead was certainly right to point to the existence of theoretical divisions among us as a *group*. More particularly, while Patrick
Murphy, Ivan Waddington, Joe Maguire and I are 'figurational'
or 'process-sociologists'[1] who work broadly within the tradition of
Norbert Elias, John Williams most certainly is not. He made this
clear in his contribution to *British Football and Social Change* when
he wrote that:

> Less successfully, and less appropriately in my view, the Leices-
> ter work also attempts to explain the peaks and troughs in
> outbreaks of hooliganism using Norbert Elias's theory of 'civili-
> zing processes'. I have already indicated in my brief review of
> the history of hooliganism at football some rethinking on my
> part of the issue of the scale and seriousness of earlier out-
> breaks of football crowd disorders. This reassessment sits
> uneasily with the 'latent evolutionism' of the theory of civiliz-

ing processes. In addition to this, the high level of generality at which the theory operates, its apparently universalistic applicability, and the sometimes rather fractious and defensive relations between 'Eliasians' and their critics, also give the theory an aura of 'irrefutability' and arguably leads, in the case of violence at football, to the underplaying of important national and cultural differences in patterns and forms of hooliganism. Finally, the theory underplays the more general importance of culturalist approaches, perhaps particularly those which examine the nature of, and shifts in, the cultural significance of the game in this country, and those structuralist perspectives which highlight key aspects of the constantly changing relationship between the state, football and the football audience.

(Williams, 1991: 177)

Later, I shall try to show in detail why John Williams' arguments, along with those of authors who have argued along similar lines, are wrong. For the moment, it is enough simply to say that the Leicester work on football hooliganism was figurational or process-sociological in conception and orientated towards the theory of civilizing processes from the outset. It was initiated by a research proposal worked out by Patrick Murphy and myself,[2] and its distinctive character, above all its attempt to combine a developmental or historical approach with a present-focused study of the structural production and reproduction of aggressive masculinity in specific community and football contexts, derived from our joint commitment to a figurational/process sociological perspective. Our work is undoubtedly flawed in many ways. It is also certainly incomplete. Nevertheless it is fair, I think, to say that it has met with a degree of success, at least if measured in terms of output. This success is largely attributable to the way in which the participant observation and reporting skills of John Williams gelled for a while with the figurational/process-sociological thrust that came from Patrick Murphy and me. But let me take a different tack.

THE DEAMPLIFICATION OF ENGLISH FOOTBALL HOOLIGANISM

To the incredulity of sections of the media and officialdom, there were substantial outbreaks of hooliganism involving mainly

English, German and Swedish fans at the 1992 European Championships in Sweden. That these outbreaks should have been greeted with incredulity is not particularly surprising for it had been widely canvassed beforehand that the English problem of soccer hooliganism had been 'solved', or at least that hooliganism at football matches in England had gone 'out of fashion'. Similar views have surfaced in the past. For example, in 1978 the authors of the joint Sports Council/Social Science Research Council booklet on *Public Disorder and Sporting Events*, partly justified their recommendation that football hooliganism was not 'a high priority research subject' with the following words:

> there is more than a suspicion that an element of fashion pervades the behaviour and that like some other youth problems such as Paki-bashing, fights between mods and rockers, and the clashes between 'teddy boy' gangs of the 50s, hooliganism may gradually subside – or media interest which plays an important part in focusing public concern upon the problem, may shift to some fresh manifestation of youthful misbehaviour.
>
> (Sports Council/SSRC, 1978: 53)

As is generally the case with observations of this sort, no consideration was given here to the possibility that more enduring structures may have underlain the succession of youth fashions described. More recently, writing in the *Independent* in 1990, Phil Shaw felt sufficiently confident that football hooliganism in England was on the wane to write in a half-page article that:

> The 'regular' Football League season reaches its climax today with all those involved, whether professionally or emotionally, hoping for a peaceful conclusion to what has been a year of surprising optimism after the numbing nadir of Hillsborough. For once, football-related hooliganism – few in the sport now call it 'football hooliganism' – has not been a burning issue. Instead, a revival of sorts has continued with League attendances up (by 4.5 per cent) for an unprecedented fourth consecutive season. Though the 95 deaths at Sheffield were not caused by hooliganism, the tragedy does appear to have prompted an improvement in crowd behaviour and, to an extent, in policing. . . . [T]he perception of progress is widely held. 'Without wishing to tempt providence, things are better

than for 20 years,' says John Stalker, former Deputy Chief
Constable of Greater Manchester Police. . . . 'It's almost as if
hooliganism is not fashionable any more.'

(*Independent*, 5 May 1990)

The words of the Sports Council/Social Science Research Council
Panel were penned just at the time when groups such as West
Ham United's 'Inter City Firm' were coming to prominence and
when the marauding of English football hooligans in continental
Europe was building up to Heysel. On Sunday, 6 May 1990, the
day after Phil Shaw's article in the *Independent*, the British people
awoke to learn from television, radio and their newspapers how,
the day before, 3,000 Leeds United supporters had gone on the
rampage in Bournemouth (*Sunday Times*, 6 May 1990). They were
also to learn of how, in addition, there had been football-related
trouble in Chesterfield, Birmingham, Halifax, Shrewsbury, Swansea, Aldershot, Cambridge, Sheffield, London and Leicester. In
Sheffield, the trouble took place at Hillsborough, the stadium
where the 95 deaths had occurred just thirteen months previously; in London, it occurred at no fewer than four matches;
and in Leicester, a group of home fans gave the lie to the idea
that all-seater stadia might form an effective counter to hooliganism by clambering over seats to attack a knot of Sheffield United
fans in what was described as 'ugly fighting' (*Guardian*, 7 May
1990).

There is evidently a widespread feeling that the hooligans will
voluntarily renounce their destructive activities in a football context independently of the sorts of structural changes that would
lead their norms of masculinity to be transformed. To my knowledge, this kind of viewpoint has received its most forceful and
sophisticated articulation from Ian Taylor. Writing in the *Independent on Sunday* (21 April 1991), he referred to what he called
'the extraordinary absence of hooliganism and other ugly incidents from English football grounds during the 1990–91 season'.
'An astonishing sea-change', he went on, 'is taking place in the
culture of some of [England's] football terraces', and he
attributed this process to the conjuncture of the BBC's 'packaging' of the 1990 World Cup with the removal of perimeter fences
from many grounds in response to Lord Justice Taylor's report
on the Hillsborough tragedy. According to Ian Taylor, the process
worked in something like the following way. The removal of

'cages' reduced the frequency of 'animal-like' responses among the fans. This interacted with the packaging of Italia '90 in which, as Taylor put it, 'the opera of Pavarotti would meld ethereally into a poetic display of European football', producing a re-emphasis on 'style'. As a result, Taylor argued, 'hooliganism [became] suddenly decidedly unfashionable, passé, irrelevant'.[3]

Significant changes are certainly taking place in English football at the moment. In 1990–1, attendances at Football League matches rose for the fifth successive season and 1992–3 witnessed the launch of the new Premier League. The growing use of face paints, bizarre forms of dress and 'inflatables' of various kinds has introduced an element of carnival to the game. The 'fanzine' movement signifies the emergence of a new and hitherto unprecedented form of football literacy (Jary, Horne and Bucke, 1991). Although still marginalized, the Football Supporters' Association has succeeded in gaining at least toehold access to the higher councils of the game. Finally, 'Football and the Community' schemes have now been established at the majority of League clubs.

It is easy to see why people who are deeply committed to the game are liable to read such changes as having made a serious dent in the hooligan problem. Nevertheless, the explanation of the putative decline of football hooliganism in terms of a nascent concern with 'style' seems to me to be flawed. For one thing, the fact that the 1990 World Cup Finals were associated in England with a hitherto unprecedented form of hooliganism, namely attacks on foreigners in this country by fans who had been watching the matches in Italy on television, shows at the very least that the BBC's packaging of Italia '90 did not immediately have the effect hypothesized by Ian Taylor. Moreover, the 'soccer casual' movement shows clearly that an interest in style and an interest in violence are not mutually exclusive.[4] And that carnival and violence are not mutually exclusive either is shown by the European Middle Ages, contemporary South America and the annual jamboree in Notting Hill. Finally, events in Sweden in June 1990 show that, even if hooliganism has become 'unfashionable, passé, irrelevant' in certain circles, this hypothesized sudden fashion shift has been far from total as far as English football supporters are concerned.

In fact, a rather different, more empirically based scenario regarding what has been happening in conjunction with English soccer since 1990 can be constructed,[5] a scenario principally involving interaction between the State and the media. It runs as follows. In 1990, following the Taylor Report (1990) on the Hillsborough tragedy, the Government was forced to shelve Part I of the Football Spectators Bill and this led to a change of tactics on its part regarding the hooligan problem. Unlike in Germany in 1988 and the build-up to Italia '90, when the Government saw it as in its interests to play up the hooligan problem, in the middle of the 1990 World Cup, because Part I of the Football Spectators Bill was no longer a viable option, they started to play the problem down. This was the case despite the fact that there were no significantly discernible differences between the levels of English hooliganism in Germany and Italy. A West German view in 1988, for example, had been that nothing happened during their hosting of the European Championships that does not happen on a normal Saturday in the Bundesliga. And there was certainly sufficient hooliganism by the English in Italy for it to have been played up by the Government had they seen it as in their interests to do so. Instead, perhaps additionally affected by the fact that the England team won FIFA's 'Fair Play Award' – which could, of course, be construed as a reward for the enduring 'gentlemanly' character of the English – and by the mood of optimism regarding English football that was engendered by the unexpectedly good playing performance of the England team in the later stages of the tournament, they decided that it was politically opportune to switch tactics and to say that the behaviour of England fans in Italy showed sufficient signs of improvement for them to support the FA's bid for the re-entry of Football League clubs into Europe.

The effect of the combined ditching of Part I of the Football Spectators Bill, the Government's support for re-entry into Europe and the more optimistic mood regarding the English game, seems to have been to make the issue of football hooliganism less newsworthy. As a result, it started to be under-reported, particularly in the national press. Nevertheless, it continued to occur both in England and abroad. It also continued to be reported, though less frequently, more *sotto voce*, usually unheadlined and nearly always just on the sports pages, often buried in some more general report. In fact, during the 1991–2 season up until the end of March 1992, Patrick Murphy and I came across twenty-three media reports of hooligan incidents of greater or lesser magnitude. Fifteen of the reports referred to incidents in England, seven to incidents in continental Europe and one to an incident in Africa. Seven of the eight incidents reported as having occurred abroad were reported in the national press, the remaining one being reported in an international paper (*Herald Tribune*). Nine of the incidents reported as having occurred in England were reported in Leicester's local media, eight in the *Leicester Mercury*, one on local radio. Seven of the locally reported incidents involved Leicester City fans and referred mainly to fights in pubs and city centres. In fact, in the part of the 1991–2 season for which we have not yet collated our newspaper data, a very serious incident occurred at Filbert Street involving Leicester City and Newcastle United fans. The latter tore out seats and threw them at Leicester fans in an adjacent pen. The Leicester fans returned the fire, using the seats and other missiles. The barrage lasted for most of the second half of the match and two Newcastle fans suffered serious damage to their eyes. At the end of the match, there was a large-scale pitch invasion by fans of both sides and riot police has to be used to keep them apart. Having witnessed this and some other incidents in 1991–2, I was not taken by surprise by events in Sweden. I think that it is also reasonable to surmise that, had the moral panic over football hooliganism of the 1970s and 1980s still prevailed, at least some of these incidents would have received the 'mindless morons', 'smash the animals and thugs' headline treatment by the national tabloids and that, in that way, the moral panic would have been reinforced.

The local radio report may be of some significance as a pointer to what is going on. That is because it involved the match commentator on Leicester City's second leg Rumbelow's Cup match with Nottingham Forest – it was played at the City Ground – requesting the permission of his director while on the air to report the terrace fighting that he observed while the match was taking place. This sheds light on the sorts of norms and values that may well be playing a part in the putative under-reporting. It may also be of some significance that one of the incidents reported in the national press referred to running battles between rival fans in London's West End in conjunction with the England–Germany match in September 1991. This incident pointed to the probability of trouble in Sweden, that is, a context where national rivalries were going to be at stake.

An implication of the above analysis is that close attention ought to be paid over the coming seasons to the complex interplay between the media treatment of soccer hooliganism and the phenomenon itself. One reason for suggesting this is the possibility that what we may be witnessing at the moment is a reprise in some respects of what seems to have happened in the interwar years. I say 'in some respects' because account always has to be taken when making historical comparisons of the fact that superficial similarities may mask structures and events of greatly different types.

That said, the Leicester analysis points to the possibility – at the moment one cannot put it any stronger than that – that the present situation is parallel in some ways to that in the 1920s and 1930s. More particularly, in the inter-war years a pattern of media reporting of football seems to have arisen in England in which praise for fans came to outweigh blame and condemnation, contributing to a positive feedback cycle which appears to have acted together with wider social changes, especially a growing incorporation of sections of the working class into dominant values, to further an already occurring tendency for spectator violence at matches to decrease.[6] It may be that we are in the early stages of such a cycle at the moment, at least as far as the media side of the equation is concerned. This discussion of the 'media–fan behaviour' equation is perhaps an appropriate point at which to begin my reply to the critics of the 'Leicester school'.

FOOTBALL VIOLENCE AND THE FIGURATIONAL PERSPECTIVE: CONTINUITIES AND CHANGES

To my knowledge, with the exception of a brief critical reference by Richard Giulianotti (1989: 14), none of the critics has so far taken account of our analysis of the complex interplay between spectator behaviour and the ways in which the media report it. One of the consequences of this is that some of them tend to miss the subtleties of our case and even claim as original to themselves arguments already put by us as part of the case they are attacking. An example is provided by the critical salvo fired against us – and Geoffrey Pearson (1983) – by Dick Hobbs and David Robins (1991: 564) for allegedly believing that 'hooliganism is as old as the game', that is, that there are no differences between the manifestations of hooliganism in different historical periods. In a supposed counter to the Leicester studies, what Hobbs and Robins suggest is that groups such as West Ham's 'Inter City Firm' are specifically modern. In the words of Hobbs and Robins, they are 'the latest in a line of young working-class men who enjoy fighting at football matches, whose lineage goes back to the season 1966–7'.

A careful reading of *The Roots of Football Hooliganism* ought to have shown Hobbs and Robins that our diagnosis of this issue is in some respects similar to theirs. We too regard 1966–7 as a watershed as far as soccer spectator violence in England is concerned. More particularly, it is our suggestion that the conjuncture of the emergence of the tabloid press and the staging of the World Cup Finals in England contributed to a pattern of sensationalistic reporting in the build-up to the Finals and afterwards which helped, as it were, to 'advertise' the game to groups like the newly rising skinheads as a context where fights and exciting 'action' regularly take place. In a word, if our analysis is pointing in the right direction, media sensationalism contributed to the pattern of football hooliganism that emerged in the mid-1960s and lasted until the 1980s, namely the pattern whereby football matches came to be used by more or less organized groups of young, primarily working-class males as a focus and context for fighting. Two whole chapters of *The Roots of Football Hooliganism* are devoted to an analysis of this watershed and developing patterns of football hooliganism since that time (Dunning, Murphy and Williams, 1988: 132–83). Hobbs and Robins do not appear to have read them. It is also, to say the least, disingenuous of John Williams to say that he has 'reassessed' the historical parts of our case for, whatever the merits and demerits of the arguments and evidence we adduced, it was always our intention to avoid both a 'flat-earth' interpretation of history in which nothing ever changes[7] and a Giddens-type 'discontinuist' thesis in which there are no discernible links and continuities with the past (Giddens, 1985: 31–4). More particularly, what we set out to do was to explore the balance between continuity and discontinuity as far as football spectator violence and disorderliness were concerned.

Principal among the discontinuities that we singled out in *The Roots of Football Hooliganism* were these: a shift from a pattern before the First World War in which attacks on match officials and opposing players predominated over attacks on rival fans, to a pattern in and after the mid-1960s in which inter-fan group fighting became the predominant form of spectator disorderliness; the emergence in the 1950s out of a previously localized situation of a more nationally standardized youth subculture and a shift within that framework through such styles as those of the teddy boys, the mods and rockers and the skinheads, with the latter being the first to choose football as a major stage for their fighting; a tendency from the 1960s onwards for football hooligan fighting to become more premeditated and organized partly as a response to official attempts to contain it; a displacement of football hooliganism from football grounds and their vicinities into contexts where the hooligans saw the controls as weak or entirely lacking, one such context being continental Europe; and finally, a move of the hooligans into the seated areas of grounds which caught the authorities on the hop, contributing to a renewed and more intensive cycle of control and displacement. Against all of these discontinuities, we laid stress on one major continuity. It is a continuity which, if our diagnosis has any substance, *is* as old as the game itself. I am referring to the fact that all these discontinuities and changes appear to be surface features which mask a relatively continuous and enduring underlying pattern, namely the fact that all these disturbances in a football context – it was not until the 1960s that the label 'football hooliganism' became the standard media and official term for describing them – involve(d) physical violence and aggression in which the principal perpetrators and their principal targets are or were working-class males and in which intensely felt local rivalries are or were at stake. But let me become more systematic.

CRITICISMS OF THE LEICESTER RESEARCH: THE ROLES OF ELIAS AND SOCIAL CLASS

The most frequently voiced criticisms of the Leicester work on football hooliganism seem to me to fall under two main headings. Ian Taylor (1987), John Horne and David Jary (1987), Richard Giulianotti (1989), Dick Hobbs and David Robins (1991) have been critical in various ways of our reliance on Elias's theory of civilizing processes. Recently, John Williams has added his name to this list. Dick Hobbs and David Robins (1991), Gary Armstrong and Rosemary Harris (1991), Richard Giulianotti (1989) and Bert Moorhouse (1991) have all voiced criticisms of our attempts to locate the core football hooligans socially and shed doubts on the concepts and categories of social class that we have used. Let me attempt to summarize these two aspects of the critique. In order to minimize the possibility of misrepresentation, I shall in my exposition quote extensively from the critics.

Writing of our work on football hooliganism, Ian Taylor argued in a paper written in 1985 that:

> The project appears to be to find evidence of violent incidents at soccer games continuously *throughout* the history of the professional game and also to locate examples of violence amongst crowds at soccer games outside England. One can see why this project is helpful to Dunning in his attempt to illustrate the evolutionary and idealist social theory of Norbert Elias – but the evidence *is* stretched ... and the theory's stress on an ongoing process of civilization *surely* is a very unhelpful framework through which to analyse the current condition of working class youth in Britain.
>
> (Taylor, 1987: 176)

Richard Giulianotti takes a rather different tack, arguing that we see football hooliganism as a rather 'self-evident', 'one-dimensional' phenomenon that is 'qualitatively the same ... the world over' and can be assessed always and everywhere according to the same criteria. 'This axiomatic approach to "a problem" the meaning of which is socially constructed,' he writes, 'ensures that the Leicester School posit an ethnocentric analysis in favour of the more "civilized", correctionist ingredients of mainstream criminology, inevitably derived from the use of Elias within the context of soccer hooliganism as the subject matter.' The interpretation of our work and that of Elias that leads Giulianotti to this conclusion is as follows:

> Elias has argued that historically the West is under the sway of a broad cultural movement towards a greater civilized and humanitarian society. It is also suggested through Elias's choice of historical evidence that the vanguard group in society pushing towards this new altruism is perennially the most politically powerful class: thus, he focuses on the development of manners in the 'Court Society' whilst the aristocracy retained power before the Industrial Revolution. This civilization process is exemplified in our increasing condemnation of physical vio-

lence: from, say, Medieval times one can clearly chart the manner in which social violence has lost its everyday toleration, and been replaced with an incipient public disdain for its various, primarily public, manifestations, derived from macroscopic pressures within modern industrial society for orderliness and routinization. From this, the Leicester School deduce that effectively the cultural condemnation of violence has yet to percolate down to the lower working classes. They are, it seems, a retardation within the overall historical teleology of the civilizing process. The inference is that given enough time, soccer hooliganism is likely to be washed out by heightened cultural altruism, though it is probable that it will loiter in other cultures and societies less advanced than ourselves.

(Giulianotti, 1989: 14–15)

Central to the critique offered by Hobbs and Robins (1991) of this aspect of the Leicester work is a reference to the fact that, during the 1980s in Britain there took place 'a deliberate weakening of the state's ability to intervene in all key areas of urban life except policing'. This suggests, they argue, 'a rather more ambiguous urban scenario than "The Unstoppable Drive of Civilization" '. Moreover, 'anomalies along the road to civilization', they suggest, such as 'the Nazi holocaust or the invention of the Stanley knife' cannot be dismissed as merely 'counter-civilizing'. They add that, in working-class communities, the monopoly of violence is held by young men and physical violence remains a common aspect of everyday life. It is not, that is to say, 'an option limited to those who have escaped the civilizing influence of the wider community but 'a fact of working class life . . . and not restricted to youth" '. However, the core of Hobbs and Robins's interpretation and critique of our reliance on the work of Norbert Elias is summed up in the following passage:

> The Leicester group consistently attempt to locate their findings in the context of Norbert Elias's theory of 'civilizing processes'. Central to this coupling of empirical work and metatheory is the belief that the working class has become increasingly 'incorporated'.
>
> According to Elias, key elites have traditionally determined social standards, and the growing complexity and interdependency of social and economic networks has increased the pressures on them to do so. The most consistent of these pressures

are those that are asserted by the growing authority of the state on one hand, and the expanding power of the 'lower social strata' on the other. Trapped between these two social movements the higher strata are forced to exercise 'greater self restraint over their behaviour and feelings'. The trend towards interdependency gives the lower social strata increased power.

It is difficult to see how the British working class have in the last two decades applied pressure on economic elites. Tacked onto a contemporary study of soccer hooliganism, Elias's notion of civilization is confused with a perceived increase in social organization. 'Stable monopolies of force' are seen as providing the base for a more stable and secure existence for the majority of the population who live in 'pacified social spaces which are normally free from acts of violence'. However, increased affluence and a 'security' born of a 'stable monopoly of force' have somehow by-passed an impoverished minority and violence for this rough 'uncivilized' group is the norm. Soccer hooligans are rough, soccer hooligans are uncivilized.

(Hobbs and Robins, 1991: 556–7).

Let me turn now to the ways in which the critics have grappled with our efforts at handling the issues related to the class locations of football hooligans. Central to the critique of this aspect of our work offered by Hobbs and Robins is the suggestion that we have 'isolate[d] a sub-group within the working class who are ... responsible for football violence'. They go on to claim that 'the assertion that the lower (and therefore rougher) working class make up British football hooligan groups is not substantiated by empirical evidence' (ibid.). If we overlook for the moment the fact that Hobbs and Robins completely ignore our reliance on statistical data collected by John Williams in Spain and on a Leicester working-class estate (Williams, Dunning and Murphy, 1989), as well as the participant observation study of the latter that he carried out (Murphy, Williams and Dunnning, 1990), we can still find their principal argument to be that 'the most "systematic and detailed" material that the Leicester group offer to support their theory of the class specificity of football hooligans was gleaned from a television documentary featuring West Ham United's elite Inter City Firm' (Hobbs and Robins,

1991: 557). This is a distortion. We were closely involved in the making of this documentary and these data did not feature in it: they were supplied to us by the director in the course of our collaboration. More to the point, however, is the fact that Hobbs and Robins argue that, while these data 'would appear to support the Leicester group's analysis, . . . a cynical eye cast over the occupations proffered by 141 self-confessed ICF members suggests that this data [sic] is not as reliable as it might be' (1991: 557). In order to substantiate this claim, Hobbs and Robins rely partly on an analysis of occupational data on football hooligans that they obtained from the London Standard which suggests, they argue, 'a wide range of occupations across the working class spectrum' (1991:58). They also rely partly on a profile of a prominent member of the ICF who was, it can be confirmed, known to us and included in our sample. Hobbs's and Robins's profile of him reads as follows:

> A self-employed decorator who worked part-time as a bouncer, he has since gone on to organise security arrangements at major sporting events, write a book, run his own mini-cab business, has appeared on several television chat shows, and acted as a script consultant on The Firm (1989), a full-length film drama based on his career as a hooligan. If this man is lower working class, we would suggest that many professional groups, if achievement, media profile and monetary reward are considered, should be classed as distinctly lumpen.
>
> (Hobbs and Robins, 1991: 558)

The critique of this aspect of our work offered by Armstrong and Harris (1991) is similar in some respects to that advanced by Hobbs and Robins. 'If the theory put forward about hooliganism is centrally concerned with the culture of men in a particular subclass', they write, 'then its significance must rest on the validity of the data on the basis of which men are ascribed to that class' (453). It follows from this, they conclude, that evidence, whether from official or unofficial sources, should be scrutinized 'most carefully'. They go on to say about The Roots of Football Hooliganism that:

> [In this book] a chart is used, from a journalistic source, that claims to give the occupations of West Ham's 'Inter City Firm', but it is presented without any assessment as to its

probable validity and to us this seems very dubious. At one extreme it lists a 'bank manager' and an 'insurance underwriter', about which occupations we are frankly sceptical. At the other extreme twelve men give their occupations as 'ticket touts', an activity that may well have been a spare time paying hobby for some of them, but to suggest that such a large proportion of the group relied on such an occupation strains credibility. Thus, to have the chart presented quite uncritically, especially since we know that 'hooligans' can demonstrate both imagination and a keen sense of humour, is unacceptable.

(ibid.)

Curiously, Armstrong and Harris do not seem to realize that our data on the social class membership of the ICF are the same as those we present on the occupations of this group, only analysed using the Registrar General's classificatory scheme.[8] However, that is less important for present purposes than the fact that, in their own words, Armstrong and Harris admit that they have 'no neat theory of football hooliganism' (1991: 456). Perhaps that helps to explain why it is difficult to ascertain a consistent line in their argument, though part of it seems to be that the Leicester studies are wrong because some football hooligans come from 'respectable' and 'middle-class' backgrounds. It does not appear to strike them that, since we do present data on such fans, either our case must be riddled with inconsistencies or they have not fully grasped what it is.

Richard Giulianotti's critique is a variation on the same basic theme. He acknowledges that we are not alone 'in premising the core feature of [our] arguments on the lower working class presence in soccer hooliganism as catalytic' but proposes nevertheless that 'the empirical weaknesses of this assertion remain'. He elaborates on his reasons for arguing this in the following way:

The Leicester school, in stressing the reproduction of values conducive to relatively more common manifestations of aggression and violence within lower working class communities, implicitly depict the microstructural fabric there (including the normative systems) as primarily self-contained. The assumption here is that working class and middle class youngsters are to be treated as effectively distinct and separate sociological entities for purposes of analysis. This can be questioned at two main levels. Firstly, though there are definite

environmental boundaries which delimit for example areas of
private housing from council house schemes, the inevitability
of these two *prima facie* distinct social groups actually interact-
ing, especially within a relatively small and socially integrated
city such as Aberdeen . . . greatly blurs this complacent schism.
Secondly, and more seriously, the assumption that the dominant values in lower working class communities remain in
essence immune from the disparaging power of more 'civilized' norms directed at it from elsewhere undermines the
Leicester school's rather conciliatory suggestion that the mass
media's 'change of reporting styles appears to have played a
part in the generation of football hooliganism as we know it
today'.

(Giulianotti, 1989: 48)

In a characteristically trenchant article, Bert Moorhouse sets his
critical sights at everyone who has so far essayed an analysis of
football hooliganism in England, claiming to have detected in
our collective work a number of 'debilitating failings'. One of
these is 'a tendency to ignore relevant debates in other areas
of social analysis, especially those concerning the complexity of
social stratification' (Moorhouse, 1991: 490). Specifically as far as
the Leicester studies are concerned, Moorhouse takes issue with
Armstrong and Harris for claiming that the Leicester research
on 'the culture of the rough working class and their propensity
to violence . . . is obviously well researched and very interesting'
(Armstrong and Harris, 1991: 452). However, he ignores the fact
that this praise is used by Armstrong and Harris as a prelude to
total dismissal, for they go on to say that: 'what we doubt is
whether [the Leicester analysis] has any particular relevance to
contemporary football hooliganism' (ibid.). Moorhouse's own
point involves a flat but unsubstantiated denial of the suggestion
that our analysis is well researched and this leads him on to the
contention that Armstrong and Harris's evidence is 'neither in
sufficient quantity nor of the correct date to cause anyone to
reject the Dunning *et al.* line' (Moorhouse, 1991: 501).

According to Moorhouse, though, 'there are plenty of other
good reasons for doing so', an assertion which leads him to
deliver what he evidently regards as the *coup de grace*. It takes the
form of a rhetorical question and is not elaborated beyond
the following sentence. 'If in Scotland', Moorhouse asks, 'the fans

of Rangers were, historically, quite violent and if part of the appeal of Protestantism was that it would secure most of the good working-class jobs available, what does this mean for any supposed association between "roughness" and "violence"?' This brings my exposition of the critiques of the work of the 'Leicester school' to a close. Before I begin to mount my counter-critique, let me first of all briefly summarize what I take the critics to have said.

Ian Taylor is the only one of the critics singled out for attention here to suggest that Elias's theory of civilizing processes is 'idealist'. However, he shares with Horne and Jary, John Williams and Hobbs and Robins the idea that it is either 'evolutionist' *tout court* or contains a tendency towards 'latent evolutionism'. Hobbs and Robins even go so far as to interpret Elias as positing an 'unstoppable drive of civilization' and suggest that the Nazi holocaust provides a massive disconfirmation of his case. They also misconstrue a reference to strata lower than the aristocracy as implying the very lowest classes when even the most cursory glance at Elias's work or a careful reading of our text would have revealed that we were referring, in that instance, to bourgeois groups. Finally, although he does not use the term 'evolutionist' in describing the Leicester work, Richard Giulianotti evidently shares this view at least to some degree because he refers to 'the overall historical teleology of the civilizing process'. He also sees the process as a 'broad cultural movement' that involves a push towards a 'new altruism'.

Central to the arguments directed by this selected group of critics against the way in which issues relating to class and the social locations of football hooligans are handled in the Leicester research is the idea that we single out what they call the 'rough working class' either as the sole or the principal locus from which football hooligans are recruited. All the critics also claim that our diagnosis is falsified by their discovery of hooligans who are 'affluent', 'respectable' or 'middle-class'. Behind this lies the idea that we equate 'roughness' with poverty in some simple and undimensional way, coupled with the notion that we see deprivation as mechanically leading to the production and reproduction of violence. Hobbs and Robins and Armstrong and Harris stand out from Giulianotti and Moorhouse in extracting our data on the ICF from their wider theoretico-empirical context and in treating them as if they were simply part of a traditional survey study, that is, without reference to the way in which we attempted to use them as part of an historical/process-sociological study in which a two-year programme of community research based on participant observation of football hooligans formed a significant component. Lastly, Richard Giulianotti suggests that we over-generalize on the basis of English data and that another of the central failings of our work consists in the fact that we treat working-class and middle-class youngsters as 'effectively distinct and separate sociological entities' and that we see lower working-class communities and their dominant values as in essence 'immune' from the power of 'more civilized norms'. I have now reached a point where I can attempt to mount a reasonably full-blown and systematic counter-critique.

'CIVILIZATION' AND THE THEORY OF CIVILIZING PROCESSES

Alan Clarke (1992: 204) has recently suggested that we pay too much attention in the Leicester research to the 'hooligan figuration' and not enough to the wider 'football figuration' of which it forms a part. By and large, I agree. My only serious reservation stems from Alan Clarke's failure to acknowledge that the Leicester work on football hooliganism was a direct outcome of my earlier work with Ken Sheard on the development of football which culminated in the publication of *Barbarians, Gentlemen and Players* in 1979.[9] In fact, it was in the conclusion to that book that the guiding hypothesis investigated in *The Roots of Football Hooliganism* was first formulated (Dunning and Sheard, 1979: 282ff.). It stemmed from the apparent anomaly posed by football hooliganism for the fact that the long-term development of football *per se* appears otherwise to be consistent with the idea of a civilizing process. Since our use of Elias's theory of civilizing processes is one of the two main aspects of our work with which the critics most persistently take issue, let me try to summarize succinctly what it does and does not say.

It seems to me that one of the problems that the critics have with the theory of civilizing processes may be connected with the word 'civilization' itself. The British Sociological Association's recent pamphlet, *Anti-Racist Language: Guidance For Good Practice*, for example, cites 'civilization' as a word which should be avoided in teaching and research. The reason, according to the pamphlet, is that 'civilization' is a term which 'derives from a colonialist perception of the world'. It is, we are told, 'often associated with social darwinist thought and is full of implicit value judgements and ignorance of Third World history'. However, the pamphlet goes on explicitly to make the following exception. 'In some cases,' it continues, 'such as the work of Norbert Elias, civilization takes on a different meaning without racist overtones.' Although the exception of Elias in this regard is welcome, it is not strictly accurate because, in Elias's usage, it is not the concept of 'civilization' which is used in a detached and non-racist way but that of 'civilizing processes'. One of the things that Elias sought at the start of *The Civilizing Process* to accomplish was to trace the socio-genesis of the term 'civilization', how it came to express the self-image of the most advanced western nations, and how it came in that connection to acquire derogatory and racist connotations not only in relation to non-western societies, but also in relation to less advanced societies in the west itself. Interestingly, Elias shows how the First World War was fought by Britain and France against Germany in the name of 'civilization' and how, in the eighteenth and nineteenth centuries, the Germans were ambivalent about the term and its referents, preferring to express their self-image through the particularistic concept of *Kultur*.[10]

Elias thus explicitly recognized that 'civilization' is a value-laden term. By contrast, the concept of a 'civilizing process' in his usage is a detached, technical term that refers to the shared complex of changes experienced by the major societies of western Europe as their development led, first of all their ruling groups and, later, more and more sections of their populations to come to have the idea of themselves as 'civilized'. A corollary of this self-image, of course, was that peoples in other parts of the world came increasingly to be seen by Europeans as 'uncivilized' and 'barbaric'. Indeed, in the eighteenth and nineteenth centuries and to a diminishing extent in the twentieth, these same epithets were commonly used by elite groups in western societies in the denotation of members of their own 'lower orders'.

A further way in which Elias sought to distance his theory from the evaluative connotations of the concept of civilization was by means of an explicit denial of the judgement that western societies represent some kind of 'high point' or 'pinnacle' in this regard. For example, he speculated that future historians will probably come to see the people of today as forming part of the Middle Ages (Elias, 1982: 57) and, in a later work, characterized even the most civilizationally advanced peoples of the present-day world as 'late barbarians' (Elias, 1991: 147).

It is not necessary in the present context to specify in detail the constellation of factual developments that Elias saw as comprising the western European civilizing process or how he sought to explain it. It is enough just to note that it is based, among other things, on a study of the development of the manners of the secular upper classes, and of state-formation with special reference to France, which involves a massive attention to detail. Accordingly, it cannot meaningfully be said either to 'operate at a high level of generality', or to constitute a 'metatheory'. On the contrary, one of its chief characteristics is its blend of the particular with the general. Moreover, Elias was clear about the fact that, like any other social development, the European civilizing process is, and always has been, based on learning and is hence reversible. In fact, it is useful to see Elias's theory as operating on two distinct yet interdependent levels. On the one hand, the theory involves an empirical generalization about the overall trajectory of personality-formation and 'interpersonal'[11] behaviour in western societies between the Middle Ages and the twentieth century. On the other hand, it involves the establishment of an explanatory connection between this empirically demonstrable 'civilizing' trajectory and the equally empirically demonstrable trajectory of state-formation. That is to say, Elias's data on what would conventionally be called the 'micro-social' or 'behavioural' level consistently reveal a dominant trend towards such things as the elaboration and refinement of manners and socially required behavioural standards; increasing social pressure on people to exercise self-control; an advancing 'threshold of repugnance' with respect to bodily functions, an advance in terms of which these functions and the bodily parts connected with them became increasingly surrounded with feelings of anxiety and shame; an advancing threshold of repugnance with respect to engaging in and witnessing violent acts; and, as a corollary of this generally advancing threshold of repugnance, a tendency to push violence and acts connected with biological functions increasingly behind the scenes.

Elias sought to explain this empirical generalization principally by reference to empirical data on state-formation, that is, regarding the unplanned establishment at the 'macro-level' of violence and tax monopolies as a result of hegemonial struggles among kings and other feudal lords. An important corollary of this long-term state-formation process which contributed reciprocally to its occurrence was the pacification of larger and larger social spaces within each developing state. This, in its turn, contributed to a growth of trade, a correlative lengthening of interdependency chains, and a growing monetization of social relations. According to Elias, as all this occurred, there took place a progressive augmentation of the power of bourgeois groups, coupled with a correlative weakening of the warrior aristocracy. At the point where the power chances of these rising and falling groups were approximately equal, kings were able to play one off against the other and uphold a claim to 'absolute rule'.[12] It was at this point, too, according to Elias, that what he called the 'courtization of the warriors' (*die Verhöflichung der Krieger*) began most significantly to take place, that is, they began to be tamed and transformed from rough and ready knights into courtiers who were polished and urbane.

It is difficult to see how such a theory can justifiably be described as 'evolutionary', even in the relatively weak sense of displaying 'a tendency towards latent evolutionism'. It is a theory concerned with potentially reversible processes based on learning which Elias sought to demonstrate as having occurred in the past. As such, it is testable at both the micro and the macro levels. It is also testable in regard to the explanatory connections that Elias hypothesized as having taken place at these two levels, by reference to specific social spheres such as sport – in fact, the Leicester studies of the development of football and football hooliganism constitute such tests – and, with the insertion of suitable *ceteris paribus* clauses, in societies outside a western context.

It is important, too, to grasp that Elias did not use his theory to make predictions about the future except for the very occasional forecast in the most general terms. That is because he regarded the future as an 'open book', that is as unpredictable at the present level of knowledge and perhaps *tout court*. Such a view followed from Elias's idea that social processes unfold as the unplanned consequences of the interweaving of aggregates of individual acts. All we can do, he argued, is establish by means of research why one past development has occurred rather than another.[13] It follows from this that it is a complete travesty to refer to Elias as having written of an 'unstoppable drive towards civilization'. As a German of Jewish descent who experienced

Nazism at first hand, whose mother died in Auschwitz and who wrote *The Civilizing Process* during the first years of his enforced exile in England, he was only too well aware that civilizing processes are fragile affairs that can easily go into reverse. Indeed, it is worth noting that the word *Prozess* in German means 'trial' as well as 'process' and that Elias was signifying by his choice of title that he saw western civilization in the 1930s as massively on trial. That he made the occasional very general forecast in *The Civilizing Process* about the future of humanity as a whole can, I think, be best interpreted as indicating his optimistic belief that, in the long term and despite all our present trials and tribulations, human beings all over the globe will be able through trial and error to learn better ways of living together than they have done up to now. Sociology, as Elias saw it, will have a crucial role to play in that process by making it more knowledge-based and hence more susceptible to planning and conscious control. But such expressions of optimism were always tempered in Elias's work by realistic awareness of the pitfalls and dangers that lie ahead such as the problem of avoiding nuclear annihilation, global ecological catastrophe and the massive tragedy that is threatened by Aids. Having, I hope satisfactorily, dispelled the idea that Elias advocated an untestable theory of 'unstoppable evolutionary progress', let me endeavour to spell out how we tried to use his theory at Leicester in the hope of contributing to the understanding of football hooliganism.

DEVELOPING SOCIAL AND FOOTBALL FIGURATIONS AND FAN VIOLENCE

I have suggested already that the Leicester research into football hooliganism was a direct outgrowth of my earlier studies of the development of football. More particularly, the hooliganism studies were suggested by the apparent anomaly in the accretion of hooliganism and crowd violence around what, if my earlier studies have any substance, is a more civilized game than the antecedents out of which it grew. Writing in 1890 of then contemporary 'survivals' of the folk antecedents of modern football, the ethnologist, G. L. Gomme, made an observation which is of some relevance in this connection. He wrote:

> It is impossible ... to contemplate these fierce contests ... without coming to the conclusion that the struggles were ...

not football games so much as local struggles; and when we observe further that locality now takes the place of clanship, the argument is forced home to us that we have in these modern games the surviving relics of the earliest conditions of village life and organization, when different clans settled down side by side, but always with the recollection of their tribal distinctions.

(Gomme, 1890)

Gomme's analysis suggests that one way of understanding football hooliganism, with its intense expressions of local rivalries, may be to see it as a kind of recurrently generated urban perpetuation of the old folk football tradition that has become superimposed upon and intermingled in complex ways with the more highly regulated and, in Elias's technical sense, more civilized modern game of soccer. What we attempted to do in the Leicester hooliganism research was to theorize and investigate the social bases of this pattern and the balance of continuities and discontinuities that has been involved in its development over time. One of the dominant continuities that we singled out in this connection involved the norms of aggressive masculinity that are typically generated in patriarchal societies and that involve fighting as part of the expectations associated with masculine roles. In other words, our starting point did not involve reference to a particular subclass or subculture but was the general observation that all males in a patriarchal society, independently of social class, will be expected to fight under certain circumstances and will have this expectation of themselves. If they do not, they are liable to be publicly regarded and to regard themselves as 'unmanly'.

Our second starting observation was the suggestion that the British civilizing process has involved a modification of these patriarchal norms of masculinity, bringing into being a dominant norm in terms of which males are expected to defend themselves if attacked but not themselves to provoke or initiate fights. It was this observation which gave rise to the principal problem that is investigated in *The Roots of Football Hooliganism*, namely that of explaining why specific groups of males should have regularly contravened this dominant norm in a football context earlier in the century, principally by regularly initiating attacks on match officials and opposing players and, from the 1960s onwards, principally by attacking rival fans. The hypothesis we proposed in this connection invokes the characteristic unevenness of the British civilizing process, an unevenness that seemed to us to stem largely from specific characteristics of the developing British class system. It is a process-sociological hypothesis, not a static one in terms of correlations between 'factors' or one that is supposed to have 'law-like' and universal applicability. It also tries to take into account the observable complexity of the dynamics of class and class relations. Let me try to summarize its bare outlines and respond to the critics as I go along.

First, we hypothesized that, before the First World War, a larger proportion of the British working class was relatively unincorporated into dominant or hegemonic values than is currently the case. Another way of putting it would be to say that the structural and cultural gap between classes was then considerably wider than it is today. Hence, we suggested, more working-class people then were likely to contravene dominant norms and one of the sites where this was manifested was in crowd behaviour at football. Second, we hypothesized that a change in the direction of greater incorporation got under way between the wars, continuing after the Second World War. This, we suggested, contributed on the one hand to growing orderliness in football crowd behaviour at least in England, giving rise to the 'it never happens here' myth, and on the other hand to a widening gulf between the growing 'more respectable' sections of the working class and the 'rougher' sections which, generally speaking, diminished up to about 1980. (It would be superfluous to repeat at this juncture my earlier discussion of our hypothesis about the part played by newspaper reporting in this process.) We defined 'roughness', not in terms of poverty and 'uncouth' manners – though there are, as we indicated, complex and mainly indirect connections – but in terms of values regarding violence and the initiation of fights. We did so because we were always mindful of the existence of the 'respectable' poor and of 'rougher' groupings in the middle and upper classes. In short, our main hypothesis was that crowd violence at football before the First World War is explainable largely by reference to the existence then of a much larger unincorporated section of the working class. The diminution of crowd violence between the wars and up to the mid-1950s, we hypothesized, is largely explainable by reference to a process of growing incorporation. Finally, we hypothesized that the emergence of the 'new hooliganism' in and around the mid-1960s and its sub-

sequent development are principally attributable to the attraction
into the game around that time of young males from the still
relatively unincorporated sections of the working class, a process
which led the moral panic which had been generated earlier
around the teddy boys and the mods and rockers to be transposed
into a football context. The 'new hooligans', of course, were
mainly skinheads and, for them, professional football came to be
a principal stage for the enactment of their violent rituals.

But what is the relevance of the theory of civilizing processes
to all this? In order to appreciate its bearing in this context, it is
first of all important to remember that Elias's theory is *not* a
theory of unilinear, progressive and irreversible evolution. We
accordingly attempted to explain the behaviour of males from
the less incorporated sections of the working class in two main
ways. First, we hypothesized that members of these groups are
characteristically less protected by the violence monopoly of the
state than are more incorporated members. As a result, they are
less constrained to be self-controlling in terms of the dominant
norms. Indeed, they regularly experience violence at the hands
of agents of the state and, in this way, their tendencies towards
violent behaviour are reinforced. Second, we hypothesized that
members of less incorporated groups are liable to live in communities that are characterized structurally by more or less close
approximations to what Suttles (1968) called 'ordered segmentation', that is to say, by a pattern involving a relatively great
degree of rigid age and sex segregation, with the consequence
that streetcorner groups or 'gangs' are liable recurrently to form.
Another way of putting it would be to say that, in relatively
unincorporated communities, more of life, including childhood
socialization, tends to take place in the streets than tends to be
the case higher up the social scale, and a pattern of street socialization is liable to contribute to the production and reproduction
of aggressive masculinity. Such aggressive masculinity derives from
the relative lack of adult control over children and adolescents
and is reinforced by the fact that such adult control as does occur
is liable to involve the frequent use of violence and, in Bernstein's
(1971) terms, resort to 'positional' controls. It tends to be further
reinforced by the conferral of peer-group prestige on males who
can fight and who show loyalty to their mates in confrontations.

All the evidence we collected, whether from official or unofficial sources, suggested that the majority of football hooligans in

England since the mid-1960s – around 70 per cent or 80 per cent – have always been employed in unskilled or semi-skilled manual occupations or unemployed. Accordingly we hypothesized, on the basis of data obtained by direct observation in Leicester, that a majority probably come from relatively unincorporated communities where an approximation to ordered segmentation is likely to prevail. However, it was never our intention to imply that such communities are always and everywhere structurally and culturally identical, or that football hooligans never come from communities of a different sort. Indeed, such as it is, the available evidence suggests that, since the 1960s, a minority of football hooligans have always tended to come from higher up the social scale. We hypothesized that such males are liable to come predominantly from upwardly mobile working-class families or downwardly mobile middle-class ones. Alternatively, they may be upwardly or downwardly mobile as individuals relative to their families of orientation. In cases of upward mobility, such males would be striving to keep in touch with their working-class roots and, in cases of downward mobility, they would be using the working classes as a reference group. A third hypothesis that we entertained is that some more 'respectable' working-class and middle-class males from 'broken homes' or who are otherwise experiencing conflict at home or school might be attracted to football hooliganism, perhaps because they have come to identify in a school, work or leisure context with the lifestyles and reputations of local 'roughs'. In short, *pace* Richard Giulianotti, we never hypothesized the degree of class segregation that he attributes to our case.

This counter-critique would be incomplete if I failed to refer to our discussion of the 'yuppie hooligans', the so-called 'new breed' who allegedly came to prominence around 1985. Our suggestion was that they are largely a media myth that stems from a misreading of the switch from the skinhead to the casual style. However, in putting this suggestion forward, we were careful to point out that it is possible even for members of the lower working class to achieve degrees of at least temporary affluence. Besides winning the pools, involvement in crime and the black economy are two of the main ways in which this can be accomplished. It is a pity that Hobbs and Robins did not take this part of our analysis into account when they used the ICF member that they call 'Big Cassie' as a supposed contradiction of our case.

Just one more thing needs to be said. In retrospect, I think that our main book should probably have been entitled *The Roots of English Football Hooliganism* because such a title might have helped to avoid the impression that we were attempting to develop some kind of universal theory. We were not. As figurational/process sociologists, we follow Elias (1974) in his insistence that universal, law-like generalizations lack reality-congruence as explanatory tools as far as human beings and their societies are concerned. It is, though, possible to offer a hypothesis at a higher level of generality than anything we offered in our earlier work. It is pretty clear by now that forms of violent fan disorderliness are a virtually universal accompaniment of the Association game. Or rather, periods of violent fan disorderliness are known to have occurred in almost every country where the game is played. Given this, it seems reasonable to hypothesize as a basis for further research that such disorders will be contoured and fuelled, *ceteris paribus*, by the major 'fault-lines' of particular countries. In England, that means social class, in Glasgow and Northern Ireland, religious sectarianism, in Spain, the linguistic sub-nationalisms, and in Italy, the divisions between north and south. The point about all these fault-lines, though, – and, of course, each can overlap with the others in a variety of ways – is that they are liable to produce structural approximations to 'ordered segmentation' or better, to express it in Elias's terms, 'established-outside figurations' in which intense 'we-group' bonds and correspondingly intense antagonisms towards 'they-groups' are liable to develop.[14] However, let me make myself perfectly clear. I do not consider this as having the status of anything other than a first working hypothesis. It needs to be tested in the crucible of systematic, theory-guided empirical research and doubtless, in that context, it would need to be modified, revised and expanded in numerous ways.

In this chapter, I have not dealt with every aspect of the Leicester case. However, I have said enough, I think, to show that most of the criticisms so far offered of the Leicester work have been pretty wide of the mark. It is not my intention in saying this to imply that I think we have 'all the answers' and have not made any mistakes. The gaps in our understanding are legion and I am sure we have made countless mistakes. It was not our intention in carrying out our studies of football hooliganism to come up with something faultless but, by means of the theorization and evidence we adduced, to push the understanding of football hooliganism beyond the levels reached by Marsh *et al.* (1978), and Taylor (1971) and J. Clarke (1978) in the 1960s and 1970s, in that way providing a basis for others to build further. However, for that to be possible, it will be necessary for our case to be interpreted more accurately than has been achieved by any of the critics I have reviewed in this chapter. Given the multi-paradigmatic and competitive character of sociology at present, I fear that such an ideal is likely to prove difficult to attain.

NOTES

1 For critique and counter-critique regarding this position and its applications to the field of sport, see Dunning and Rojek, 1992. A masterly introduction to the work of Elias is provided by Stephen Mennell (1990).

2 Our proposal for a study entitled 'Working Class Social Bonding and the Sociogenesis of Football Hooliganism' was submitted to the old Social Science Research Council in 1978 and funded by them from 1979 to 1982.

3 *Independent on Sunday*, 21 April 1991. In fairness to Ian Taylor, I have to say that this was a newspaper article rather than a sociological one and that, besides lacking space in such a context for a full elaboration of his case, some of what he wrote may have been editorially or sub-editorially changed.

4 See, for example, Jay Allan (1989).

5 There is not sufficient space here for me to consider the other scenario which has been quite widely canvassed, namely that the putative decline in football hooliganism resulted from the 'Acid House Phenomenon' and the taking of drugs such as 'ecstasy' which allegedly provide more of a 'buzz' than fighting at football. The issue of drugs and football is clearly one that requires further research but it seems to me that this is just another of those unidimensional explanations which may perhaps be of some relevance to a total explanation but which fail to plumb the depths of the phenomenon.

6 See chapters five and six of Dunning, Murphy and Williams (1988).

7 One could argue that the analysis in Pearson (1983) involves a 'flat earth' interpretation of history because, as he presents them, patterns of hooliganism and the 'respectable fears' they generate do not appear to change over the ages.

8 See note 37 of Armstrong and Harris (1991: 457).

9 E. Dunning, and K. Sheard (1979). Although primarily concerned with rugby, this book also deals in considerable detail with the correlative development of soccer.

10 See Elias (1978a), chapter one: 'On the Sociogenesis of the Concepts of "Civilization" and "Culture" '.
11 Norbert Elias himself would not have used the term 'interpersonal' because of what he took to be its *homo clausus* connotations, that is the fact that it presupposes an 'interaction' between wholly closed and separate human beings. For Elias, we are *homines aperti* and inextricably intertwined with others from birth to death. One of the principal aspects of this intertwining or 'interdependence' is, of course, revealed through language. Elias made great play of the fact that, as a species, human beings are, as it were, 'biologically programmed' for the processes of social learning through which we become fully human.
12 Elias is clear about the fact that the 'purest' form of absolute rule developed in France. Of all the major European countries, the process of state-formation in Britain diverged most strongly from that model. See his Introduction to Elias and Dunning (1985).
13 See Norbert Elias (1978b), especially chapter 6, 'The Problem of the "Inevitability" of Social Development'.
14 See Elias (1978b), especially chapters 4 and 5.

REFERENCES

Allan, J. (1989) *Bloody Casuals*, Glasgow: Famedram.
Armstrong, G. and R. Harris (1991) 'Football Hooligans: theory and evidence', *Sociological Review*, 39, 3: 427–58.
Bernstein, B. (1971) *Class, Codes and Control: vol. 1. Theoretical studies towards a sociology of language*, London: Routledge and Kegan Paul.
British Sociological Association (no date) *Anti-Racist Language: Guidance For Good Practice* (no date).
Clarke, A. (1992) 'Figuring a Brighter Future', in Dunning and Rojek (eds) (1992).
Clarke, J. (1978) 'Football and Working Class Fans: tradition and change', in R. Ingham (ed.) *Football Hooliganism: the wider context*, London: Inter-Action Imprint.
Dunning, E. and C. Rojek (eds) (1992) *Sport and Leisure in the Civilizing Process: critique and counter-critique*, London: Macmillan; Toronto: University of Toronto Press.
Dunning, E. and K. Sheard (1979) *Barbarians, Gentlemen and Players: a sociological study of the development of rugby football*, Oxford: Martin Robertson.
Dunning, E., P. Murphy and J. Williams (1988) *The Roots of Football Hooliganism*, London: Routledge.
Elias, N. (1974) 'The Sciences: towards a theory' in R. Whitley (ed.) *Social Processes of Scientific Development*, London: Routledge and Kegan Paul.
—— (1978a) *The Civilizing Process, Vol. 1. The history of manners*, Oxford: Blackwell.
—— (1978b) *What is Sociology?*, London: Hutchinson.

—— (1982) *The Civilizing Process, Vol. 2. State-formation and civilization,* Oxford: Blackwell.

—— (1991) *The Symbol Theory,* London: Sage.

Elias, N. and E. Dunning (1985) *Quest for Excitement: sport and leisure in the civilizing process,* Oxford: Blackwell.

Giddens, A. (1985) *The Nation State and Violence,* Cambridge: Polity.

Giulianotti, R. (1989) 'A Critical Overview of British Sociological Investigations into Soccer Hooliganism in Scotland and Britain', *Working Papers on Football Violence,* No. 1, Department of Sociology, University of Aberdeen.

Gomme, G.L. (1890) *The Village Community,* London.

Hobbs, D. and D. Robins (1991) 'The Boy Done Good: football violence, dangers and continuities', *Sociological Review,* 39.

Horne, J. and D. Jary (1987) 'The Figurational Sociology of Sport and Leisure of Elias and Dunning: an exposition and critique', in J. Horne, D. Jary and A. Tomlinson (eds) *Sport, Leisure and Social Relations,* London: Routledge and Kegan Paul, 1987.

Jary, D., J. Horne and T. Bucke (1991) 'Football "Fanzines" and Football Culture: a case of successful "cultural contestation" ', *Sociological Review,* 39, 3: 581–97.

Marsh, P., E. Rosser and R. Harre (1978) *The Rules of Disorder,* London: Routledge and Kegan Paul.

Mennell, S. (1990) *Norbert Elias, Civilization and the Human Self-Image,* Oxford: Blackwell.

Moorhouse, H. F. (1991) 'Football Hooligans: old bottle, new whines', *Sociological Review,* 39, 3: 489–502.

Murphy, P., J. Williams and E. Dunning (1990) *Football on Trial,* London: Routledge.

Pearson, G. (1983) *Hooligan: a history of respectable fears,* London: Macmillan.

Redhead, S. (1991) 'Some Reflections on Discourses on Football Hooliganism', *Sociological Review,* 39, 3: 479–86.

Sports Council/Social Science Research Council Panel (1978) *Public Disorder and Sporting Events,* London.

Suttles, G. (1968) *The Social Order of the Slum: ethnicity and territory in the inner city,* Chicago: University of Chicago Press.

Taylor, I. (1971) 'Football Mad: a speculative sociology of football hooliganism', in E. Dunning (ed.) *The Sociology of Sport: a selection of readings,* London: Frank Cass.

—— (1987) 'Putting the Boot into Working Class Sport: British soccer after Bradford and Brussels', *Sociology of Sport Journal,* 4: 171–91.

Taylor, the Rt. Hon. Lord Justice (1990) *The Hillsborough Stadium Disaster: final report,* London: HMSO.

Williams, J. (1991) 'Having an Away Day: English football spectators and the hooligan debate', in J. Williams and S. Wagg (eds) *British Football and Social Change: getting into Europe,* Leicester: Leicester University Press.

Williams, J., E. Dunning and P. Murphy (1989) *Hooligans Abroad,* London: Routledge.

Chapter 7

An analysis of football crowd safety reports using the McPhail categories

Jerry M. Lewis and AnneMarie Scarisbrick-Hauser

INTRODUCTION

After each major British football riot or crowd tragedy, an official report of the inquiry into the event has been issued. As Lord Taylor (1990: 4) notes, 'It is a depressing and chastening fact that mine is the ninth official report covering crowd safety and control at football grounds.' These reports have been a source of data and policy recommendations. They have also been a source of great controversy particularly in regard to the policy recommendations.

While these reports have been very useful, they have generally not clearly defined the concept of 'hooligan' or 'hooligan behaviours' or attempted to distinguish these aberrant behaviours from those culturally derived elements of the football spectating phenomenon. It is to this latter issue that this paper is addressed using Clark McPhail's (1991) book, *The Myth of the Madding Crowd.* In it he argues that crowd scholars have not very carefully delineated the behaviour that they purport to study. This paper first describes the typical elements of an official report, followed by a description of the McPhail categories. Identification of these categories is then examined in selected British football crowd inquiry reports. The paper concludes with suggestions for the use of these categories in future football research and implications for football policy-making.

Despite many years of study in the area, our initial observation is that the definitions of 'hooligan' and 'hooligan behaviours' are, for the most part, tautological, value-ridden and of little use to collective behaviour scholars in their present form. It is the goal of this paper to address that issue.

Clark McPhail (1991) argues that collective behaviour scholars have not carefully delineated the phenomenon they wish to study. As a means of undertaking this study, he developed behavioural categories as a guide for analysing crowd behaviours. The purpose of this paper is to investigate the application of these categories and show that the categories developed by McPhail could be very useful, in official inquiries about crowd safety. While this is of more interest to the researcher, it should also be of interest in an 'applied sense' to the policy-maker.

This paper is divided into four sections. First, we describe the elements of a selected number of recent British football disaster inquiry reports; second, we describe and discuss the McPhail categories and their application to the football (soccer) situation; third, we apply the McPhail categories to the findings in our selection of recent British disaster inquiry reports; fourth and last, we discuss the implications of our conclusions for policy-making.

It may be argued that we present the 'American' point of view in this paper. We note at the onset, that the first author has spent at least fifteen years examining sport spectator phenomena (Lewis, 1989). The second author is an Irish citizen, a physical educator and sociologist, whose doctoral dissertation dealt with the Hillsborough tragedy(Scarisbrick-Hauser and Lewis, 1990). Both authors are familiar with the world of football and experienced in the use of multiple methods or triangulation. Both authors have conducted site visits, participation observations, personal interviews, analysis of public documents. We also feel that our 'outsider' quality allows us to bring a unique perspective to football inquiry reports.

In contrast to the American football season, the British football season runs from the middle of August to early May. The majority of the games are played on Saturday afternoons with the matches beginning at 3.00 p.m. and ending around 4.45 p.m. The typical English FA Premier League club (there are four divisions in total) will play between fifty and sixty matches a year, most of them in league competition. Football supporters avidly follow the fortunes of their club in League and Cup matches.

Since the mid-1960s, British soccer has had a number of tragedies associated with it. Venues such as Bradford, Birmingham, Hillsborough, Heysel, and Ibrox have become symbols for soccer horrors. Some of these tragedies were directly related to soccer 'hooliganism' (Heysel and Birmingham) while others were indirectly related (Bradford and Hillsborough). The causes of soccer hooliganism as well as the proposed solutions have been widely debated (Taylor, 1990). Whatever the cause or solution, hooliganism has had a profound effect on English soccer, ranging from major changes in architecture of stadia to the selling of match programmes. At least nine official reports have been published since the Shortt Report of 1924. These reports have described the official view of the causes of the disaster and offered many recommendations for the improvement of safety and better crowd control strategies in English football stadia. Let us take a look at the typical elements of one of these official reports.

OFFICIAL INQUIRY REPORTS

After each football tragedy, an inquiry chairperson is appointed and instructed to investigate immediately the causes of the disaster and make recommendations as to the future of sports. These inquiries typically issue reports which have wide-ranging impacts on policy-making as well as guiding research. It is usual to find a wide-ranging policy mandate in these reports. For example, Lord Taylor was instructed to conduct an inquiry into the Hillsborough tragedy and 'make recommendations about the needs of crowd control and safety at sports events' (Taylor, 1990: 1). We suggest that the content presented in the official reports is more legal than behavioural. For example, taking a look at the Hillsborough final report presented by Lord Taylor, we find that roughly ten pages of the report are specifically devoted to the Hillsborough disaster (the interim report was devoted to a more detailed coverage of the disaster). The remainder of the report is concerned with future crowd control strategies and crowd safety at sports events.

The purpose of this paper is to suggest a strategy for evaluating the behavioural descriptions and analyses of crowd safety reports. This strategy is based on the categories developed by Clark McPhail. We begin with a detailed review of the McPhail categories of crowd behaviour (McPhail, 1991: 164).

THE McPHAIL CATEGORIES

Clark McPhail, of the University of Illinois in Urbana, USA, has conducted a number of research projects and reviews of the relevant literature in which he has brought into question the explanations of crowd behaviour by collective behaviour scholars. One of his main concerns is the failure of these scholars to indicate adequately and exactly what they are explaining. He suggests that if scholars do not know what the dependent variables are, how can they define what the independent variables are or how they influence the dependent variables.

McPhail has developed thirty-four categories of behaviour that purport to describe the activities of crowd members in any crowd.

Table 7.1 Some elementary forms of collective behaviour-in-common

Collective orientation	*Collective vocalization*	*Collective verbalization*
	1 Ooh, ahh, ohhing	
	2 Yeaing	
	3 Booing	1 Chanting
1 Clustering	4 Whistling	2 Singing
2 Arcing, ringing	5 Hissing	3 Praying
3 Gazing, facing	6 Laughing	4 Reciting
4 Vigiling	7 Wailing	5 Pledging

Collective gesticulation (nonverbal symbols)
1 Roman salute (arm extended forward, palm down, fingers together)
2 Solidarity salute (closed fist raised above the shoulder level)
3 Digitus obscenus (fist raised, middle finger extended)
4 #1 (fist raised shoulder level or above, index finger extended)
5 Peace (fist raised, index finger and middle fingers separated and extended)
6 Praise or victory (both arms fully extended overhead)

Collective vertical locomotion	*Collective horizontal locomotion*	*Collective manipulation*
		1 Applauding
		2 Synchro-clapping
	1 Pedestrian	3 Finger-snapping
	clustering	4 Grasping, lifting,
1 Sitting	2 Queuing	waving object
2 Standing	3 Surging	5 Grasping, lifting,
3 Jumping	4 Marching	throwing object
4 Bowing	5 Jogging	6 Grasping, lifting,
5 Kneeling	6 Running	pushing object
6 Kowtowing		

Source: McPhail, 1991: 164.

These categories have been developed both theoretically and empirically by McPhail and his graduate students.

As can be seen in Figure 7.1, the categories are divided into seven major groups including collective orientation, vocalization, verbalization, gesticulation, vertical locomotion, horizontal locomotion, and manipulation. Each of these groups has subcategories which we will now discuss.

Collective orientation

This category refers to the classification of orientation towards direction. McPhail (1991) writes that collective orientation 'provides a crude indicator of a range of objects' which that crowd (gatherings in McPhail's terms) might be giving attention. Collective orientation is made up of four subcategories including 'clustering', 'arcing/ringing', 'gazing/facing' and 'vigiling'. 'Clustering' refers to a process where from two to six individuals have a common or convergent direction of attention. In the terraces at soccer stadia it is possible to observe small groups of supporters all orienting themselves in the same direction, though not necessarily in the direction of the game. McPhail notes that there are also pedestrian and conversation clusters.

'Arcing/ringing' refers to the process where small groups of people create an arc or a ring around a focal point. Typically 'clustering' and 'arcing/ringing' go hand in hand. The 'arcing/ringing' process is done in concert with clustering. For example, when a group of police officers goes into the terrace to retrieve the ball or snatch a hooligan one can observe this 'arcing/ringing' process as a support attempt to observe the actions of the bobbies. The category of 'facing' is not clear in the McPhail categories. The last category of collective orientation is 'vigiling'. A possible example of a 'vigil' might be a crucial penalty kick to resolve a tie where both teams' fans assume an expectant air before the kick.

Collective vocalization

This is the process where two or more persons engage in common vocal sounds. McPhail defines subcategories of behaviour under 'collective vocalization' including ooh-ahh-ohh-ing, yeaing, booing, whistling, hissing, laughing and wailing. Ooh-aah-ing is often heard at football matches when a player attempts a goal from a long distance and supporters are able to track the ball as it heads towards the goal mouth. Yeaing is often heard when a penalty kick is successfully scored. Of course, booing is a staple of all sporting events and English soccer is not an exception. Booing can occur almost anytime during a match but is likely to be stimulated by poor refereeing of offside calls. It also occurs when a player mishandles an effective pass such as a cross from a team-mate. Lastly, booing can occur at the interval of match (half-time) when a team has been playing at below expected levels. This is rare, however, as most booing is reserved for linesmen. Whistling happens at some English soccer matches in a very unique manner. The winning team's supporters will begin to 'whistle' to encourage the referee to end the match. In contrast to American sport, the timekeeper is the referee who ends the match with three short whistle blasts. One also sees this pattern at European matches in general.

McPhail notes three other patterns of crowd behaviour – hissing, laughing, and wailing. Thinking about the typical football match, we can all identify these behavioural patterns. I have never seen hissing or wailing at an international soccer match, although in cultures where public wailing is the norm, this may happen.

Collective verbalization

This describes two or more people engaged in co-ordinated vocal sounds (but not speech). McPhail notes several subcategories of collective vocalization including chanting, singing, praying, reciting, pledging. At football matches one sees both chanting and singing and they may be properly treated together. The chanting and singing have both positive and derisive components. The positive represents the support provided by supporters to their teams. For example, when a team scores, soccer fans will begin to chant 'We are going to Wembley... We are going to Wembley', referring to the FA Cup tournament completed in the spring. Or fans will chant the name of the player who scored the goal. If a team suddenly begins to play well, the supporters will begin to chant, 'Here we go, here we go, here we go'. While chanting is the norm, singing does occur. For example, fans will sing, 'You'll Never Walk Alone' from *Carousel*. It begins 'When you walk through the night . . .'. Liverpool supporters are particularly known for this song.

There are also derisive aspects of chanting but not of singing. For example, when a team scores for the first time, its supporters will begin to chant the score 'One-nil, One-nil, One-nil'. This will usually evoke a response from opposing supporters. Or, if fans from one team are perceived as particularly quiet, the opposing fans will begin to chant, 'Where is Arsenal? Where is Arsenal?' or the appropriate team name. This will usually stimulate a response from the opposing fans.

One particular form of chanting is reserved for police. When supporters are moved from the trains or bus parks in the conga line or – as one commentator called it, a military exercise – fans will chant the elephant walk at police. This is the chant that one associates with elephants at a circus: 'de dump de dump de dump'. Generally police ignore the chant, but a few shout, 'knock it off'.

Sometimes derisive chanting can be very ad hoc. For example, at one match it was observed that a soccer ball was being brought to the field by a parachutist. Fans from both teams began to chant 'Manchester, Manchester, Manchester' referring, quite cynically, to the team that had lost players in a plane crash in the mid-1950s. Neither set of fans chanting were from Manchester.

Collective gesticulation

'Collective gesticulation' occurs when two or more persons co-ordinate their physical gestures. This is often done in connection with 'collective vocalization' and 'verbalization'. McPhail describes six types of collective gesticulation including the 'Roman salute', 'solidarity salute', '*digitus obscenus*', '#1', 'peace' and, 'praise or victory sign'. Two categories of gesticulations occur at British soccer matches, '*digitus obscenus*' and praise or victory signs. We begin with '*digitus obscenus*'. There are two forms of '*digitus obscenus*' in British football – the reverse peace sign and the 'wanker'.

In the American anti-Vietnam war movement, the 'peace' sign was displayed by a hand sign. The palm was forward with only the index and middle finger raised. The reverse of this 'peace' sign has the same meaning as '*digitus obscenus*' in the US. How-ever, it is often taken much more seriously by British football fans than in the American sport culture. A British football supporter could be seriously fined for giving it in a crowd situation, while this would not be true in North America. The other gesture is the sign of the 'wanker' which is well known by readers of this volume. This sign is not part of the sports culture of North America.

The victory sign is used when one's team scores a goal. This is usually accompanied by both chanting or singing and jumping up and down.

Collective vertical locomotion

'Collective vertical locomotion' refers to co-ordinated vertical behaviour involving two or more crowd members. McPhail delineates six types of behaviours including the obvious 'sitting', 'standing', 'jumping', 'bowing', 'kneeling', and 'kowtowing'.

Although the construction of many stadia is changing to accommodate 'all-seating arrangements', in regard to sitting and standing, many supporters stand at matches in the terraces. By far the most serious problems of fan hooliganism and crowd crushes have come from fans in the standing terraces (Popplewell, 1985; Taylor, 1989).

The only time fans sit in the terraces is at half-time when they take a break. Other than this, all of the activities are carried out while standing behind the barriers and on the terraces. Care has to be taken as it is possible to fall as some of the terraces are quite steep.

'Jumping' is a very important form of fan behaviour. The behaviour involves small groups of football supporters with their arms around each other jumping up and down, chanting or singing. It is sometimes, incorrectly in our view, interpreted as soccer hooliganism. Soccer supporters who 'jump for joy' are, for the most part, male and under the age of 25. Soccer supporters are identified by a scarf, badge or favour, or hat. Sometimes they wear all three (Morris, 1981: *passim*). The techniques of 'joy-jumping' are to jump up and down very fast. At the same time, supporters chant and wave their arms. The physical activity involves the entire body. It is always done in concert with other fans. It generally involves small groups of fans but there can be large groups of up to 200–300 fans jumping for joy.

The most avid football supporters stand at the end of the pitch in the terraces. Most of the 'jumping for joy' takes place in League matches among the visiting supporters – the most avid fans, they travel with the team to away matches and represent from 10 to 15 per cent of the supporters in the stadium. Thus we can identify that a small proportion of the fans at the match are jumping for joy. Their fervour does seem intense.

We would suggest that joy-jumping happens at important moments in a match and in highly predictable ways. Away supporters will rehearse their jumping for joy before the match begins. This usually happens when they first arrive at the stadium, before the match, after they have walked from the train station or the bus parks. The jumping for joy announces the presence of the 'away' supporters to the home fans. However, jumping for joy most often takes place after a goal is scored. But it has to be a special type of goal. Jumping for joy occurs when one's team scores its first goal or when a goal ties or puts one's team ahead. Joy-jumping may also happen when a highly skilled goal is scored such as a dramatic header after a corner kick. The last three factors mentioned by McPhail, bowing, kneeling and kowtowing were not observed at English football matches.

Collective horizontal locomotion

'Collective horizontal locomotion' takes place when two or more people co-ordinate their movements in space. McPhail proposes six types of collective horizontal movement including 'pedestrian clustering', 'queuing', 'surging', 'marching', 'jogging' and 'running'. It is possible to observe all of these behaviours at an English soccer match. Pedestrian clustering involves small groups of people moving together, talking or simply orienting towards an external object.

When the terraces are not completely filled, you can observe small groups of supporters moving back and forth in pedestrian clusters. An unfamiliar phenomenon to American sports spectators, queuing is very British and happens several times during a match although it involves more than six people. For the 'away' supporters queuing begins when the train or bus arrives at the home stadium – for example, Arsenal, a London club would travel in groups of supporters by train or bus to within a mile of the Aston Villa ground in Birmingham. From there they would be moved in conga line to the Villa Park ground. The first queue is getting into the conga line with police serving in an outrider position. The next queue would be for the purchase of tickets. This is followed by a queue to be searched – generally only young males are frisked for weapons and throwing materials such as milled lids (Lewis, 1982). Next, there is the queue for food and drink. Lastly, after the match, a queue is formed for the return conga line back to the train station or bus park.

'Surging' is a very important pattern in the terraces. The movement can be horizontal (side to side) or vertical (back to front). It is one of the major sources of danger in the British football stadia. These stadia are located, particularly in the top two English divisions in run down sections of the cities. Many were built from the turn of the century to the 1920s and consequently do not have the amenities one seems to have in many American stadia. In walking up and down one has to take care not to fall even when no fans are present. Falling becomes a particular problem when the terraces are one-half to three-quarters filled and supporters begin surging. It is a truism among the police that packed terraces are safer than partially filled ones. Not only fans but police are afraid of falling in the terraces. One of the authors was sometimes warned by the constables not to fall because he was likely to be kicked by some of the football supporters. Marching as we have noted takes place in the conga line and is part of the social control process. Jogging and running can be combined for analytical purposes. Jogging rarely occurs, however. Running happens in two ways at an English soccer stadium. First, when fans attempt to run on to the field to interrupt play – called a pitch invasion. This is fairly rare because the architecture of stadia mitigates against pitch invasions, and law-enforcement officials take such invasions very seriously. Running occurs outside the stadium usually when cries of 'fight' are heard and the police have failed to establish proper segregation and movement procedures.

Collective manipulation

'Collective manipulation' refers to the process of two or more people co-ordinating their hand activities. McPhail defines six categories of collective manipulation including applauding; synchro-clapping; finger-snapping; grasping, lifting, waving object; grasping, lifting, throwing object and grasping, lifting, pushing object. Applause was seen at matches but generally after a good try for a goal and never when a goal was scored.

Desmond Morris (1981: 259–60) has a very complex description of synchro-clapping. It happens in four different ways. First, to welcome the team on to the field at the start of the match. Second, to provide a beat for the songs. Third, to encourage players to speed up their play and fourth to encourage players to perform in a more interesting manner. It is in this latter two formats that we have observed synchro-clapping.

Grasping, lifting, waving objects (GLW) is a very important part of fan behaviour at soccer matches. It is called the scarf display. This is where hundreds of soccer supporters take off their scarfs, hold them over their heads and sway back and forth. It is a tremendous display of positive fan support. Grasping, lifting, throwing objects (GLT) occurs rarely in co-ordination. Usually throwing of objects such as coins, milled can lids, and so forth involves just one individual who is vocally supported by others. Once we heard about fans who in a group threw bananas at an opposing player. Grasping, lifting and pushing (GLP) rarely occurs at British football matches. However, we have observed that American fans engage in this activity, particularly following championship victories. For example, fans have been known to overturn cars in celebration riots (McPhail, 1991: 170; Lewis, 1982). In another study Lewis (1992) found, by using field notes and secondary material, twenty-eight of the thirty-four categories delineated by the McPhail model.

COMPLEX COLLECTIVE BEHAVIOUR-IN-COMMON.

Although McPhail has described his behavioural categories as separate entities, he emphasizes that these elementary forms of collective behaviour rarely happen alone. Typically they occur in some system of combination. He notes that 'people frequently engage in two or more of these behaviours which are performed in the same direction or at the same tempo or velocity, or are otherwise judged common to the two or more persons on one or more of these dimensions' (McPhail, 1991: 171). We now present an application of the McPhail categories to a selection of British inquiry reports.

AN ANALYSIS OF CROWD INQUIRY REPORTS

First, we identified all nouns and verbs that indicated meaningful behaviour in the parts of the reports that described the crowds. For example, words like queue, throwing, running were coded. Next, we determined if the context of the words in terms of the sentence and related sentences referred to at least two football spectators. Lastly, we matched the mentions of behaviour with the McPhail categories. The data are reported in Tables 7.2 and 7.3.

Table 7.2   McPhail categories in inquiry reports

Collective categories	Hilllsborough*	Bradford**	Birmingham***
ORIENTATION			
Clustering	.	x	.
Arcing/ringing	.	.	.
Gazing/facing	.	x	x
Vigiling	.	.	.
VOCALIZATION			
Yeaing	x	.	.
Booing	.	.	.
Whistling	.	.	.
Hissing	.	.	.
Laughing	.	.	.
Wailing	.	.	.
VERBALIZATION			
Chanting	.	x	x
Singing	x	.	.
Praying	.	.	.
Reciting	.	.	.
Pledging	.	.	.
GESTICULATION			
Roman salute	.	.	x
Solidarity salute	.	.	.
Digitus obscenus	.	.	.
#1	.	.	.
Peace	.	.	.
Praise/victory	.	.	.
VERTICAL LOCOMOTION			
Sitting	.	x	x
Standing	.	x	x
Jumping	.	.	.

Table 7.2 (continued)

Bowing	.	.	.
Kneeling	.	.	.
Kowtowing	.	.	.
HORIZONTAL LOCOMOTION			
Ped. clustering	x	.	x
Queuing	x	.	x
Surging	x	.	x
Jogging	x	.	.
Running	.	x	x
MANIPULATION			
Applauding	.	.	.
Synchro-clapping	.	.	.
Finger-snapping	.	.	.
GLW	.	x	x
GLT	.	x	x
GLP	.	.	x
ADDITIONAL CATEGORIES			
Climbing	x	x	x
Falling	x	.	x
Kicking	.	.	.
Public urinating	x	.	.

*   Source: Taylor, 1989: 4–14.
**   Source: Popplewell, 1985: 4–10.
*** Source: Popplewell, 1985: 31–9.

In the three crowd actions we were able to identify twenty-six out of the thirty-four categories receiving at least one mention in the inquiries dealing with a crowd crush, fire or hostile outburst. These data are reported in Table 7.2. The Birmingham hostile outburst received mention in thirteen categories, the Hillsborough crush in seven categories and the Bradford fire in six categories.

We then coded for frequency of behaviour. These data are reported in Table 7.3. Most of the behaviour is associated with the Birmingham hostile outburst. The crowd action represents over half of all the mentions, with GLT accounting for most of these.

Last, we identified four additional behaviour categories that need to be considered in future studies. Those listed in Table 7.2 and 7.3 include: climbing, falling, kicking, and public urinat-

Table 7.3   McPhail category frequencies†

Collective categories	Hillsborough*	Bradford**	Birmingham***
ORIENTATION			
Clustering	3	0	2
Gazing, facing	0	1	2
VOCALIZATION			
Yeaing	2	0	0
VERBALIZATION			
Chanting	0	1	3
Singing	1	0	0
GESTICULATION			
Roman salute	0	0	1
VERTICAL LOCOMOTION			
Sitting	0	1	1
Standing	0	1	4
HORIZONTAL LOCOMOTION			
Ped. clustering	1	0	5
Queuing	1	0	4
Surging	4	0	6
Jogging	1	0	0
Running	0	1	4
MANIPULATION			
GLW	0	2	1
GLT	0	2	18
GLP	0	0	3
ADDITIONAL CATEGORIES			
Climbing	1	1	13
Falling	2	0	1
Kicking	0	0	0
Public urinating	2	0	0

*   *Source*: Taylor, 1989: 4–14.
** *Source*: Popplewell, 1985: 4–10.
*** *Source*: Popplewell, 1985: 31–9.
†   Empty categories are omitted.

ing. It is essential that climbing be included in future analyses using the McPhail categories, particularly in the context of British football.

In summary, we did not find as much behavioural description

as the inquiry policy positions warranted. Our analysis of the official reports indicated that the amount of space devoted to behavioural factors that may have contributed to the disaster was disproportionate to space given to proposing global changes in football.

CONCLUSION AND RECOMMENDATIONS

This paper has shown that the McPhail categories of behaviour are useful in the evaluation of the official reports of English football disasters. We think that a research approach should be combined with the legalistic strategy that one finds in official inquiry reports. This approach would focus on a detailed description of the behaviour of football fans in tandem with policy-making. This would locate the policy components of inquiries in social science perspectives rather than legalistic/political agendas.

Next, we want to comment on the use of official inquiry reports by collective behaviour researchers. In football studies, a long hard look at football spectators' behaviour outside the reference of a disaster inquiry might lead to a more fruitful definition of this term, 'hooligan'. There is too much taken-for-granted knowledge associated with the concept of 'hooligan'. Perhaps a better term would be 'football spectator behaviour'. Finally, we would suggest that culture be included as a variable which may influence football behaviour research. A distinction needs to be made between the culturally acceptable behaviour patterns observed at football matches and those patterns which have ambiguous outcomes and are presently defined by the global term, 'hooligan'. The McPhail categories would facilitate this.

REFERENCES

Lewis, J. M. (1982) 'Fan Violence: an American social problem' in M. Lewis (ed.) *Research in Social Problems and Public Policy*, JAI Press (2): 175–206.
—— (1989) 'A Value-Added Analysis of the Heysel Stadium Soccer Riot', *Current Psychology* (8): 15–29.
—— (1992) 'An Analysis of English Soccer Games Using the McPhail Categories', American Sociological Association meeting, Cincinnati, Ohio, August.
McPhail, C. (1991) *The Myth of the Madding Crowd*, New York: Aldine de Gruyter.

Morris, D. (1981) *The Soccer Tribe*, London: Jonathan Cape.

Popplewell, O., Lord Justice (Chairman) (1985) *Inquiry into the Crowd Safety and Control at Sports Grounds: interim report*, London: HMSO.

Scarisbrick-Hauser, A. and J. M. Lewis (1990) 'Ritual Responses to the Hillsborough Soccer Tragedy', American Sociological Association meeting, Washington, D.C., August.

Taylor, P., Lord Justice (Chairman) (1989) *Inquiry into the Hillsborough Stadium Disaster: interim report*, London: HMSO.

—— (Chairman) (1990) *Inquiry into the Hillsborough Stadium Disaster: final report*, London: HMSO.

Chapter 8

Football hooliganism in the Netherlands

H. H. van der Brug

INTRODUCTION

Football is a very popular sport in the Netherlands. This is proved by the great number of practitioners, but also football is very much in demand as a spectacle. The extent of this interest is shown, for example, by the ratings of TV football. In 1985 38 per cent of the Dutch population stated that they put on their television especially for a football match, while 17 per cent even stayed at home for football on television (van der Brug, 1986).

The Netherlands–Denmark match for the European Championship in 1992 in Sweden, drew 10.2 million television spectators (76 per cent of the Dutch population over six years old) (*De Volkskrant*, 24 June 1992). With respect to this, it is illustrative that popular television films such as *Dallas* score lower: only 6 per cent of those interviewed said that they would stay at home to watch *Dallas*. It is obvious that fewer people are willing to face all types of weather to encourage their favourite team in the stadium. Nevertheless, 22 per cent of the Dutch population visited at least one football match as a spectator in 1985. However, this was usually to watch amateur football. At present approximately 4 per cent of the Dutch population go to professional football matches now and then (van der Brug, 1986).

The highest division (the first division) in Holland, which consists of eighteen clubs, draws most spectators, about 6,000 on average per match. However, for some time now there has been a declining interest in attending these matches (see Table 8.1).

This is why several clubs continually find themselves in a difficult financial position. Only PSV Eindhoven has sufficient financial resources to be able to counter the increasing competition of Italian and Spanish clubs in an international sense. As in most other countries, football in the Netherlands draws spectators from all classes in society.

Table 8.1   Dutch professional football first division attendances

Season	Total attendances	Mean number per match
1967–8	3,665,725	11,979
1972–3	3,013,107	9,847
1977–8	2,712,409	8,864
1982–3	2,584,390	8,446
1987–8	2,039,682	6,666
1988–9	1,880,413	6,145

THE DEVELOPMENT OF SOCCER HOOLIGANISM IN HOLLAND

It was as early as 1889 that a soccer match played in Rotterdam had to be stopped as a result of the inappropriate conduct of the attending public. With respect to spectator behaviour, Miermans (1955) also reported a couple of fights during football matches in the Netherlands between 1920 and 1940. Yet there are hardly any serious indications that the Netherlands experienced more than simply sporadic outbursts of violence by spectators at Dutch football matches before the Second World War.

Throughout the 1970s, a growing number of incidents occurred at Dutch first division football matches. In the early 1970s, these incidents were only sporadic. In most cases, the referee was the target of disturbances that were not too serious. Often, the official would have made a debatable decision leading to the defeat of one of the sides playing. Nearly always the incidents occurred directly before or directly after the final whistle. During the season 1971–2, for example, there were only seven incidents. In five of these cases, it was the referee who was the target of the disturbances. Usually, the violence in question consisted of throwing beer cans or other objects in the direction of the referee. Only occasionally was there a different target, for example the players from the opposing team. In these instances, the players concerned would have done something considered improper by the crowd, for example committing a foul, scoring from an offside position, or forcing a penalty. In those days, the behaviour of the players led to violence from the crowd only within the context of a change in the score, in terms of victory or defeat. In any case, this observation contradicts a derived variant of the theoretical principles of Bandura (1979), according to which the observation of violence may lead to violence from the person observing it. Nevertheless, there was a clear relation between the course of a game and the incidents. It was always the supporters of the losing team who started the disturbances.

Later this situation changed. Incidents no longer exclusively occurred during the second half or after the match. On the contrary, spectator disorder broke out more and more regularly before the match had even started. Outspoken rivalries developed between groups of young supporters. Besides the match on the pitch, a parallel contest took place between the so-called 'Sides' – groups of fans so called after the ground section where they were usually located. The heart of this competition was to outstrip the other Side in toughness, taking risks, and raising hell. Songs, insults, and other provocations were meant to arouse their opponents.

During the course of the 1970s the 'Sides' increasingly equipped themselves with knives, belts, bike chains, nunchakus, hammers, screwdrivers, knuckledusters, etc. The notorious Sides were FC Utrecht Bunnikzijde, Ajax F-Side, Feijenoord Vak-S, and Midden-Noord of FC Den Haag. Throughout this decade these young people were clearly recognizable by their club colours and club symbols on caps, shawls, and other pieces of clothing, as well as by their flags and other emblems carried by them.

By then, soccer hooliganism within stadia was kept under control by all sorts of measures such as security fencing and intensive policing. These strategies had two different effects. Inside the stadia, players of the opposing team now became the main target of unruly fans, because the effective segregation of supporters made it more difficult to attack the opposing fans. Goalkeepers were particularly prone to getting it in the neck. Initially, attacks on goalkeepers often had a ludic character, for example throwing rolls of toilet paper into the penalty box. However, these attacks became more and more violent, the goalkeeper being pelted with objects of an increasingly serious kind, such as stones, beer bottles, darts, fire-crackers, etc. By this stage, on a number of occasions highly dangerous bombs had been thrown on to the pitch.

This latter tradition continues up to the present. Unfortunately, it has to be stated that firework and smoke bombs have been increasingly replaced by fragmentation bombs and strikers. As we know, the fragmentation bomb which was thrown by a Dutch spectator on to the field during the Netherlands v. Cyprus fixture on 28 October 1987 almost led to the expulsion of the Netherlands from the European Championships. Furthermore, in 1989 Ajax were banned for one year from European competition because of the throwing of iron bars by fanatical F-Siders at a European club fixture.

Compared with the years from 1970 to 1980, the period after 1980 shows an enormous increase in violence outside the stadia. Supporters often raise hell in the inner cities and sometimes the residents are not spared. Shops are looted, passers-by are robbed. In addition much havoc is created, especially in trams, trains and buses. In this connection, it is important to mention that the supporters often arrive well in advance of the game. As the relevance of the disorder to the actual game decreases, disturbances by supporters have become a phenomenon that stands on its own. This is also shown by the composition of the Sides. In the early years of football hooliganism most Siders were greatly involved with their club, but by now this involvement has considerably decreased. The numbers of people that travel to away matches are a clear indication of this tendency. In contrast to matches which promise little excitement, high-risk matches when a team with a violent Side is playing are attended by far greater numbers of young people. It often turns out that young people take to supporting another team when things at their first club become a bit dull. The changes in the nature of incidents are shown in Table 8.2.

THE CAUSES OF FOOTBALL HOOLIGANISM

According to some theories (Veugelers, 1981), exactly the same process happened in Holland as had taken place in England, in that hooliganism came to be seen as an attempt by some to preserve traditional working-class culture. Apart from the fact that this latter aspect forms a weak link in Taylor's theory (1970), Veugelers overlooks the differences between the two national football cultures. English soccer still has a number of characteristics that – judged by the standard of Taylor (1970) and Clarke (1973) – are closely linked to male working-class values: rather

Table 8.2 The objects of violent spectator behaviour according to three time periods

Supporters' target	1970–75 no.	%	1975–1980 no.	%	1980–87 no.	%
Referee	32	(48.5)	20	(10.3)	10	(2.2)
Players opposite team/trainer/ bombs/ fireworks	10	(15.2)	59	(30.4)	94	(20.3)
Others in stadium/police	1	(1.5)	8	(4.1)	28	(6.1)
Supporters of opposite team	13	(19.7)	54	(27.8)	132	(28.6)
Vandalism in stadium/ misconduct	2	(3.0)	6	(3.1)	56	(12.1)
Vandalism, violence outside stadium/ misconduct/ discrimination	1	(1.5)	21	(10.8)	104	(22.5)
Creating havoc on the train	7	(10.6)	26	(13.5)	38	(8.2)
Total	66	(100)	194	(100)	462	(100)

Source: van der Brug, 1989.

uncomplicated, attacking football on the pitch. Proportionally, there is a lot of standing room off the pitch. Unlike continental football, English football is characterized by 'man-to-man combat' and physical struggle. Moreover, in Holland the gap between working-class and middle-class culture is much smaller. Though it is possible to indicate some similarities between the development of Dutch and the development of English football, the differences between the two must not go unmentioned. In addition, there is a significant point to be made in comparing Dutch and English football. If the observation is correct that working-class values were better preserved in English football than in its Dutch counterpart, it is still hard to see why hooliganism first appeared in England, and in its most extensive and serious form. This could have something to do with the point made above that in England the gap between working- and middle-class culture is much wider, but this still does not explain why in a country like France, which resembles England in this respect, hardly any football rowdyism occurs, while in Holland it is the order of the day.

A lot remains unexplained, when taking the ideas of Taylor, Clarke and their epigone Veugelers as a starting point. More is known of the situation of Dutch youth after World War II. Social changes have led to a cultural crisis for young people as a whole, and as a result the traditional pattern of values has lost part of its meaning. Many of these new activities were gradually going to escape social control by the traditional authorities. In addition doubts arose concerning what was considered to be desirable conduct and what was not. We have already seen that football hooliganism became increasingly detached from the game itself, and more and more a part of the crisis we have identified. Football hooliganism shared the same causes as vandalism and juvenile delinquency: the absence of effective parental control and a problematic school career. This may be shown by testing an explanatory model with the aid of the so-called Lisrel-analysis (van der Brug, 1986; Bakker, Whiting and van der Brug, 1990).

It falls outside the scope of this article to go into the methodological details of Lisrel-analyses, but the model has explained more than 60 per cent of variations in the variable under examination (football hooliganism). It also should be mentioned that research among the Dutch supporters at the European Championship Finals in Germany (van der Brug and Meijs, 1988a) and later research among hooligans (van der Brug and Meijs, 1989) gave the same results with respect to the significance of parental control and school career for football hooliganism.

In Table 8.3, based on the later research, the educational level of father and son are shown (van der Brug and Meijs, 1989). For our respondents we see that the educational level is very low and far from the 'normal' distribution of youngsters of that age in Holland. The educational level of fathers, on the other hand, is not unusually low. For persons of that age it is not far from the distribution for the Dutch population as a whole. So we see that the social background for Siders in Holland differs from what is the case in England, where it seems to be more homogeneously working-class. So, contrary to the norm in the Netherlands, our respondents (football hooligans) are of a lower educational level than their fathers.

Table 8.3 Educational level of respondents and their fathers

Level of education	Father %	Respondent %
Primary	30.5	33.5
Junior Secondary Vocational	32.2	41.1
Junior General Secondary	20.0	17.5
Senior General Secondary	10.8	6.1
Higher Vocational/University	6.4	1.9
	n = 247	n = 247

Source: van der Brug and Meijs, 1989.

It seems that in Holland there is a relationship between individual downward mobility and participation in football hooliganism, a situation which is quite different from the pattern in Britain, where the explanatory factors are much more collectivistic and highly related to social class.

DUTCH SUPPORTERS AND THE NATIONAL TEAM

Many Dutch supporters are known to have attended the European Championship Finals (10–25 June 1988) in Germany. Many violent confrontations were expected between groups of supporters from the various countries. The greatest problems were anticipated during one of the matches from the qualifying rounds: England against Holland. But remarkably enough, Dutch football hooligans in particular remained calm.

By way of two questionnaires (before and after the matches), we approached 184 young people about their behavioural intentions, expectations about what would happen, participation in violent behaviour, and so on. The intention to take part in football hooliganism was certainly present, as the survey clearly showed (van der Brug and Meijs, 1988). In particular, several respondents expected that the match against England might lead to disturbances, and a number of them were quite prepared to participate in confrontations with English supporters. Consultations as to how this would be handled in Germany had been held between representatives of various clubs before the matches. However, most Dutch supporters travelled to Germany separately. This meant that the Dutch supporters who were violently inclined were split up into small groups. English and German hooligans, on the other hand, formed relatively homogeneous groups. In the case of the Germans, this was because contacts between their clubs had led to agreements to provoke confrontations with the English, who did not travel to and from Germany like the Dutch, but stayed in the tournament's host nation between matches. This led to some degree of organization among the English themselves and to their forming a clear target for German aggression. Dutch football hooligans, on the other hand, were concealed in an enormous crowd of Dutch supporters, so big it prevented violent Dutch supporters from organizing. An additional factor was that younger club supporters, who are known to be frequently responsible for starting incidents, were under-represented in Germany. The category of football hooligans with a marginal interest in football, who only attend high-risk matches in the Netherlands, was also absent. These football hooligans are generally less concerned about missing matches, and therefore strongly inclined to take risks. The fact that the supporters in Germany definitely did not want to miss any matches helped to inhibit their violent behaviour.

In the qualifying competition for the 1990 World Cup Finals in Italy, we conducted a study of the behaviour of supporters at away matches against Finland and Wales (van der Brug and Meijs, 1990). In addition we asked a sample of youngsters who are often involved in football hooliganism about their intentions of attending matches at the 1990 World Cup Finals. Dutch hooligans did travel to both of the matches, in Finland and Wales. The mean age of these fans was rather high (25), so the younger club supporters were evidently under-represented at the away matches in question. It seems that this also was the case for hard-core hooligans. While some of the supporters at the European Championship Finals in Germany had intended to become involved in hooligan incidents, we could not find any indication of the same attitude being prevalent among those going to Finland and Wales. We found that amongst hard-core Siders from Amsterdam (Ajax), Eindhoven (PSV), Den Haag (FC Den Haag), and Rotterdam (Feijenoord), a substantial percentage of hooligans reported an intention of going to Italy to see several matches (van der Brug and Meijs, 1989).

From the comparable data which we have obtained, it is possible to say something about respondents' expectations and intentions of becoming involved in incidents. The data presented relates to four matches: the Netherlands v. England at the European Championship Finals in Germany; Wales v. the Netherlands during the qualifying phase for the 1990 World Cup Finals; the Netherlands v. England in the first round of the 1990 Finals; and the Netherlands v. Germany in the second round of this tournament (van der Brug and Meijs, 1991). Did we expect problems in connection with these games? The findings are presented in Table 8.4.

Table 8.4 Expectations of incidents at four matches involving the Dutch national team

Prospect of incidents	v. England in Germany %	v. Wales in Wales %	v. England in Italy %	v. Germany in Italy %
Impossible	13.5	40.0	8.7	3.0
Possible	66.5	58.3	67.4	23.5
Fights certain	20.0	1.7	23.9	73.5
	n = 174	n = 86	n = 92	n = 34

Source: van der Brug and Meijs, 1991.

Expectations in connection with the Wales-Netherlands match did not run high. For both matches against England, and the match against the Germans, things were clearly different. Only a few supporters ruled out the possibility of incidents taking place during these matches. A substantial percentage was (almost) sure that incidents would occur during the three other matches. This holds especially for the Netherlands–Germany game. A strong correlation appears between fans' expectations of football-related disorder at matches (see Table 8.4) and the bad record of opposing fans for football hooliganism. These correlations were .25 for the England match in Germany, .29 for the match against Wales, and for the matches in Italy against England and Germany respectively .57 and .38. Respondents with a hooligan record expected more strongly than others that incidents would take place during the above matches. In this connection one may think of 'mirror perception', and the relationship between self-opinion and the opinions of similar others. This term was chosen because the perception of the latter group is regarded as mirroring one's own outlook; thus, in order to see them you look at yourself. But other factors play a role as well. Before the match in Wales, for example, Dutch football hooligans proved to have read and heard more about possible incidents during that game (tau =.35), while in addition they had heard more about the rumour of English hooligans coming to the game (tau =.39).

Now, what may be said about the actual intention of engaging in football hooliganism during those matches involving the Dutch national team? This data is presented in Table 8.5. Since the question asked was slightly modified, the data on the Netherlands-Germany match is not included in this table.

Against Germany, approximately 27 per cent indicated that they did not want to be involved in incidents at all, 27 per cent did want to be involved, while the remainder made certain conditions on their potential involvement. We may deduce from this data that – in any case against Germany – there was clearly a violent intention amongst these fans.

Table 8.5 Expectations of personal involvement

Attitude to be adopted	v. England in Germany (fractions)	v. Wales in Wales (fractions)	v. England in Italy (fractions)
'I don't want to have anything to do with it.'	.52	.75	.46
'Only watch what happens.'	.26	.24	.27
'Yes, see who's stronger.'	.22	.01	.27
	n = 174	n = 86	n = 92

Source: van der Brug and Meijs, 1991.

There is hardly any difference between the willingness to engage in violent activities at the games against England in Italy and Germany. In Wales, however, this willingness was much less prevalent. The latter finding was not simply the result of a lack of willingness in general to engage in hooliganism. As many as 21 per cent of the supporters in Wales stated that they might be involved in incidents in the future, while 26 per cent said it would be unlikely but not impossible. Were the supporters of Wales no real challenge? Or had the safety measures that had been announced in England and Wales caused this lack of readiness to undertake action?

In Germany and Italy, where a clear willingness to engage in violent actions could be found, the following pattern appeared. In Germany most people who did not want to have anything to do with incidents of hooliganism had, of course, no hooligan record (sixty-one respondents), but the fact is that twenty-five who do actually participate in football hooliganism in the Netherlands said exactly the same thing. Of the remaining 48.5 per cent, 26.3 per cent did not want to be involved – except for watching what was taking place (ten persons in this category are not hooligan, but thirty-four are). The other 22.2 per cent answered 'Yes, I would like to see who is stronger.' All these respondents turned out to have a record of hooliganism.

In Italy the findings are quite similar. First of all, there is the correlation between the scale 'football hooliganism' (see Table 8.4, p. 182) and respondents' own involvement in the incidents at the match between the Netherlands and England. The correlation is very strong (tau =.65; p < .001). Here too we see, however, that a large number of the respondents who do not want to have anything to do with incidents have in fact a record of hooliganism (51.3 per cent). It is possible, though, to draw the other conclusion, namely that people who do not take part in hooliganism in the Netherlands are not planning to do so in Italy either. Our data gave only one exception to that rule.

It should be pointed out, however, that the category for football hooliganism in the Netherlands – but not in Italy – mostly concerns respondents with low scores on the scale 'football hooliganism'. It never concerns the hard-core hooligans. Finally, it seems important that a good many participants at the Dutch matches only wanted to watch the goings-on in Italy. But this is, of course, a circumstance in which one may be slowly manoeuvred into a position in which participation is inevitable.

As in Germany in 1988, a lot of problems were expected with groups of supporters at the 1990 World Cup Finals, in particular at one match during the first round, namely England v. Netherlands. In addition, supporters from other countries were expected to keep their end up. After all, it had been the German supporters who had had a major share in the disturbances that occurred during the 1988 European Championship Finals in Germany. (How would supporters from the former GDR behave?) In addition, supporters from Spain, Italy and Yugoslavia were repeatedly involved in disorder. In spite of these facts, no major incidents occurred. Apart from serious riots in Milan involving German and Yugoslavian supporters, and some incidents caused by English fans, nothing really negative happened. The latter incidents, which took place in Sardinia, were blown up by the media to gigantic proportions.

The Dutch high-risk supporters kept very quiet, as they always do with matches involving the national team. This had previously been the case during the 1988 tournament in Germany, and at the away matches during the qualifying round for the World Cup Finals in Italy. Only the home game against Germany in the qualifying round led to serious fights between German supporters and Dutch fans; a number of the Dutch fans involved never go to football matches. A number of explanations for the quiet behaviour of the Dutch supporters in Germany were advanced by us on the basis of our survey in Germany (van der Brug and Meijs, 1988).

The Dutch hooligans were hidden in an enormous crowd of Dutch supporters with a positive attitude towards the tournament. This crowd was too big to be attacked by the English or German hooligans, and at the same time prevented violent Dutch supporters from organizing. Those hooligans with only a marginal interest in the actual football game were missing, in particular those who attend high-risk matches in the Netherlands. In addition, the younger Siders were under-represented in Germany. These supporters are generally less concerned about missing matches and therefore strongly inclined to take risks. This had obviously not been the case with Dutch high-risk supporters in Germany.

At the away matches during the qualifying competition for the 1990 World Cup Finals, the situation was somewhat different from the German tournament. There were some supporters who sometimes engaged in hooliganism in the Netherlands, but never in its more serious forms. The intention of becoming involved in incidents at away matches of the Dutch national team was absent. Striking features of these matches were the relatively high average age of the Dutch high-risk supporters present, and a contextual factor, namely the positive attitude of the Dutch supporters in general. The latter aspect implies a primitive form of support of the Dutch national team as well as an intention to celebrate during each match, an attitude leading to the type of behaviour which is also typical of Danish football fans and Dutch spectators at skating matches. This positive attitude of Orange supporters shows a strong connection with their composition as a group, which is to a considerable extent dominated by spectators who seldom attend football matches in the first division of Dutch professional football. They are averse to football hooliganism in all its forms and they are the ones who set the tone of support for the national team abroad.

The potential for violence in Italy was quite similar to the situation in Germany in 1988. A substantial number of Dutch supporters had a so-called hooligan record, while many high-risk supporters were not entirely averse to being involved in incidents. However, in Italy these fans proved highly intimidated by two circumstances. First, there were the repressive actions of the Italian police followed naturally by the fear of severe sanctions such as imprisonment or deportation. Second, they were afraid of the English hooligans whose reputation had been heightened by exaggerated reports in the media.

In addition, a number of high-risk supporters took the view – and with good reason – that English hooligans outnumbered them and were better organized. When the Netherlands played against Germany in Milan, the same applied to the German hooligans. They too were better organized than their Dutch counterparts. It is striking that this corresponds with the situation in Germany in 1988. As an explanation we then argued that while the Dutch travelled to and from the host nation between matches, the English stayed in Germany throughout, so that the latter were able to get organized to some extent. As for the Germans, co-operation between their various Sides was easier to realize in their home country.

In Italy the situation was quite similar. The match against the English took place in Sardinia, the 'home-town' of the English supporters, and the same went for the German supporters in Milan. The Dutch supporters came to the games by various means of transport from various places. There was little time to get organized. In spite of that we take the view that co-operation between Dutch high-risk supporters from various Sides comes about only with the greatest difficulty. National solidarity does not prevail over the group identity of the particular Side. Talks prior to both tournaments (European and World Championships) have hardly led to any results in terms of concerted action.

Dutch police travelling alongside supporters have exerted a positive influence on the behaviour of Dutch supporters in Italy. They were reasonably accepted by the Dutch high-risk supporters, even if these supporters knew they were being watched closely. The functions of the police among the supporters are wide and their task consists of providing information, mediating and directing. The fact that many supporters have confidence in them after seeing them work in Italy, will definitely contribute to the effectiveness of their actions in the Netherlands.

FOOTBALL HOOLIGANISM AND THE MEDIA

The many emotional descriptions of football hooliganism in the media raise the question of the influence of such reporting. An important shortcoming of the many observations about the relationship between the media and football hooliganism is their poor empirical basis. With reference to this an attempt has been made to investigate the significance of the media for the supporters themselves (van der Brug and Meijs, 1988). What is, according to these supporters, the influence or the effect of the media reports on their behaviour and the reputation of their Side? In all there were fifty-three respondents from different Sides in Holland. The question of whether the sample survey consists of a sufficient number of hooligans to carry out an adequate analysis can be answered positively on the basis of a scale named 'football hooliganism' (Mokken Method), which consists of statements that represent various types of behaviour, such as fighting with supporters of the opposite team, done by 92 per cent of the respondents at least now and then, throwing fireworks on the field (22 per cent), carrying weapons (30 per cent), throwing stones (58 per cent), and so on. The scale consists of nine items.

There are two methods of improving one's status: a person or persons is/are captured or written about individually; or, in an indirect manner, a Side is described so that one may identify oneself with the Side. In the latter case it may be important that the Side with which one identifies receives greater attention than other Sides. Table 8.6 demonstrates the very strong influence of the media on the Sides' reputation variables.

Table 8.6 Scale of media influence on reputation

Statement	diff.	coeff. H (i)
'Some boys do everything to appear on *Studio* [Dutch TV programme] or in the *Nieuwe Revu* [Dutch weekly].'	.45	.59
'It is fun when everybody can watch on TV that we were surrounded by police while we went to the stadium in Venlo.'	.49	.66
'A real —Sider thinks it is important that his Side appears in the newspapers more frequently than other Sides.'	.64	.76
'The more we get into the newspapers, the greater it is.'	.68	.66
'It is fun when the —Side is mentioned in the newspaper or on television.'	.70	.82
'Side supporters think it is important that newspapers write about their Side.'	.77	.85
Scale coefficient	H = .72	N = 47

Source: van der Brug and Meijs, 1988b.

As we see as a result of the scale-construction, seeking prestige appears to be an important motivating factor for participation in football hooliganism. The scale 'media influence on reputation' shows a strong relationship with the scale 'football hooliganism' (Kendall-tau =.48; p<.001).

The prestige which can be acquired from 'deeds of heroism' that are represented in the media, or by the fact that the Side with which one identifies is creating a furore, can be motivating for football hooliganism. It is obvious that when such prestige is thought to be important, one is inclined to display a type of behaviour which contributes to this prestige, thus hooliganistic behaviour. But, of course, such a conclusion is not necessarily a safe one. In order to trace this further, a scale was constructed consisting of items that represent such behavioural tendencies.

The statements in the scale and the reactions to these statements suggest that information preceding a match can be motivating for football hooliganism. This is, for example, shown by reactions to the statement that supporters who are a part of the

Table 8.7 Scale of media-influenced behaviour of supporters

Statement	diff.	coeff. H (i)
'When I see and hear on television that a Side calls us names, I become angry and I will remember it.'	.31	.40
'When I read in the newspaper that the Hague Side has constructed the bomb, I think it becomes time that we show our reputation.'	.49	.52
'When I read in the newspaper that the Side of the club that will pay us a visit are fighters, we'll give them a special reception.'	.51	.47
'When I read in the newspaper that there will be extra police, it makes the coming match more interesting.'	.78	.72
Scale coefficient	H = .51	N = 49

Source: van der Brug and Meijs, 1988b.

other Side are fighters, or that a different Side has constructed a bomb. Reporting about extra police can attract supporters because the latter group will expect that this means that something interesting is going to happen. Media reports on violent behaviour encourage a similar type of behaviour (imitation). The above scale of 'media influence' is highly correlated with the scale 'football hooliganism' (tau =.48; p<.001). There is no doubt whatsoever that the media have some effect on football hooliganism.

MEASURES TO FIGHT FOOTBALL HOOLIGANISM

Ever since the early 1970s football hooliganism has gained a firm foothold in the Netherlands, in spite of an intensive policy to suppress this undesired social phenomenon. Though the past few years show a slight drop in football hooliganism, the events at a number of games played recently indicate that these 'outbreaks of football violence' are far from being kept under control.

The first policy document on this matter saw the light in 1977. In this document hard and emphatic police action was advised against, in favour of preventive measures. Policy-makers were especially pleased with an FC Den Haag initiative worthy of imitation. The club had founded a young supporters' association, and its membership card admitted its holder to all sorts of facilities, for example video shows. In general the project group involved was an advocate of clubs developing a positive attitude towards their supporters. The relationship between supporters and clubs was to be tightened. This view has set the agenda ever since. The interim report of the Roethof Committee (1984) is characterized by considerations of similar import. These ideas seem to be derived from the English sociologist Ian Taylor (1970), who contended that football hooliganism was the result of the alienation of supporters from clubs, a process which had commenced in the 1960s. However, this theory is highly contestable. In so far as such a breach can be identified in England, the gap between clubs and players on the one hand and the supporters on the other was much smaller than in most other West European countries. Nevertheless, football hooliganism in England is a more serious phenomenon than anywhere else in the world. Besides, one can also ask how effective the FC Den Haag policy has been? Doesn't Den Haag have one of the most violent Sides in the Netherlands?

In 1981 a report was published by the 'Safe Stadia Committee' of the KNVB (the Dutch Soccer Association). This report made out a case for better coordination of the police forces involved, and for stadia being forced to comply with certain safety standards. They advised setting up a 'Safety Bureau', in order for information to be gathered, and local and supra-local consultations to be stimulated. Measures taken initially were in the field of techno-prevention, for example steel fencings, segregation of supporter groups, searching fans at the gates, restrictions on the selling and drinking of alcoholic beverages, etc. These measures, if taken in isolation, cause spectator movement to other places, which can only mean that problems will increase in the long term. Pratt and Salter (1984), referring to the situation in England where the same types of measures were taken, pointed out that hooliganism could even increase as a result of the segregation of supporters. The target sections have developed into true fortresses to be defended. As a result pseudo-subcultures (Ends) have developed which have served as a sort of institutionalization of football rowdyism. The Netherlands showed a similar development.

In 1985 the consultative body, the National Consultations on

Football Hooliganism was installed. It brought together senior men from the Ministries of Home Affairs, Justice, Transport and Communications, and Welfare, Health and Cultural Affairs, as well as representatives from the local authorities, the police, the railway police, and the Dutch Soccer Association. The 1986 interim report states that by then the co-ordination of police policy and the various local authorities had improved. At the Information Point for Football Hooliganism, which was set up only recently, data is stored about undesirable conduct of supporters.

Early in 1987 a research project by the Criminality Prevention Bureau, carried out by order of the Ministry of Welfare, Health and Cultural Affairs, was published. The Bureau concluded that, in concert with youth welfare work, a number of projects could be developed aiming at the hard-core hooligans. According to the authors, these hard-core hooligans include supporters who regularly attend matches, and who are often involved (directly or indirectly) in incidents inside or on the way to the stadium. However, this description is not without problems, something already indicated by the authors themselves. In my opinion, the main problem is that this finding concerns two different patterns of behaviour, namely regularly going to a match on the one hand, and involvement in incidents on the other. Of course these two behavioural aspects are inter-related. However, a not too spectacular correlation also implies that the two variables are to a certain extent independent. In other words: there are also young people who participate in football hooliganism, but who do not regularly enter the stadium. This is obvious from the fact that many more Siders come to high-risk matches than to the games where nothing exciting is expected to happen. Furthermore, many 'supporters' change clubs, when little that is sensational occurs. It remains to be seen whether those young people are responsive to this type of positive policy aimed at supporters. In addition, such a policy approaches football hooligans as a separate group. This implies the danger of turning the Sides into institutionalized bodies, a development started earlier thanks to all sorts of techno-preventive measures. In spite of these objections a positive policy towards supporters is the main policy instrument to reduce football hooliganism in the Netherlands.

A rather encouraging indication of the appropriateness of this approach is the research evaluation of social programmes and

youthwork in relation to the problem of football hooliganism
(van der Brug, van Dijk, Hilhorst, Meijs and van Uffelen, 1991).
There is some evidence for a diminishing tendency for participation in football hooliganism in the period 1988–90. This is
especially so compared to clubs without social programmes (Table
8.8).

Table 8.8   Incidents in relation to supporters from clubs with and
without social programmes (first division)

Social programmes	1988–9 Incidents		1989–90 Incidents	
	no.	%	no.	%
With social programmes	161	75.9	139	58.6
Without social programmes	51	24.1	98	41.4
Totals	212	100	237	100

Source: van der Brug et al., 1991.

Although the results are not conclusive in view of the shortness
of the programmes at the moment of the evaluation, they support
an approach which is not only based upon techno-prevention.

CONCLUSIONS

Those expecting a definitive answer as to the causes of football
hooliganism, let alone the type of policy to be followed to reduce
it, may be disappointed about the current knowledge in this
specific field. Nevertheless, football hooliganism is increasingly
regarded as a complicated social phenomenon.

In the Netherlands football hooliganism is initially attributed
to rough play on the pitch. Though players' violent behaviour
may add to the aggression of the crowd, this theory is too simple
an explanation for hooliganism. The same applies to the train of
thought according to which the 'degeneration' of Dutch professional football would be to blame.

It seems to be more advisable to consider the development of
Dutch professional football as a configuration in Elias's sense:
phenomena with a certain interdependence. The relations
between and within these configurations only to a limited degree

result from the actions of individuals; they have their own, unpredictable dynamics. By the early 1970s, the 'result' had become the dominant value within the configuration of Dutch professional soccer to which all other normative limitations were made subordinate. 'Fair play' was replaced by a more instrumental value, which implies that only the final result counts. This has been obvious from the behaviour of club directors, coaches, and players, as well as from the behaviour of the spectators. This value was clearly expressed by Rinus Michels, the former coach of the Dutch National team, when he said that 'football is war'. In fact, his statement reflected the roots of the behaviour of all those involved. Thus, we have the club director insisting on the sacking of the trainer fired after bad results, the coach ordering his team to play according to a result-directed system, and the players sometimes resorting to gross instrumental violence in order to reach the desired result. But this value also determines the conduct of some groups of spectators, and not exclusively of the so-called hooligans. It is not just the kids who treat the opposing team to catcalls before the kickoff. Our research has shown (van der Brug, 1986) that over the years, football crowds have increasingly resorted to this sort of behaviour. They have also become more accommodating about serious fouls upon the players.

Towards the end of the 1970s, football hooliganism became increasingly isolated from the course of game. A causal pattern had come to exist that showed great similarities with other forms of vandalistic and delinquent behaviour. Concomitant circumstances in this connection are the absence of effective social control by the parents and an unfavourable school career. In Holland there is some downward social mobility among football hooligans related to worklessness, short-run hedonism, alcohol and drugs.

It seems tempting to judge the development of Dutch professional soccer in terms of social disintegration. Two additional processes fit into this idea: social differentiation would then be the result of growing cultural diversification, which implies that the different sectors of our society, all with their own patterns of norms and values, are increasingly growing apart. Within professional soccer, according to this view, a pattern of norms and values has developed that is completely separated from similar social systems. Though it is undoubtedly correct that the development of professional soccer is characterized by serious forms of decay of social standards, this view completely passes over a similar decay of moral principles in many other departments of our society. Furthermore, two other circumstances remain unaccounted for. In the first place, why have traditions of football hooliganism developed particularly in the Netherlands, England and Germany, but to a much lesser degree in other European countries, where professional soccer has shown a similar development? And secondly, why do some clubs show the development of a tradition of hooliganism, while other clubs do not?

In Holland there is some evidence for the positive influence of the police in travelling to away matches with fans, and for the positive influence of social programmes in relation to football hooliganism.

REFERENCES

Bakker, F. C., H. T. A. Whiting and H. van der Brug (1990) *Sport Psychology, Concepts and Applications*, New York: John Wiley and Sons.

Bandura, A. (1979) 'A Social Learning Theory of Aggression', *Journal of Communication* (28): 12–29.

Brug, H. H. van der (1986) *Voetbalvandalisme, een speurtocht naar verklarende factoren*, Haarlem: De Vrieseborch.

—— (1989) *Voetbalvandalisme in Nederland*, Amsterdam: Stichting Het Persinstitut.

Brug, H. H. van der and J. Meijs (1988a) 'Nederlandse supporters bij de EK in Duitsland', *Onderzoeksverslag*, Rijswijk: Ministerie van WVC.

—— and —— (1988b) 'Voetbalvandalisme en de media', *Tijdschrift voor Criminologie* (4): 336–47.

—— and —— (1989) *Effectevaluatie Voetbalvandalisme en Jeugdwelzijn*, Amsterdam: Stichting Het Persinstituut.

—— and —— (1991) *Dutch High-Risk Supporters at the World Championship Football in Italy*, Amsterdam: Stichting Het Persinstituut.

Brug, H. H. van der, A. G. van Dijk, N. Hilhorst, J. Meijs and R. P. van Uffelen (1991) *Eindrapport experimenten voetvalvandalisme en jeugdwelzijnwerk*, Rijswijk: Ministerie van WVC.

Clarke, J. (1973) 'Football Hooliganism and the Skinheads', *Centre for Contemporary Cultural Studies*, University of Birmingham: CCCS.

Giltay Veth, N. J. P. (voorzitter) (1981) 'Rapport van de Commissie Veilig Voetbalbezoek', Zeist.

Hartsuiker, J. P. (voorzitter) (1977), 'Rapport van de Projectgroep Vandalisme van Voetbalsupporters'.

Landelijk Overleg Voetbalvandalisme (1986) 'De eerste helft, een tussenbericht over de werkzaamheden van het Landelijk Overleg Voetbalvandalisme in het eerste jaar', 's-Gravenhage.

Miermans, C. (1955) *Voetbal in Nederland: maatschappelijke en sportieve aspecten*, Assen: Van Gorcum.

Pratt, J. and M. Salter (1984) 'A Fresh Look at Football Hooliganism', *Leisure Studies* (3), no. 2: 201–20.

Taylor, I. R. (1970) 'Football Mad: A Speculative Sociology of Football Hooliganism', in E. Dunning (ed.) *The Sociology of Sport*, London: Frank Cass.

Veugelers, W. (1981), 'Wie zijn de echte voetbalsupporters? Oorzaken en achtergronden van het voetbalvandalisme', Psychologie en Maatschappij.

Chapter 9

Tackled from behind

Gary Armstrong and Dick Hobbs

While football hooliganism is a problem, we can observe the
generation by police, media and politicians of a moral panic on
a par with that detailed by Hall *et al.* (1978). We do not deny
that football-related disorder both in and around grounds has
caused death and injuries. The first death related to football
hooliganism occurred in August 1974. One writer (Smith, 1983)
found 'several more' in the 1975 and 1976 seasons, six murders
between 1979 and 1982, and dozens of injuries through slashings.
However, the author did not consider it necessary to chronicle
actual evidence for these claims. Yet, whatever the true extent
of the problem we would argue that casualties from football
hooliganism compare favourably with, for instance, national statistics on homicides in 1989 and, in the same year, nearly 800
fatalities on the roads as a result of drunk driving. It is our
contention that the police response is disproportionate to the
problem, and that covert policing is the primary tool of a police
force seeking to promote and extend both the tactics and ideology of a pervasive and intrusive surveillance culture.

It is the attitude of the police which is the primary focus
of this chapter – in particular, their obsession with hierarchical
structures and organization coupled with their unshakeable faith
in their own intelligence gathering. We listen to various police
witnesses informing the unknowing public of the hooligan gangs.
One example is Mr David Phillips, then Chair of the Association
of Chief Police Officers (ACPO) on Football Hooliganism, whose
1987 lecture at the European Conference on Football Violence
was the product of three sources: 'my own observations; our
considerable football intelligence and what I have read and heard
from others'. The hooligan, conference learned, had the follow-

ing characteristics: a lack of interest in football, little knowledge
of the game, his use of which was simply to pursue gang aims.
Individuals in the gang were recognizable by being 'restless' and
at away games 'hiding in nooks and crannies... looking for
opportunities to exploit', and 'one can recognize those who have
won their spurs'. (How, we were not told.) Mr Phillips described
hooligan 'challenges, campaigns' which presented opportunities
to 'win battle honours', marked by a 'high level of organization'.

Psychological notions were introduced; 'the whole grounds are
a volatile mix capable of ignition'. The level of sound in the
crowd can cause 'paralysis', and because of this the hooligans
deliberately organize chanting and clapping. 'The hooligan wants
to be part of a large group, he is a would-be leader, a sort of
"warlord".' Chanting in unison heightens his sense of power; 'the
most violent are those that do this chanting'. Having generated
such an atmosphere the hooligan can perform his deeds. This
combination of psycho-babble and uninformed self-opinion was
the extent of his knowledge.[1]

Until the introduction of the Public Order Act 1986, football
hooligans were invariably dealt with by the legal process, by use
of minor charges contained in the Public Order Act 1936
(Coalter, 1984; Cook, 1978; Trivizas, 1980, 1981). The first use of
serious public order charges against football fans was, we believe,
in November 1973 in London. Three fans were charged with
affray after attacking a 15-year-old rival. The Metropolitan Police
were quoted as saying that this new measure would be used in
future (*Sheffield Star*, 16 November 1973). The situation became
more grave, so that the very serious charge of riot was served
upon a Chelsea fan in 1985, normally meriting a maximum sentence of ten years. However, Judge Argyle sentenced the fan to
life imprisonment. The facts of the case were that outside the
ground the youth was arrested and on the evidence of one police
officer was charged. His actual action was that of attempting to
kick a rival fan. His attempt failed and there were no injuries.
Although welcomed by various MPs and police representatives,
the life sentence was reduced, in the Court of Appeal in May
1986, to three years.

However, the initial prosecution was a portent of things to
come. The state responded to hooliganism from 1986 onwards
by making use of little used conspiracy charges. In total, thirty-
six football fans in London were charged with 'conspiracy to

cause an affray' in 1987. This is significant because as Kettle and Hodges (1982: 20, 187–8) have written, 'The conspiracy theory is just about the oldest card in authority's pack', being the same charge as that used against the emerging labour movement in the nineteenth century and in the 1960s against political activists. The authors chronicle the period from the 1780 Gordon Riots to the 1981 inner-city riots, and show how both media and police have consistently sought to uncover plots and ringleaders. In addition, Bunyan (1977) notes that charges of incitement and conspiracy do not require proof of any actual crime having been committed.[2]

PAST ATTITUDES TO COVERT POLICING

Significantly, attempts both to control movements of fans and to infiltrate travelling supporters with plain-clothes police was originally requested by the Football Association in 1981. The FA also asked the Foreign Office for names and addresses of England supporters arrested at a match in Switzerland in order to blacklist them. The FO refused, arguing it would be an infringement of liberty (Croker, 1987). On a domestic level the FA recommended plain clothes police be used in the mid-1960 and again in the early 1980s. The suggestion of co-ordinating information on football hooligans was repeatedly made by football authorities but refused by the Home Office, claimed the then Secretary of the Professional Football Association, Mr Graham Taylor (*The Times*, 11 May 1983).

Covert policing can be a powerful device in presenting criminal behaviour as being especially problematic. Brought to the attention of the public, it serves to stress the seriousness of the threat and the danger to which the officers are exposed. The boring, routine, essentially administrative, nature of everyday detective work (Manning, 1980) is ignored in favour of the low-life glamour of the policeman who temporarily goes over to the other side. The selective presentation of covert policing is especially effective in the constant competition for resources which takes place both inside and outside of the police. It is also a potent political tool for the dramatization of the fight against crime, particularly in the fight against violent, seemingly self-indulgent, crime. For, as in the case of football hooliganism, votes and finances are to be gained from being seen to do something about such apparent evil. During the 1980s a tactic previously associated with attempts to apprehend armed robbers or terrorists was applied to football supporters. It had become in Marx's (1988: 1) terms 'a cutting edge tactic'.

British society has an ambiguous relationship with covert policing and has traditionally avoided adopting any form of police work other than the uniform patrol as its primary rhetorical device. The motivation for this selectivity is to be located in the socio-economic climate that prevailed in the era immediately before state policing was introduced in Britain.

Localized, pre-industrial precedents for latter-day policing agencies conformed to a community ethos with a strong emphasis on an overt accessible presence (Critchley, 1978). By the Middle Ages, the preservation of the King's Peace was firmly established as the primary function of the police, establishing via statute 'a direct link between the authority of the constable and the power of the monarchy' (Hobbs, 1988: 17).

Formal social control in Britain became bonded to the maintenance of the prevailing social order. This principle was reinforced by the Statute of Winchester in 1285 which introduced three measures; the watch, indicating the involvement of the citizenry in routine patrol and order maintenance; the practice of hue and cry that enforced all citizens to participate in the apprehension of criminals; and the requirement for all men to keep weapons in their homes in support of hue and cry (Critchley 1978: 6). Social control was localized, overt and, via the majesty of the law, retained powerful links with the highest authority in the land (Styles 1987: 21).

By the time that the Government was forced by increased disorder to consider a unified state-funded police force in London, the role of the police had been taken up by many disparate professional, semi-professional and amateur organizations (Armitage, 1937; Ascoli, 1979; Critchley, 1978; Dilnot, 1929; Radzinowicz, 1956). These organizations were funded from a variety of state, local government and private sources, but they all shared an essentially *preventative* function. Resistance to reorganizing these various constables, watchmen and runners into one coherent structure was vehement and leant heavily upon the belief that policing and republicanism went hand in hand. While musket volleys and sabre charges were regarded as appropriate ways of dealing with provincial unrest (Silver, 1967), such bloody behaviour on the streets of London, where a sedate, rational, ordered commercial world was rapidly emerging, was hardly good for business (Miller, 1977; Reith, 1956: 157).

Consequently a form of identifiably civil control was needed, one that did not embody the republican threat of the insidious French informer and *agent provocateur,* yet was essentially non-militaristic in its practice. The model that Parliament eventually bought in 1829 was the preventative, uniformed 'impartial socio-legal-sanitary inspector' (Miller, 1977). The emphasis on prevention in the political rhetoric that preceded the 1829 Police Act is especially crucial. The Police Act was sold to Parliament as creating 'a vigorous preventative police consistent with the free principles of our free constitution (Robert Peel, quoted in Radzinowicz, 1956: 362). Consequently,

> the early police presence was far from the threatening, insidious, unseen spy from the French system and, in forming a fully professional force of paid constables, visually accessible to all, the clientele were also easily distinguishable, and the internal binding of the organization assured.
> (Hobbs, 1988: 34; see also Manning, 1977: 128–9)

The political and organizational tone for British policing was therefore set, and there was apparently no room for covert operations. Yet it rapidly became apparent that a detective function in some form was necessary. Initially this took the form of a small, low-key 'Detective Branch' which came into being in 1842, and was severely restricted by organizational rules from indulging in any practice that so much as hinted at covert activity. For instance they were forbidden to mix with criminals (Critchley, 1978: 60; Hobbs, 1988: 40–1).

By the time the CID was formed in 1877, the overt nature of British detective work was finally established and even subsequent corruption tended to be the result of administrative or licensing discrepancies (see Ascoli, 1979: 210; Sherman, 1974: 98). Any hint of undercover work was met with outrage, and the fear of 'foreign' or 'continental' policing inspired the tag of *agent provocateur* being applied to such un-British activity (Prothero, 1931: 100).

Indeed the British detective was expected to display qualities that were not only unsuited to covert operations but also remarkably similar to the attributes that one might require of any member of the 'lower orders'. As Clarkson and Hall-Richardson (1889: 266) explain

> Englishmen possess pre-eminently qualities which are essential to good detective work such as dogged pertinacity in watching, thoroughness of purpose, an absence of imagination and downright sterling honesty.

Covert policing remains an essentially 'un-British' enterprise, as an officer who infiltrated a gang of armed robbers explained to us:

> I had been in the field for over a month, was on the edge of a real result. So I go to a final briefing before we nick 'em, there's two of us and as we walk down this corridor in the [Scotland] Yard a uniform governor sees us, calls us back and tells us get a shave and put a tie on.
>
> (fieldnotes)

TAKE ME TO YOUR LEADER

The image of hooliganism presented by the media changed in the early 1980s from that of the anarchic rabble to the highly organized group which met in pubs to plan violence, which wore items of clothing identifiable as 'uniforms', and which was under the control of 'generals' and 'lieutenants'.

There exists a long history of media-induced belief that public disorder is manipulated by sinister forces; collective activity is often presented as the evil few controlling the naive but impressionable majority. The process has been neatly summarized by Chibnall (1977: 28):

> The professional imperative of personalisation encourages their identification and isolation as objects for the projection of negative popular fantasies. A whole social demonology is established and the genre of exposé journalism is enriched by stories of the form 'we name the men behind the . . .'.

Similarly, Northam (1988: 32) notes the riots of 1981 were blamed on left-wing groups: 'social explanation is exhausted with the discovery of a villain'.

The first media portrayal of football hooliganism's 'organization' and 'leadership' arose with the trial of the 'Cambridge casuals'. In May 1985 the British public discovered through massive media coverage the 'new' way football hooligans operated, basically of how fights now took place in city centres and around public houses, and how the participants now wore clothes which did not conform to the stereotypical image of the football fan.

One incident in Cambridge in February 1984 between local fans and Chelsea visitors resulted in the home hooligans receiving enormous publicity over a year later when those arrested in the incident stood trial. The outcome of this lunchtime fight was a Chelsea fan receiving a bad wound to the neck after being hit by a bottle. Another sustained a broken jaw, and one policeman sustained damaged vertebrae. Others required hospital treatment for minor injuries, caused by pool cues and bottles taken from pubs and used in the fight. Twenty-four fans were jailed for their involvement, twenty-three receiving between fifteen months and four years. Most were in their twenties, quite a few were married, some with children. Several others had no previous convictions and were considered 'good' characters in their work (one, much to media fascination, in his local church).

The media coverage transformed the Cambridge fans into a militaristic, highly organized unit which caused havoc throughout England. Nobody was safe from their excesses and one man ('the general') was behind it all. 'General' Muranyi was a 25-year-old window cleaner, who had been barred from the local ground by the club in 1983 for causing trouble, and had served a six-month prison sentence for 'unlawful assembly' related to football hooliganism. His other offences were 'possessing an offensive weapon' and 'assaulting police'. After this incident he was charged with and pleaded guilty to 'riot'. Sentencing him to five years' imprisonment, Justice Millard said,

> You are the General, the Colonel and Majors are not before the court. You know who they are and so do they. . . . By your actions you have ruined the lives of several of your co-defendants. Some of them weaker characters than you and lads of good character. . . . This was organized, planned violence which endangered life.
>
> (*The Times*, 22 May 1985)

Led by a 'general', organized on military lines, their uniform was described in *The Times* as 'Pringle label sweaters, jeans and Nike training shoes – so they could easily identify their comrades during disorders'. 'Look-outs' were posted to seek out and divert rival fans to the pubs upon whose arrival the gang would run out and attack them in a 'pincer movement'. *The Times* claimed that their violence was immense, 'they caused havoc in football towns and cities throughout the country', and, because they 'made every match day a problem', a special team of detectives was used against them.

MAN-TO-MAN MARKING: TACTICS

Undercover operations against football hooliganism were pioneered at Scotland Yard's Public Order branch in 1985. Volunteer officers were, in some cases, given new – false – identities and in some cases false addresses and told to live the life of hooligans. Some did this very well, and in two cases which were never publicized, two undercover police officers who had apparently infiltrated hooligan groups were arrested by uniformed officers (Armstrong, forthcoming).

The mass arrests of suspected football hooligans in dawn raids involving dozens, sometimes hundreds of police officers began in March 1986. The format was similar wherever the 'dawn swoop' was carried out – the hooligans had been 'kept under surveillance' and 'infiltrated' over varying lengths of time. Dossiers were written on various individuals regarded by police as ringleaders, many of whom initially were charged with conspiracy either to cause an affray or to commit violence. The charge was significant, showing there was no hard evidence to link individuals with any particular acts of violence; essentially what they said in a variety of contexts, and artifacts found in their homes were used as evidence against them.

The procedure for arrest was quite simple; officers on dawn raids would take various artifacts from the accuseds' houses, and these would then be displayed to a compliant media often invited along by police. Those arrested were revealed as the generals or notorious core hooligans.

Between them, the police and media had almost written a script which only necessitated changing the name of the football hooligans involved, so that on each raid the public was informed that the arrested had the following characteristics in common:

1 Led at least part of a vicious gang that had caused havoc throughout Britain for months/years.

2 Had a name for their hooligan gangs, were highly organized, and organized and plotted their attacks in great detail.
3 Used calling cards (always exhibited) which they pinned on victims of their violence.
4 Used a terrifying array of weapons (always exhibited) which included not only items such as a chain-mace, shotguns, bows and arrows, but also pool cues, bread knives, carpet knives and other articles found in nearly every household in Britain.
5 Often possessed literature linking them to the politically extreme-right organizations. When this could not be found and displayed, a Union Jack flag or the Cross of St George was sufficient. With these would be displayed any photographs fans might have had of one another and scrapbooks of press releases related to hooligans.

In effect nothing was safe from being exhibited. On one occasion, even a bottle of toilet cleaner and Leicester University's book *Hooligans Abroad* were shown to the media as incriminating proof of the owner's dangerousness. What follows is a brief chronicle of these raids and the mass arrests which enhanced the claims made for police intelligence-gathering and covert surveillance.

Lincoln: New Year's Eve 1986

Arrests here did not involve highly publicized 'dawn raids' and 'exhibits' but the construction of the gang was portentous. This followed disturbances in Lincoln city centre on New Year's Eve (31 December 1986) which resulted in injuries to 25 police officers, 27 shops being looted and damages of over 20,000. A mob of 150 attacked 70 police who had to use riot shields and bring in reserves from another nearby force. One hundred and fifty youths were later arrested; 67 appeared before the Crown Court on a charge of affray: 34 pleaded guilty, 22 were found guilty and 11 were acquitted. The trouble was blamed on Lincoln football hooligans, the LTE (short for Lincoln's Transit Elite). The *Daily Telegraph*, reporting on the end of the trials in March 1988, told how trouble began when a group of 20 was refused admission to a pub. When hundreds gathered to see in the New Year they were encouraged to attack police by the LTE who staged a mock fight to draw out police. The *Daily Telegraph* added:

The so-called LTE is known to police as a notorious, well

organized gang of about 70 hooligans. Only those with previous criminal records are accepted as new members, and they travel to Lincoln City's away matches, invariably starting fights with rival supporters.

However, the first police operation to make headline news across the nation occurred three months later.

Chelsea: Operation Own Goal

On the morning of 26 March 1986, seven Chelsea fans were awakened in their beds by police and arrested in front of media cameras. The arrests were the culmination of months of intelligence gathering and surveillance work by plain-clothes officers. The operation disclosed how football violence was planned in advance and orchestrated by ringleaders aged 19–34, smart in appearance and in good jobs, even 'family men' who apparently would not take partake of alcohol or engage in violence, but who, having organized events, drifted away when trouble began. They were, in effect, sinister Godfathers, who duped their foot-soldiers and left them at risk of being maimed or arrested. The prosecution told of battle plans, codes, decoys and coded maps. Ambushes were arranged after which rival fans were seriously wounded and were left unconscious with calling cards which declared 'You have been nominated and dealt with by the Chelsea Headhunters.'

Articles taken from their homes included (according to the *Daily Mirror*, (27 March 1986)), a crossbow, daggers, iron bars, coshes, screwdrivers, scalpel blades, craft knives, a high-velocity catapult, and National Front literature. The front page headline read 'Mace of Evil' and pictured a police sergeant holding a chain-mace found in one of the houses. Breakfast TV saw the presenter holding the mace, asking the watching public, 'What kind of person carries this at a football match?' The answer was quite simply no one. The object was never taken out of the house as it belonged in a collection of military memorabilia. The *London Evening Standard* (26 March 1986) added to the arsenal, talking of a Samurai sword with a two-foot blade and an Ulster Loyalist flag being found. Those under arrest were 'organizers . . . holding regular "conferences" to plan campaigns of violence weeks and sometimes months in advance'. Confusion over the police role arose very quickly. While nearly all papers wrote of undercover infiltration, the man in charge of the operation, Superintendent Hedges, is quoted in the *Daily Mirror* as saying that the officers travelling with supporters had been in uniform. 'It was no undercover operation.' Certainly it was a limited operation. None of the officers travelled to away games with the fans, for fear of being found out. In effect their infiltration was little more than standing in pubs and putting names to faces filmed on video.

Birmingham: Operation Red Card

Operation Red Card ended in January 1987 when 180 police officers swooped into the homes of 67 youths suspected of belonging to a hooligan group called the 'Zulu Warriors', supporters of Birmingham City. Twenty-one were remanded in custody for one week; others were bailed not to go within one mile of a football ground; 49 were charged. Nearly all the arrested pleaded guilty to offences that included 'conspiracy to commit violent disorder', violent disorder and affray; as well as burglary, theft, wounding, conspiracy to assault police and endangering life on a railway train. Fifteen were jailed, the maximum sentence being thirty months.

West Ham and Millwall: Operation Full-Time

A few days after Red Card came Full-Time for the fans of West Ham's Inter-City Firm and Millwall Bushwhackers. A total of 26 suspected hooligans were arrested at dawn by 250 police officers after a five-month surveillance and infiltration operation. In June, seven Millwall fans were released and the conspiracy charges against them dropped. In court, the prosecution offered no evidence and the case was dismissed.

Leeds 1987: Operation Wild Boar

Wild Boar resulted in the arrest in Leeds of 11 youths aged 17–30. After being infiltrated by four police officers between December 1986 and April 1987, all were charged with conspiracy to make an affray. Two undercover officers did on occasion travel on the coaches with the fans. In court they called it the 'aggrobus' with a leader known as 'The General' (*Guardian*, 19 April 1988).

The so-called 'Leeds Service Crew', which had been described in the media since the early 1980s, was a title given to them by the British Transport Police. There was no such thing as membership and no such group as the 'Yorkshire Army', a name also used in prosecution evidence.

After a nine-week Crown Court trial, 6 of the accused were jailed, 3 for four years, 2 for two and a half years and 1 for eight months. Another received a fifteen month Youth Custody order and another was ordered to do 150 hours of Community Service. One alleged ringleader, jailed for four years, was an ex-para-trooper (hence the nickname 'The General') who had served in the Falklands War and was found to be suffering from Post-Traumatic Stress Syndrome. The Judge recommended some form of psychiatric treatment for him as part of the sentence.

West Ham and Crystal Palace: Operation White Horse and Back Yard

On 27 April 1987, 46 youths in the south-east of England were arrested in an operation involving 250 police officers. The youths were mainly supporters of West Ham (10) and Crystal Palace (32). In July of the same year, charges against all the accused were dropped by the Crown Prosecution because of what was referred to as 'unsafe' evidence.

Millwall: Operation Dirty Den

In April 1988 two Millwall fans, reportedly 'Bushwhackers', a hooligan subgroup, were accused of causing 'havoc and mayhem' at football grounds over a six-month period, and were convicted of conspiracy to make an affray. Four others were cleared after a three-month trial. The jury was divided and a fight broke out amongst them when sentence was passed.

Cardiff: November 1987

Eleven Cardiff City supporters arrested in the ground during a match at Swansea in August were charged with Riot, the first time such a charge was ever brought against football supporters. However, the charge was dropped when the prosecution realized the near impossibility of it standing up in court.

Luton: Operation Spoonbill, March 1988

A dawn raid on seventeen homes involving 70 officers led to the arrest of eight youths and the display of a variety of 'weapons' – craft knife, lead shot, baseball bat, chains, distress flare, a scrapbook of press cuttings, an academic book about football hooligans and a bottle of toilet cleaner. The eight arrested, aged between 24 and 28, were accused of belonging to a gang called the MIGS (short for Men In Gear). All were charged with conspiracy to commit acts of disorder. Five were remanded in custody for a week. Police told reporters that they had discovered that sales of ammonia and bleach in a town centre store had doubled and shops had sold out of craft knives. How they ascertained this was not explained. A few months later the conspiracy charge against all eight accused was dropped, although five were to be charged with a lesser public order charge.

Wolverhampton: Operation Growth, March 1988

At the end of March 1988 came the biggest dawn raid yet and one which was to produce the most convictions. In an operation called GROWTH (Get Rid of Wolverhampton's Troublesome Hooligans), 250 officers arrested 67 young men after raiding 68 houses. Further arrests raised the number to 77. The raid was the result of an undercover operation by 15 officers who secretly filmed fans from vehicles at both home and away games. The cause of the Operation was, according to the Chief Superintendent of Police behind the idea, 'dreadful scenes tantamount to riots at several Wolves away games'. The accused were aged between 17 and 36 and, at one stage, included a 33-year-old policeman who was questioned about his involvement when off duty. Charges against the fans ranged from conspiracy to riot, violent disorder and criminal damage, to theft and burglary. What the latter charges had to do with football hooliganism is open to question. Whilst some fans were remanded in custody, others were bailed on condition they did not attend any professional sporting event or go within one mile of the Wolves' ground and the city centre on match days. By December 1988, 65 fans who had pleaded guilty were convicted of various offences; 40 received immediate or suspended jail sentences. All received five-year exclusion orders from football grounds. The Chief Superintend-

ent explained to the *Independent* that his officers had taken great
care in recording notes of everything they saw following the
collapse of other similar trials. He praised the courage of his
officers who had 'endured great risk' to gather the evidence.

Manchester City: Operation Omega

The following month, April 1988, 26 Manchester City fans were
arrested at dawn by 100 officers after a six-month undercover
operation entitled Operation Omega. The group was named 'The
Young Guvnors', calling cards were found as were knives, coshes
and body armour. (The fact that this last item belonged to a
youth who was a competent Thai boxer and was part of his
training attire did not strike the police and media as relevant,
and it was confiscated and photographed.)

Bolton Wanderers: Operation Gamma 1989

The Greater Manchester Police continued where other forces left
off. Arising out of their inquiries came another raid, this time
on the fans of Third Division Bolton Wanderers. Although conspiracy charges were no longer used, the usual script was applied
and in May 1990, 34 fans pleaded guilty to various offences. Nine
were jailed, the heaviest sentence being for three years. The
Bolton gang was described as having constituent gatherings called
the 'Tonge Moor Slashers' and 'Billy Whizz Fan Club', named
after amphetamine sulphate which they took before violence.
'Ringleaders' had 'armies' of 200–300 followers for away games
where they had 'intelligence' gained from communication with
other fans about which pubs to ambush rivals in. Some were
involved in Protestant extremism and made Nazi salutes, and
weapons were found in the dawn raid. A dawn raid on Bolton
fans in February 1990 saw six youths arrested for singing and
gesticulating in the course of a recent match.

Manchester United: November 1990

With the subject barely making news any longer, the Greater
Manchester Police executed yet another dawn raid in November
1990. This time their targets were Manchester United supporters,
33 of whom were arrested in a variety of locations – Lancashire,

South Yorkshire, Bedford and the Midlands. Amongst those arrested were two teachers and a police civilian worker. The Assistant Chief Constable of Greater Manchester Police claimed it was the culmination of a fifteen-month investigation.

Bradford City: Operation Ointment, April 1992

A total of 11 fans of Bradford City and Stockport County were arrested in a dawn raid to be questioned by police following fights between the two sets of fans in Stockport town centre in April and October 1991.

TRIAL, TRIBULATIONS AND THE COMPARISON OF NOTES

Problems arose when the show trials did not follow the script. In May 1988, three months into the trial of 11 West Ham fans at Snaresbrook Crown Court, the Judge stopped proceedings and ordered the jury to clear all the defendants on the charge of conspiracy to cause an affray. The charges covered a two-year period from 1986–8 and were formulated in part from documentary evidence seized from the fans' homes and in part from a four month undercover operation involving seven officers. The 60 hours of video evidence were of little utility. Evidence given orally contradicted that written and two of the officers involved were under suspension at the time of the trial due to allegations against them regarding a pub assault. The Defence brought in a retired forensic scientist who stated that pages in police log books had not been written at the same time. What was written was either untrue or inaccurate. The Judge's correction came after the prosecution offered no evidence. One of the accused, 'Cassie', claimed afterwards that the police had 'set criminals to catch criminals, and got found out'.

A week later charges were dropped against eight Chelsea fans at Knightsbridge Crown Court when the defence discovered that eight pages of a police log book had been tampered with. Three of the officers involved had been part of 'Own Goal' operation the previous year. The media, though, could declare 'at no time were they recognized when they infiltrated the fans again' (*Evening Standard*, 19 May 1988). This was untrue, firstly because there is some doubt about whether the police did in fact 'infiltrate' the group and, secondly, Chelsea fans knew precisely the police officers' identities having watched court proceedings a year earlier (fieldnotes).

The police had *not* fully infiltrated the gang, but had merely listened on the periphery to stories about them and arrested those whose names seemed to match. In court, one youth accused of various violent offences, was rightly found not guilty. In fact the man who was really guilty had, in the early part of the trial, listened to the evidence from the public gallery, realized it was his activities that were being discussed and fled the country, only returning when the trial was over. His name differed from that of the accused by a single vowel (fieldnotes).

After an eighteen-week trial which had cost over £2m, four Chelsea fans, variously leaders of the 'Chelsea Mob' or the 'Headhunters', were convicted of conspiracy to cause affray between January 1980 and March 1986. They were found guilty of orchestrating violence by meticulous planning, their roles being described as 'Field Marshals' who would leave the scene when the fighting began. The group was accused variously of using code-named travel arrangements to avoid police, as well as starting 'mock' fight decoys to draw police from an area when they would subsequently attack rival fans. The group would ambush rival fans and would leave their victims calling cards which stated 'You have just been nominated and dealt with by the "Chelsea Headhunters".' One of the accused was jailed for ten years along with other Chelsea fans. Justice Schofield stated 'You were strutting about like a little tin-pot leader whose vanity and arrogance has no bounds', and remarked that he was undoubtedly the ringleader acknowledged as such by the Chelsea Mob. The *Daily Mirror* (9 May 1988) called him the 'Field Commander' who 'waged a six-year campaign of terror against other fans and innocent bystanders'.

A trial two years later could similarly be regarded as a success for the police, and saw five people jailed for conspiracy after all the accused had pleaded guilty. In June 1989, in Manchester, sentence was passed on 21 men aged between 15 and 27, the charges against them varying from theft and impersonating a police officer to wounding the match referee and conspiracy to riot between the months of August 1987 and February 1988. In total, five admitted conspiracy to cause violent disorder when all charges of conspiracy to riot were dropped by the prosecution;

only one had all charges against him dropped (interestingly he was a 26-year-old probation officer). Custodial sentences were handed out to eight of the offenders, the heaviest sentence being 21 months (then 18, 15, 12, 9 and three terms of 6). Others received Community Service Orders and fines, and all were banned from attending football matches, some for up to fifteen years. One unreported but fascinating aspect of this trial was the fact that the four so-called undercover police officers all gave evidence in Crown Court behind a screen in order to disguise their identity.

At a similar trial in Manchester of 19 Manchester United fans in April 1992, the High Court ruled that the prosecution could not appeal against the judge's refusal to allow undercover police to give evidence behind screens. The fans were to face charges ranging from conspiracy to riot to violent disorder. The prosecution QC had argued that the lives of officers would be at risk because criminals and drug dealers could sit in the courts and recognize them. Significantly the case against the accused was dropped.

NOTABLE FAILURES: THE ROLE OF COVERT POLICING ASSERTED AND ACTUAL

Those subjected to the first 'dawn swoops' were released from prison in November 1989. Three men jailed for a total of twenty-seven years were freed when the Appeal Court ruled that the undercover police officers did not write their evidence when they claimed they had. Chief Justice Lane said their statements were falsified and unreliable and 'the creditworthiness of the officers involved in making them has been destroyed'. None of the six officers behind Own Goal was prosecuted, although the Met. Commissioner, Peter Imbert, said he could 'brook no part with officers who do this'. An internal investigation by Scotland Yard did not bring about charges. The failure of the operation was blamed on 'administrative inadequacies, lack of experience and in some cases unacceptably low levels of supervision' by the Met. Police Commander who compiled a report in October 1988. An article in the *Evening Standard* (17 November 1989), claimed the young officers chosen had no proper CID training, and whilst they could 'blend unobtrusively with the dangerous and vicious thugs' they 'did not understand the vital importance of the paperwork' for a successful prosecution, and explained how whilst eavesdropping in noisy pubs they could only scribble details in toilets on scraps of paper. Instead of logging this later in the station, 'after working long hours in isolation they went home to their wives and families and left the notes until morning'. Details left out were later put in and their log books accordingly altered. Scotland Yard's own forensic scientists decided to check the evidence and discovered the discrepancies which caused the collapse. However, this was not all that was wrong with the police case. Photographic evidence contradicted written statements and oral evidence contradicted written evidence. A Met. Commander explained the unreliability of the police infiltrators' evidence by claiming they drank heavily with the group because they were unable to turn down drinks (Graef, 1989: 165–6). This was stretching credibility too far as an excuse for incorrect notebooks; after all, wasn't the police claim originally that such hooligans stayed sober to co-ordinate the Infantry? Much was made by various sections of the press about the failure of the trials. To make matters worse, one of the jurors for Own Goal was a single mother who was photographed enjoying a celebratory drink with the acquitted. Furthermore, as Richard Littlejohn in the *Evening Standard* (20 May 1988) pointed out the jury foreman was a 25 year-old disc jockey. The editorials of the *News of the World* and the *Daily Mail* called for a change in the jury system, as did an article by Christopher Monkton in the *Evening Standard.*

One interesting question emerged which had hitherto been ignored by the media – how and what did the police infiltrators do? One of the defendants in the Operation Full-Time trial told a journalist that the plain-clothes policemen who stood with them at matches urged them to 'organize bigger groups to cause violence' and added, 'They were worse than the hooligans. They wanted trouble' (*Independent*, 28 June 1988).

One undercover operation which was relatively successful, was in Leeds, West Yorkshire. Operation Wild Boar did involve the successful infiltration by police of Leeds fans; undercover officers going into pubs, to matches, on the coaches and even staying the night in a flat of two of those arrested in the the dawn raid. Two of the officers were from Wakefield, and that they were able to infiltrate was attributed to two things by the fans with whom we spoke. Since Leeds fans came from all over Yorkshire and England, they realized their own group of supporters had a wide catchment area and so never had a situation where in a pub or coach someone would always know the name and background of everyone there. Second, was the fact one of the core members in the dock, Ord, an ex-paratrooper, was convinced that he knew the two officers as 'Donny Whites' (Doncaster based Leeds fans) and was persuasive in telling others that they were his mates and that they were all right.

On the morning of the dawn raid, both officers were sleeping in the flat of one of the accused, which he shared with another defendant. In the court, the defence solicitors were suspicious of the police evidence and were particularly interested in the fact that one of the undercover officers had been arrested in the course of his work at Bradford railway station by a uniformed officer stationed locally. The arrest was genuine, with the detective taken away in a van, having a charge sheet made out and being put in a cell, until a 'phone call between Bradford and Leeds police stations sorted the matter out. He was not charged with any offence, although the charge sheet stated he was arrested for 'threatening behaviour'. The uniformed officer, when in the dock, claimed that he arrested the detective for not having a train ticket. The defence solicitors thought this story nonsense and questioned the arresting officers at length about what the detective was really doing to merit arrest. The uniformed officer, though, stuck to his story and the truth did not come out. Later, when talking to the Leeds supporters, all were angry that the operation had been carried out against them. They maintained the undercover officers had constantly encouraged them to break away from police escorts on the way to various matches and to fight, even trying to arrange fights themselves. In court the two officers were accused by one defendant of urging violence against blacks (*Guardian*, 20 May 1988).

The one trial that produced a large number of convictions was Operation Gamma. The result was proclaimed as one which had resulted from close liaison between carefully trained undercover officers and lawyers for the prosecution – although how it was that experienced (that is, older) police officers achieved undercover infiltration with the young lads was not made explicit. None the less it was claimed that the seven-month operation put officers under 'immense personal and psychological pressure', and, that to help them carry out the operation they were given reconstructed identities which included false names, addresses and numbers in the telephone directory. Their observations were handed over to senior officers immediately after they had been written and then examined by lawyers.

PAY WHILST YOU WATCH

The policing of football supporters is a political issue which has seen the normalization of surveillance and control without a political protest. When applied to other citizens, voices are raised. During the miners' strike commentators of the liberal left questioned certain procedures which, when used on football supporters, produced silence. Consequently, in May 1984, the Home Office announced that the police had a right to photograph, without their consent, those who were detained in custody, provided they did not use force to do so. The Home Office explained that pictures were only to establish who was arrested, where and when, and were automatically destroyed if no charges were brought. When charges were preferred, photos were destroyed after the case if requested (*Guardian*, 21 May 1984). The collection of photographs and their circulation as 'potential troublemakers' precedes that of 1980s' policing tactics for industrial disputes. In fact, police collecting 'mug shots' of suspected football hooligans for a 'rogues' gallery' was an idea not totally new to the 1980s. In the *Daily Mirror* (4 May 1973) a report told of how at two grounds in the country, Coventry and Ipswich, police were keeping photograph albums of such fans and passing them on to other police forces.

Despite Home Office safeguards, photographs of convicted and suspected hooligans are kept in police stations throughout the country. With these snapshots, usually taken secretly from a distance, are various dossiers on the individuals which are often the product of hearsay brought to the police and collated by uniformed Football Intelligence officers. The opprobrium with which hooligans are greeted justifies this fact for the public. To assist in the control of hooligans, the police have acquired a considerable array of new technology. Elements of the media went into rapture when the 'Hoolivan', a specially equipped vehicle, was unveiled to assist crowd control outside football grounds in August 1985. In the *Sunday Times* (August 1985) an article by Roger Ratcliff described how the new surveillance could 'identify hooligans from a distance of 150 yards' (how, he did not say) and that it contained a rogues' gallery of known offenders, and pictures of 'those wanted for questioning about previous incidents'; in other words, in contravention of the 1984 commitment, photographs of those not convicted are held on police files. The article tells how the Hoolivan was developed in 1983 and was tested at Chelsea in 1984 without publicity. The technological capabilities allowed it to be linked with the CCTV of football grounds and be in constant radio contact with officers inside and outside grounds.[3]

We need to note also how other surveillance was a product of private donations to the police. From the mid-1980s, various businesses financed the creation of a new morality around football which was combined with a grossly nostalgic image of the past. Thus banks, supermarkets, and newspapers promoted via publications and prize money, the better behaviour of fans. The most notable of all was the Football Trust, which gave the police millions of pounds to assist in surveillance and the building of dossiers on people. Following the closed circuit TV monitors they installed in all English Premier and First Division grounds came their financing of mobile video-recorder cameras which police used both inside and outside grounds. Thus, thousands of people are now held on police files thanks to the generosity of the 'Spot the Ball' competition companies that constitute the Trust.

Another form of surveillance is of course the deployment of plain-clothes police at football grounds. Initially termed 'spotters', these officers would travel to away games and point out 'their' hooligans to local police. This process was then extended to an international context when police plain-clothes 'spotters' were sent to West Germany for the 1988 European Championships to assist in the control of English hooligans. Previously they had been used for an International in Yugoslavia. This police operation was funded by the Football Association.

This is of particular significance in the context of the use of both covert policing and associated surveillance tactics in other situations: Northern Ireland (Brewer and Magee, 1991; Hillyard, 1981; Ryder, 1989; Sim, 1987); during the inner city riots of the early 1980s (Kettle and Hodges, 1982); and as strategic devices during the 1984–5 Miners' Strike (Geary, 1985; Green, 1990; Samuel et al., 1986). These examples of the extension of covert policing were carried out quietly, with no attempt to stress the change in emphasis of police tactics. For while, certainly in public order operations, uniformed officers remained at the leading edge of police activity, this activity was increasingly being informed by intelligence-gathering techniques that were the antithesis of the original preventative and discriminate police mandate. However, the 'new police undercover work' (Marx, 1988) had yet to be sold to the general public as integral to good police practice. Sectarian strife, the eruption of urban populations and the most divisive industrial dispute of the twentieth century all involved massive conflicts. Their very complex natures led to unresolved debates and, most importantly, to the role of the police being fundamentally questioned.

Football hooliganism however is a relatively uncontentious target for covert policing and it has been argued that the key to selling covert police practice as 'good' practice, thereby normalizing the concept is the creation of the undercover cop as cultural hero (Marx, 1988: 33). The hero must face peril, and we contend that this is why covert work with organized groups of hooligans is trumpeted publicly as essentially dangerous, even while routine covert work which is carried out quietly on less contentious targets goes on without acclaim despite the occasional death (see Cater and Tullet, 1990: 274–85).

The success of the covert operations against football hooligans has been varied, with many of the early covert efforts ending in stunning and embarrassing failure. The success of more recent operations is due to the selection of charges, for it can be seen that charges, of conspiracy tended to be unsuccessful in gaining a conviction, while less substantive charges got 'results'. As Marx has noted, 'the law's requirements shape police means', and the difficulty of obtaining convictions for conspiracy led the police to turn to other legalistic means in order to gain what even politicians were regarding as a good result. As Reiner (1985: 88) has noted, 'police officers experience external pressure for "results" more or less so at different times according to particular moral panics or trends in crime statistics'. Certainly during the 1980s with crime rising at an unprecedented rate, any political party staking claim to a law and order mandate had to be seen to be tough on crime (Crook, 1993; Downes and Ward, 1986). This was exemplified by Colin Moynihan, Minister for Sport, who stated in 1988, 'Football hooligans are worse than animals, a cancer in an otherwise healthy body.'

HOOLIGAN CONSPIRACIES: THE INTERNATIONAL DIMENSION

Established following the 1988 European Championships in Germany, the National Football Intelligence Unit became fully operational in March 1990. The Unit consisted of six full-time police officers with a civilian employee led by a Superintendent, seconded from the Greater Manchester Police, a force well to the fore in anti-hooligan operations, having executed three dawn raids on local fans. The Unit was given a budget of £500,000, and a brief to gather hooligan and 'hooligan-related' intelligence. The information collated came from a variety of sources, primarily the local police Football Intelligence officers who follow nearly all football clubs. These officers were able to inform the NFIU how local hooligans operated and what they did. Other information came from overheard gossip and informers. All local information was collated in London and then computerized and coded as to how reliable the Unit considered the intelligence. It was then distributed nationally. By 1992, 6,000 names and mugshots were held on the computer files.

The Unit was well grounded in the ideology of hierarchical conspiracy. Prior to the 1990 World Cup Finals, Superintendent Appleby, head of the Unit, told of the following, impending atrocities:

> One thousand have pre-arranged a series of clashes . . . two years liaising with each other . . . culmination of two years planning . . . apex of their hooligan careers . . . arrangements are in hand to effect meetings in Sardinia . . . . Our intelligence is that planned violence is in the pipeline between the Dutch and English. . . . Terribly violent people who get a lot of pleasure out of inflicting harm on other people . . . potential is pretty staggering.
>
> (*ITN News*, 13 March 1990)

It is interesting that the equivalent police officer in Holland, with whom Appleby had liaised for the previous six months, knew nothing about this and was furious with this claim (Armstrong, forthcoming). Contacted the following day by dozens of reporters, he had to confess to knowing nothing about either the conspiracy or the announcement. Diplomatically, Chief Inspector

Peter Van Essen gave the following reply in an interview with one of the authors.

> We, the Dutch and English, visited each other's grounds very recently. We don't have information that the fans are having a conspiracy to create public disorder in Italy. We would like to make clear that whenever the Dutch played abroad in the last three years they behaved well and that includes games against England in West Germany and at Wembley. The British press for both games were predicting massive disorder, but nothing happened.
>
> We are trying to assist the British police to prevent anything happening. If we had knowledge about such a conspiracy it would have been used to prevent the incident happening. If I was so sure of it I would ensure I was in a position to use the information to prevent it. It should not be a matter for the media. The Dutch are convinced that information on conspiracy can only come from them and they deny all knowledge of a conspiracy. We cannot imagine what provoked the British police into saying what they did. In my opinion they have no justification. I am reluctant to link it to self-interest.
>
> (fieldnotes)

In the meantime the media caught the spirit of the day. The *Sun* in an exclusive back-page headline, reported 'We'll Bomb England World Cup Fans', and added '31 days to go and the aggro has started'. Journalist Brian Woollnough told of British police having urgent talks with the Sardinian police to prevent a 'total bloodbath' and quoted a spokesman of the Dutch Supporters' Association telling of a build-up of tear gas and bombs to throw at the English in revenge for having the reputation as Europe's most fearsome fans. The article declined that in response 150 highly trained officers with machine guns from Holland would be going to the grounds. However, in an interview with the Dutch police we found that they had no knowledge that their officers were to attend in such large numbers or be so well-armed. In fact, six unarmed officers attended the tournament (fieldnotes).

Meanwhile the Home Secretary sent to the Italian authorities the names and photographs, supplied by the NFIU, of 100 English hooligans, the 'hard men'. The Italian authorities could then decide whether to exclude those named or not. Soon after, on the night of 30 May on British TV, Superintendent Appleby announced the 'Hooligan Hotline' launched by the Home Office, manned by his Intelligence Unit and open twenty-four hours. Home Office Minister, Earl Ferrers, whose responsibility covered the seven-strong Unit was quoted in the *Guardian* as saying, 'I would ask anyone with information, no matter how minor or seemingly unimportant, to ring.' Callers were allowed, whilst remaining anonymous, to give names and information about movements, intentions and persons they knew who were attending the Finals. This was not the first time such a ploy had been used. The West Midlands Police had operated a similar hotline in 1988 and two clubs, Manchester United and Leeds, had telephone facilities for people to ring in with information about both hooligans and people who swore in the ground so they could be banned. By coincidence, in the same issue of the *Guardian* in which the hotline was advertised (with phone numbers), the letters page contained one entitled 'Safeguard for Every Citizen', written by twelve members of 'Charter 88', various peers, professors, solicitors and journalists (all members of the Labour Party). The letter sought a written Bill of Rights in which liberties would be coded in law. This aspiration arose out of, in their words, 'our faith in social justice and individual freedom; our belief in the right of the citizen against power, public or private'. This admirable quest for safeguarding liberties contrasted with their silence concerning football fans.

Meanwhile, the Unit was given further publicity when the Assistant Chief Constable of Manchester, Mr Malcolm George, Secretary of the Chief Constables Committee on Football Hooliganism was quoted as saying, 'We have a lot of good intelligence in this country about plans being made that will involve the Dutch – plans for hooligan activity' (*Independent*, 31 May). Over 1,000 names and photos held on the unit's dossier were to be made available to the French and Italian police and to seaport and airport officials.

Some of the 100 'hard men' listed were deported back to Britain, even those with no criminal record. Meanwhile, as fans gathered, Superintendent Appleby told the *Sunday Times* (20 June 1990) they were now 'awaiting leadership'.

The big planned showdown with the Dutch came to nothing. The claims of Superintendent Appleby were not repeated by the media as the match passed without incident between the two sets of fans, although incidents before the game between England fans and the Italian military were ugly and regrettable (see Buford, 1991). The final match against the Egyptians was peaceful; the fans prepared for the next match against Belgium in Bologna.

It was before this game that the most significant incident involving England fans occurred, albeit miles away from any of the tournament's venues and days before a match. England fans staying in the resort of Rimini before their match against Belgium in Bologna were involved in skirmishes with Italian youths. Riot police moved in to tear-gas a crowded bar, beat those who ran out seeking refuge and then arrested and deported any Englishman they could find. The Rimini deportations brought praise and condemnation and became, to an extent, a party political issue. The Shadow Sports Minister, Denis Howell, protested that 'we should not convict by mass libel of this sort people who claim they are innocent and haven't been given the opportunity to prove it'. The reply of Sports Minister Moynihan was that Howell had 'echoed the plea of the louts who comprise the football effluent tendency'. Innocent people were arrested in bars or streets two miles away from where the incident took place, and deported, their crime that of being English. They were deported without being allowed to pick up luggage and, in some cases, passports. On arrival at Gatwick Airport, they were photographed without their consent by police officers of the NFIU and photographs and personal details were placed on the police computer. The information was then sent by police to local newspapers in the areas where the fans had given their addresses so further condemnation of them could be written without proof of guilt. None was charged with any crime but all were subject to Deportation Orders which banned them from returning to Italy. One month later, the Italian authorities rescinded the orders. There was no evidence to suggest that any of these events was a product of organized violence and hierarchical leadership.

That this deportation was calculated by the Italian and British Police was almost certainly proved when the defence committee for the deported fans found that the plane that brought them back to England had been chartered in advance and was detained in Rimini until sufficient fans to fill its seats had been arrested. As a result, while some were detained overnight, 25 more were arrested in hotels the next morning to achieve a total of 237 –

exactly the number of seats available on the plane. Mr Howell stated bluntly, 'I think Scotland Yard police, under the orders of the Government in the shape of Colin Moynihan, had organized it with the Italian police' (*Footie* magazine, August 1990). Confusion reigned. A total of 60 English fans had been arrested in Italy and over 300 deported. But less than one month later, Mr Johanssen, President of UEFA, said after an Executive Committee meeting which allowed English clubs back into European competition, 'I think isolation is not a good thing. . . . English fans are no worse than others.'

The police have persisted in their model of hierarchical hooliganism and continued also the pursuit of the conspiracy theory. In November 1990, police revealed to a committee of MPs a 'Mafia-style command system running football violence in Britain'. This is very significant because it illustrates how, despite the collapse of the show trials and the absence of any evidence to support their script, the police can still sing the same song without questioning. Every submission to the Committee from various police representatives had elements of the organized/hierarchical gang construct (HAC, 1990: 9, 15, 32, 36, 130, 531). The NFIU submission was more extreme, telling of hooligan 'status' being gained by attacking rivals and police, acting boisterously in motorway cafes, urinating on food in pubs, and pulling up or down women's clothing (ibid.: 9, 3, 38). As for organization, such gangs had various 'post-holders', including intelligence officers, photographers, armourers, transport managers' (ibid.: 32, 49), all in a 'dedicated and highly disciplined central command' (ibid.: 53, 49). Away from football, it was alleged, such people commit offences to finance their football activities. Interestingly details of the NFIU's computer information was revealed (ibid.: 38). With over 6,000 names of 'hooligans', it is interesting to note that the offences that brought them to the attention of the Unit are just over 1,500 for violence, yet over 4,000 for non-violent offences including drugs (470), fraud (446), auto-crime (497) and others (747). What the latter four offences have to do with football hooliganism is a mystery. Not a scrap of evidence was produced to substantiate these claims, but, nevertheless, the document *Policing Football Hooliganism* produced by the Home Affairs Committee is now the latest word on the subject. The British police, in this document, recommend to European police that they learn by example how to deal with the problem.

In January 1991 a conference audience in London was addressed by two members of the NFIU about the hooligans' domestic and international activities. Superintendent Appleby reiterated his Unit's knowledge of hooligans in 'organized, dedicated teams of violence' who carry Stanley knives which are 'used all the time', and told of the 'new weapons' in their arsenal which included cattle prods which give a high voltage electric shock. Where and when this latter, potentially lethal weapon had ever been used he did not say (fieldnotes).

Expanding on his theory of conspiracy between the Dutch and English supporters for the World Cup, Appleby told the conference of the following. There had been four hooligan conferences – two in Walsall, one in Victoria, London, the other in Tenerife. The first, in Walsall, involved hooligans from twelve clubs with two representatives each. All stayed one night in a hotel and took in a local match as part of their meeting; he claimed to have officers on the spot who knew what was being planned. Later there was a meeting in Victoria between 'twelve hooligans of Utrecht and London thugs', but then 'so paranoid about secrecy were the hooligans that as a result the next meeting was in Tenerife'. He did not say if this involved the Dutch, but in fact there were no details at all about this meeting.

Because of all he knew, Appleby explained, 'I deliberately went public, and took a chance and told them what was going on. It worked. Once they knew I knew they changed their plans.' We were never told what the plans were (see also HAC, 1990: 26, 32 and 46, 36). It has been impossible for us to verify the existence of these meetings or the consequences. We did learn however that Tenerife was brought to the notice of the police at Christmas 1989 when twelve fans who had met over the years following England, went away for a week's holiday. As part of their fun they sent a postcard to the police (fieldnotes).

More was to follow in August 1992, despite an apparent tail-off in hooligan activity. A national, 24-hour 'Hooligan Hotline' was established by the Unit, which was now incorporated into the new National Criminal Intelligence Service. We can only speculate on whether this was a response to a 21 per cent rise in football-related offences in season 1991–2, the first rise in four years. Later still, the Unit found a new *raison d'être*, in December 1992. It established what one journalist called a 'Special Task Force' to curtail the new Nazi hooliganism in Britain, and examine their links with European counterparts (*Mail on Sunday*, 13 December 1992). We soon learned of how the hooligan had turned his attention to rape and armed robbery (*Sunday Times*, 27 December 1992). We await with interest evidence to emerge to support these claims. When it does so we will have to deal with the problem of whether to define these criminals as organized rapists or organized football hooligans.

CONCLUSION

Football hooliganism has made it possible for the British police to introduce and normalize covert tactics and strategies of surveillance. While there has been a traditional antipathy to covert policing, the creation of a moral panic around the phenomenon of soccer-related disorder served to market a solution that, as we have indicated above, has symbolic rather than pragmatic utility (Manning, 1977). Whilst this is accepted and is not a political issue when imposed upon football supporters, when conducted on others moral indignation sets in.[4]

The police, as an institution have status. What they say and the way they define a situation is taken as authoritative by many politicians and news editors. Douglas (1987: 92) describes the attributes of institutions, which in this case are applicable to the police, when she explains how they 'channel our perceptions into forms compatible with the situations they authorise', how they are endowed with a 'rightness' and 'narcisstic self-contemplation', offering solutions based only from the 'limited range of their own experiences' which means more control, greater power, and more surveillance.

Discipline, to borrow from Foucault (1977), can be imposed by three principal methods: hierarchical observation, normalizing judgement, and examination. With the introduction of 'hooli-vans', CCTV and handheld cameras, heralded as a 'good thing' and a 'cure' and financed by private pressure groups, surveillance has been normalized. The population at large has welcomed the movement because, obviously, if you are doing nothing wrong you have nothing to fear. But when the 'hoolivans' and the videos are used on other groups in society, will it be too late to ask questions concerning civil liberties, and the privatization of law and order? The use of surveillance and computer-held intelligence should be a worry to everyone. For the latter, one needs to ask what goes into it and what information is considered appropriate; 'intelligence', as Campbell (1980: 87) noted, can be nothing more than gossip (see also Ackroyd *et al.*, 1977: 151–96; Bunyan, 1977: 74–101; Manwaring-White, 1984). When, as is the case, profiles of individuals are held by the NFIU because the person is 'known to keep the company of hooligans', we have entered the danger zone that threatens to affect societal groups other than the terrible, tattooed, effluent tendency.

The motivation for targeting hooligans relates to their position as a subgroup of society who, unlike for instance black youth or strident trade unions, would be unlikely to gather sympathy from any source. For instance, the Football Supporters Act 1991 introduced three offences specific to football grounds – throwing missiles, racist chanting and running on to the pitch. All three of these offences were more than adequately dealt with by existing legislation (Public Order Act 1985, Sections 1–5). The police officers had utilized this legislation at soccer matches with no specific problems in gaining convictions. The law, therefore, is used in this context as a symbolic device for indicating the strategic intent of Government to locate and isolate a societal group already marginalized by their behaviour. The pragmatic reality of promulgating a law that has no actual effect in terms of prevention, arrest or conviction, is of secondary consideration to the public relations benefits gained from talking tough about crime.

Furthermore, the public cannot rely on the sociological 'experts' to provide a cynical eye. Leicester University researcher John Williams (1991: 25) tells readers of the 'good work' of the NFIU whilst suggesting it 'should be open to inquiry from representatives of responsible supporter organizations' (ibid.: 31), whoever they might be. Basically, if you want to know what knowledge the State holds on you, join the supporters club. The academic and police 'experts' then have a power base; as Dandeker (1989) argues, 'expert status' is a form of surveillance because experts are presumed to have access to specialized knowledge. This dangerous liaison between police and academics casts doubt upon the validity of much of this expert knowledge.

Aided by electronic evidence (Marx, 1988: 134–5), computerized predictive profiles (often based on non-criminal data), the use of private resources (provision of electronic equipment, funding police officers for overseas trips) a moral order is created based on an ahistorical notion of post-traditional leisure pursuits (see Henley Centre for Forecasting, 1991).

As Marx (1988: 57) has noted, the new surveillance is highly supportive of 'stage management and scripted scenarios' and the dramatized contest of soccer matches is difficult to ignore. It constitutes in many ways a Hollywood type film-set for the performance of both hooliganism and covert policing, complete with cameras, microphones, monitoring screens, playback facilities, producers, directors and the full galaxy of major and minor actors, from extras (uniformed police, non-violent spectators) to stars (undercover police and 'top' hooligans). This is real method acting with a backdrop as purpose-built as any film set, a cast of thousands and the occasional corpse to provide narrative focus.

NOTES

1 For remarkably similar thesis of crowd behaviour see Smith and Way (1977).
2 Further, he specifies that the first time conspiracy was used in connection with a public order offence was in Britain in 1973. An Anti-Internment League march marking the anniversary of Bloody Sunday in Derry turned violent, and four marchers were charged with 'conspiracy to cause threatening and riotous behaviour' (Bunyan, 1977: 35–51).
3 In the *Mail on Sunday* (24 November 1985), Andrea Waind, guest of the 'Hoolivan' for an afternoon, described officers talking about taking 'the front runners for intelligence', basically describing the mass photographing of young men walking as part of a group of visiting fans. 'Intelligence' means in fact that their identity was recorded. Waind subsequently described how a later Hoolivan model could take 500 photographs in one afternoon, and had a communication system that cuts out outside noise, so, as one officer explained, 'you can't hear bricks hitting you'.
4 In December 1990, plain-clothes police officers were sent to stand incognito in pubs in Humberside. Three other forces, Bedford, Dorset and Dumfries and Galloway publicized freefone telephone lines along which observers could inform on law-breakers. The issue in question was drink-driving, an extension of tactics of covert policing to a more serious but more widely committed offence. Despite drunken driving killing 800 people annually in Britain, the editorial of the *Independent* found the tactics troubling, and called it an unnecessary, big brother, police state activity.

REFERENCES

Ackroyd, C., J. Margolis, J. Rosenhead, and T. Shallice (1977) *The Technology of Police Control*, Harmondsworth: Penguin.

Armitage, G. (1937) *The History of the Bow Street Runner 1729–1829*, London: Wishart.

Armstrong, G. (forthcoming) *Fists and Style*, Ph.D. Thesis, University College London, Department of Anthropology.

Ascoli, D. (1979) *The Queen's Peace*, London: Hamilton.

Buford, B. (1991) *Among the Thugs*, London: Secker and Warburg.

Brewer, J. and K. Magee (1991) *Inside the RUC*, Oxford: Clarendon Press.

Bunyan, T. (1977) *The History and Practice of the Political Police in Britain*, London: Quartet.

Campbell, D. (1980), 'Society under Surveillance', in P. Hain (ed.) *Policing the Police 2*, London: Calder.

Cater, F. and T. Tullet (1990) *The Sharp End*, London: Grafton.

Chibnall, S. (1977) *Law and Order News*, London: Tavistock.

Clarkson, C. T. and J. Hall-Richardson (1889) *Police*, London: Leadenhall Press.

Coalter, F. (1984) *Crowd Behaviour at Football Matches: a study in Scotland*, Edinburgh: Centre for Leisure Research.

Cook, B. (1978) 'Football Crazy?', *New Society*, 15 June.

Critchley, T. (1978) *A History of Police in England and Wales 1900–1966*, London, Constable (first edition 1967).

Croker, T. (1987) *The First Voice You Will Hear Is . . .* , London: Collins Willow.

Crook, F. (1993) 'One Brutal Exception Does Not Prove the Rule', *Independent*, 23 February.

Dandeker, S. (1989) *Surveillance, Power and Modernity*, London: Polity.

Dilnot, G. (1929) *Scotland Yard*, London: Geoffrey Bles.

Douglas, M. (1987) *How Institutions Think*, London: Routledge.

Downes, D. and T. Ward (1986) *Democratic Policing*, London: Labour Campaign for Criminal Justice.

Foucault, M. (1977) *Discipline and Punish: the birth of the prison*, New York: Pantheon.

Geary, R. (1985) *Policing Industrial Disputes: 1893 to 1985*, Cambridge: Cambridge University Press.

Graef, R. (1989) *Talking Blues: the police in their own words*, London: Fontana.

Green, P. (1990) *The Enemy Without*, Milton Keynes: Open University Press.

Hall, S., J. Clarke, C. Critcher, T. Jefferson, and B. Roberts (1978) *Policing the Crisis*, London: Macmillan.

Henley Centre for Forecasting (1991) *F.A. Blueprint for Football*, Oxford: Henley Centre.

Hillyard, P. (1981) 'From Belfast to Britain', in *Politics and Power 4: Law, Politics and Justice*, London: Routledge.

Hobbs, D. (1988) *Doing the Business*, Oxford: Oxford University Press.

Home Affairs Committee (HAC), (1990) *Policing Football Hooliganism: memoranda of evidence*, London: HMSO.

Kettle, M. and L. Hodges (1982) *Uprising*, London: Pan.

Manning, P. (1977) *Police Work*, Cambridge, Mass.: MIT.

—— (1980) *the Narcs Game*, Cambridge, Mass.: MIT.

Manwaring-White, S. (1984) *The Policing Revolution*, Brighton: Harvester.

Marx, G. T. (1988) Undercover Police: surveillance in America, Berkeley, California: University of California Press.

Miller, W. (1977) *Cops and Bobbies*, Chicago, Ill.: University of Chicago Press.

Northam, G. (1988) *Shooting in the Dark*, London: Faber.

Prothero, M. (1931) *The History of the Criminal Investigation Department at Scotland Yard*, London: Herbert Jenkins.

Radzinowicz, L. (1956) *A History of the English Criminal Law and its Administration*, vol. 3, London: Stevens.

Reiner, R. (1985) *The Politics of the Police*, Brighton: Wheatsheaf.

Reith, C. (1956) *A New Study of Police History*, London: Oliver and Boyd.

Ryder, C. (1989) *The RUC: a force under fire*, London: Methuen.

Samuel, R., B. Bloomfield and G. Boanas (1986) *The Enemy Within*, London: Routledge.

Sherman, L. W. (ed.) (1974) *Police Corruption*, New York: Anchor.

Silver, A. (1967) 'The Demand for Order in Civil Society', in D. Bordua (ed.) *The Police: Six Sociological Essays*, New York: Wiley.

Sim, M. (1983) *Violence in Sport*, Toronto: Butterworth.

Smith, M. and K. Way (1977) 'Soccer Violence: what lies behind the aggro', *Psychology Today*, March.

Smith, M. D. (1975) 'Sport and Collective Violence', in D. W. Ball and J. W. Loy (eds) *Sport and Social Order: contributions to the sociology of sport*.

Styles, J. (1987) 'The Emergence of the Police – explaining police reform in eighteenth and nineteenth century England', *British Journal of Criminology*, 27 (1): 15–22.

Trivizas, E. (1980) 'Offences and Offenders in Football Crowd Disorders', *British Journal of Criminology*, 20.

—— (1981) 'Sentencing and the Football Hooligan', *British Journal of Criminology*, 21.

Williams, J. (1991) 'Football Spectators and Football Spectator Behaviour', in F.A. *Blueprint for Football*, Henley: Henley Centre.

Williams, J., E. Dunning and P. Murphy (1985) *Hooligans Abroad*, London: Routledge.

Chapter 10

Taking liberties
Hibs casuals and Scottish law

Richard Giulianotti

INTRODUCTION

The point of departure of this paper is the arrest, trial and
conviction of two men for the Scottish legal offences of mobbing
and rioting, attempted murder, serious assault, and assaults at a
public house (The Well) and disco (The Kronk) in Dunfermline
in September 1990. The convictions appear to have been secured
on the initial premise that the football hooligan gang, the 'Hibs
casuals', were the collective perpetrators of the disturbance, and
that being commonly recognized as prominent figures if not
'leaders' within this movement, the two accused were certainly
present. The paper argues that the convictions were unsound
for two inter-related reasons. First, the social construction of
speculative, hyperbolic knowledge about the gang, emerging
prior to the trial, undoubtedly influenced the presentation and
evaluation of admissible evidence. Second, various technical
irregularities during the trial beset the accumulation and presentation of Crown evidence, undermining strongly the safety of the
verdict.

The trial is seen as the culmination of a media-led police and
public campaign into the nature and practices of Hibs casuals.
The 'knowledge' sustaining these investigations frequently signi-
fied the gang as 'beyond normal hooliganism', a quasi-Mafia
outfit, imbued with a rigid internal hierarchy, code of honour,
and concerned in extortion and drug-running activities, all of
this being coated by a patina of violence and *vendetta*.

'HARD TO BE HUMBLE': THE SOCIO-HISTORICAL HABITUS OF THE SCOTTISH SOCCER CASUAL

The 'casual' has been the dominant subcultural identity within Scottish soccer since the early 1980s, and contrasts with prior hooligan forms in a number of ways. Earlier soccer subcultures had evinced an affective, *mechanistic* relationship to the club supported, and the latter's surrounding locale. Gang names of young fans were often localist in nature (Young Leith Team (Hibs), Gorgie Boys (Hearts)), and their affiliates were usually festooned in club colours and motifs. In contradistinction, Scottish casual movements connote a more formal, *organic* mode of subcultural identity, relative to the club's home locale and the wider catchment area of support. Names of casual gangs habitually pertain to the prospective mobilization of town- and city-wide movements: Aberdeen Soccer Casuals, Capital City Service (Hibs Casuals, the CCS), etc. More conspicuously, Scottish casual attire eschews club colours in favour of the expensive designer sports and menswear worn in the south as part of the nation wide youth culture predominant in the early to mid-1980s (Redhead and McLaughlin, 1985; Redhead, 1986; Hills, 1991). Relative to earlier soccer subcultures, the casual appears both economically and stylistically upmarket. To the police seeking to enforce segregation of fans inside and outside grounds, this abandonment of club-based colours indicates a clear-headed instrumentality behind the casuals' pursuit of violent confrontations. Currently, the most active casual movement in Scotland follows the Edinburgh club, Hibernian (Giulianotti, 1994a).

Both popular and academic commentators on British hooligan subcultures have identified a curious, late 1980s mutation of the casuals' violent identity. The 'rave' music phenomenon, and use of the 'hug drug' ecstasy (MDMA), is regarded as the catalyst for a perceived, but most contestable, decline in British football hooliganism, post-Heysel (Hills, 1991; cautiously confirmed by Redhead, 1991). Notwithstanding arguments on the *de*amplification of football hooliganism by media and politicians (see Dunning, Giulianotti, this volume), I am not alone in feeling the uniqueness and ubiquity of this development may be overstated. Armstrong (forthcoming) uncovers an analogous suspension (and not inversion) of soccer-based rivalries at 1970s Northern Soul discos. There is also evidence that Scottish casual formations adopt distinctive orientations toward the rave phenomenon. Some (such as Dunfermline casuals) may embrace the style via a pluralist, 'multiple self' interpretation of the range of 1980s subcultural identities. In contradistinction, Hibs casuals have sought to reaffirm the centrality of soccer-based enmities, a continuity in gang identity which seems to be enabled by their sharing of an exceptional, boundary-premised social ontology (Giulianotti, 1994a).

The ambiguities surrounding the relationship between the casual and raver identities provide the backdrop to the disturbances at The Kronk rave disco. Before assessing the trial's procedure, two factors must be discussed. First, there are the general 'vocabularies of motive' or 'techniques of neutralization' which are recognized or delegitimized by the Scottish criminal code in its dealings with public disorder (Mills, 1940; Sykes and Matza, 1957). Second, there are the particular layers of knowledge enveloping the Hibs casuals prior to the trial itself.

BEYOND REASONABLE DOUBT: THE SCOTTISH LEGAL SYSTEM AND THE ERADICATION OF FOOTBALL HOOLIGANISM

The Scottish legal system possesses three tiers of criminal court: District, Sheriff and High Court of Justiciary, in ascending order of power. The culpability of the accused is computed in atomistic terms. Individuals are summoned or indicted to account for allegedly illegal actions, real or intended, in terms of personal motive and rationale. Dispensation of justice may be categorized as *restitutive* or *repressive*, in dealing with 'normal' or socially 'pathological' crime respectively, to reinforce the wider *conscience collectif* (Durkheim, 1964).

One definitive feature of the Scottish criminal code is its insistence upon corroborating evidence against an accused for a successful prosecution to be tenable – a necessity not formally recognized in the English penal code. However, as one leading Scottish sheriff recently indicated, this requirement is no guarantee of safe conviction. Legal commentators may have allowed the Scottish system of corroboration to receive 'a better press than it deserves, in that juries may find the weakest of corroborating evidence to convict, as assisted by the evidence of unscrupulous police officers' (MacPhail, 1992: 148).

The most important figure in Scottish jurisprudence is Hume, the great eighteenth-century empiricist, who argued that recourse to experience was the only sound proof of a proposition (Camic, 1983: 64). Hume contended that the morality of an act is revealed through evaluation of its 'utility' (Stroud, 1977: 183), in an incipiently sociological sense. However, Hume also posited as an ontological fact the subservience of reason to the ends of 'passion' (Hume, 1962: 415–16). Thus, the Humean imaginary offers 'passion' as a vocabulary of motive to the formally and/or morally accused – we all, it seems, know and understand what it is to 'lose the head'. Such an observation becomes a commonplace when the mental blackout is wrought by intoxication, whether this be environmental (for example the *crime passionel*) or biochemical (for example alcohol) in cause. Hume is commonly accredited with a critical, upright stance over the use of alcohol-consumption as a mitigating circumstance in criminal cases. But this temperance is eroded by his experience- and passion-orientated philosophy, which confirms the socially routine consumption of alcohol, and the palpableness of its effects according to the dominant Scottish Calvinist imaginary. Thus, in cases of 'normal' crime more attuned to restitutive justice, Hume prevaricates cryptically: 'many other instances may be imagined, which seem to offer the like reasons for mitigation of the ordinary pains' (quoted in Christie, 1990: 13). Accordingly, Scottish law remains deeply ambivalent about the validity of alcohol-consumption as a 'mitigating circumstance' in criminal case defences.

Traditional, or 'normal' Scottish hooliganism, if not the everyday experience of football-watching north of the border, is strongly associated in the public imagination with alcohol-consumption (Holt, 1989: 259–60; Giulianotti, 1994b). At the 1980 Scottish Cup Final, this narrative attained its apogee with the televised pitch battle at Hampden between Rangers and Celtic fans. Media inquests into the causes of the disorder drew attention to the mountains of empty bottles and cans subsequently collected from the field and terraces (cf. Roadburg, 1980: 270–1). Backed by the findings of the 1978 McElhone Report, the 1980 Criminal Justice (Scotland) Act formally barred access to football for those either possessing alcohol or in any way 'under the influence'. The legislation was almost automatically hailed as having extinguished Scottish football hooliganism's inflammatory spark (Crampsey, 1990: 216–17; Forsyth, 1990: 120–1). Thus,

having reified the dominant discourse on soccer-related disorder
in the drunk, 'bleezin' or 'skittled' condition, at the legal and
popular levels the 'problem' came to be regarded as physically
eradicable through vigilant policing. Indeed, the underlying
rationale of the 1980 legislation was posited as educative, giving
rise to a new and restitutive social contract between police authority and the newly abstemious fan, imposed from above. But this
accord also repressively re-enforced the cognitive and penal
boundaries against the post-1980, 'pathological' hooligans that
stood outside. A new discourse now oversees the denial of naming
and 'vocabularies of motive', in favour of the personification of
instrumental wickedness. The 'so-called casual', 'stone cold sober
just plain bloody evil' (Grampian Police Chief Superintendent),
whose 'activities have escalated well beyond what can be classed
as "normal" hooliganism' (Association of Chief Police Officers
[Scotland] evidence to Home Affairs Committee (HAC), 1990:
53).[1]

Having officially 'recognized' and 'eradicated' the psycho-social
bases of 'legitimate' Scottish hooliganism by the early 1980s, the
sudden emergence of a completely new hooligan 'style' generated
a cognitive problem within Scottish legal and public discourses.
The Scottish casual thus inhabits the obscene cognitive void
which Baudrillard (1988: 178–9) terms 'simulation'. Simulation
is 'a third-order simulacrum, beyond true and false, beyond equiv-
alences, beyond the rational distinctions upon which function all
power, the entire social stratum'. For Baudrillard, the habitual
law-and-order response to this unknown object's realer-than-real
challenge is a 'discourse of crisis' – in which wild conjectures and
impulsive responses come to dominate public 'knowledge' of the
object. Perhaps the best illustration to date of this process was
an MP's endeavour in 1985 to introduce a 'Private Members'
Bill', which would imprison any soccer-related offender for a
minimum three months.[2] The (ultimately abortive) legislation
had been inspired by the reported activities of Aberdeen casuals
during the movement's halcyon days in the mid-1980s
(Giulianotti, 1993a) Hibs casuals, by contrast, may be said to
have undergone a more protracted and excessive 'discourse of
crisis' since 1990.

HIBS CASUALS AND THE DISCOURSE OF CRISIS: A MONSTROUS CABAL

Since the mid-1980s, peaking after the events in Dunfermline but before their formal criminalization in the courts, the increasingly loquacious discourse of crisis surrounding the Hibs casuals precipitated a 'fatal strategy' of investigation by police, media and security intelligence.[3]

A series of speculative investigations by the popular media framed the formation as a quasi-Mafia, according to three principles: nomenclature, internal structuration, and collective practice. Some of the reportage was premised upon released or leaked police reports speculating on the gang's criminal machinations. The most serious allegation pinned two murders on the gang, though neither death was characterized by a soccer-related input.

Nomenclature

In the course of a three-day investigation by Edinburgh's *Evening News*, the gang's established *nom de guerre*, 'Capital City Service', was wrongly stated to have been replaced by another gang title, The Family. Rather than interpreting this to be a gang claim of surrogate kinship for its affiliates (cf. Armstrong and Harris, 1991), The Family was mediated to denote the trading name of a quasi-Mafia network. This contention was 'corroborated' by two further purported gang names. 'The Mob' (*Sun*, 18 January 1990) was literally capitalized upon, though the term is routinely used by Scottish casuals when discussing their own or opposing collectives (Giulianotti, 1991: 526n.). The additional (in fact rarely used) signifier 'The Brotherhood', was also introduced to reports, though the empirical and symbolic referents for this sobriquet are far adrift of the *fratellanza*.[4]

Organization

Official and popular constructs of organized crime networks tend to acknowledge both their communal, mechanistic origins and tentacular organization. The latter is witnessed by a rigid division of labour, and conventional bureaucratization of the criminal collective. This transition from tradition to modernity gels with the deep-seated cultural conviction that modern crime, financial and/or violent, is 'cabalistic' in nature, 'having been well planned in advance as part of some conspiratorial plot' (Cohen, 1980: 63). Macroscopically, criminal gangs are then read off as organized into an exclusivist, ordered segmentation framework, structured in the form of *la Cosa Nostra*.[5] But the uncivilized genus of organized crime is publicly confirmed by gang regressions into capricious and brutal acts of retribution, most obscenely through the cultural atavism of *vendetta*.

Some reports on Hibs casuals have displayed less equivocation on the presence of an internal hierarchy, and ruthless protection of economic and cultural spaces. Edinburgh's *Evening News* exclaimed on its front page:

> The Hibs casuals' main gang, formerly called Capital City Services, has re-grouped and changed its name to The Family. It is run on Mafia-style lines with a Godfather figure and Family zones throughout Lothian.
>
> (*Evening News*, 13 October 1990)

More substantively, another report stated

> There is also evidence of a rank structure in the Casuals. Members are given specific tasks by the leader who selects more aggressive members to be known as the Frontline. They are responsible for organising fights and collecting 'taxes'. Others organise travel or the printing and distribution of leaflets and calling cards.
>
> (*Evening Times*, 17 September 1990)

To continue the metaphor of cultural and moral decadence, the newspaper identified the gang's leaders as an Edinburgh solicitor, and two homosexuals approaching middle age! In reality, no matter the number of individuals imprisoned or who have their activities put 'on ice', through attendance centre orders or being released on bail, the Hibs casuals have not become extinct. The formation's continuation, and personal testimonies from 'top boys', indicate an absence of leaders, though a presence of 'core figures'. It is this culture of shared identification and solidarism, through continued and repeated intra- and inter-action with opposing casuals and subcultures, rather than any organizational discipline, which is the main resource of the Hibs casuals.[6]

A stylized historiography (purporting to be subculturally informed) of Scottish soccer's seedy side added, 'Hibs casuals have turned parts of Edinburgh's city centre into a week-end war zone and have been implicated in protection rackets, drug rings and criminal damage' (Cosgrove, 1991: 136). The conspiratorial argument found an understated affine among senior police officers in Scotland:

> The organisation of this element [the casuals], their planning capabilities, mobility and communications, together with their propensity to carry weapons are features which have galvanised the police into sophisticated counter measures . . . . Experience has shown that the activity of this casual element is not restricted to match days, but seems to erupt sporadically throughout. Although the casual element has resource implications on match days for the police, the service must be prepared to prevent, or react to, outburts of activity at other times.
>
> (ACPO [Scotland] evidence to HAC, 1990: 53)

We have, therefore, a clear indication of the extra-football activities of the Hibs casuals established in the popular and police imaginations.

Practices

Two of the major criminal activities characteristic of organized crime in popular and official discourses are the importation and sale of narcotics, and the protection racket. The reasoning here is commonly of the *post hoc ergo propter hoc* variety. For example, the arrival of immigrants in the United States, and the speculative appearance of drugs within their perceived territories, entails that the former have simply 'caused' the latter (cf. Ianni and Reuss-Ianni, 1976: 186–201). However, extended, ethnographically informed analyses of Italian-American criminal groups suggest an ambivalence towards the sale of drugs, for instrumental as much as ethical reasons (Abadinsky, 1983: 128–9).

Popular knowledge of Hibs casuals adds a racketeering inflection to the perceivedly generic mutation of casual violence into drug-orientated practices. One edition of Scotland's top tabloid, the *Daily Record* (27 January 1992), led with a report on 'The Match Day Drug Dealers!', which exclaimed that 'Hibs casuals organise a big slice of the Edinburgh Ecstasy market'. The editorial response was in belligerent mood:

A new menace appears on the terraces at football matches –
the drug, Ecstasy. Casuals, who have already brought the game
into disrepute, are pushing the drug among younger fans. Real
fans, football authorities and police should team up. And boot
this sick new craze right out of the park.

(ibid.)

This report, and the predictable 'corroboration' offered it by the
Evening News (27 January 1992), oxidized a narrative already
inflated by the leaking of a police document to the Glasgow
Evening Times in September 1990. This story encouraged the *Evening News* (13 October 1990) investigation to spotlight 'police
fears that casuals are involved in major drug dealing'. Inspired
by police speculation that remained unsubstantiated in court
convictions, the report posited as evidence: 'Homes of Hibs casuals
have already been raided and cannabis found' (ibid.).

Reliable information attributing the supply of Edinburgh's
hard, soft and psychedelic drug trade to the machinations of
Hibs casuals is a scarce resource. Inevitably, there is a variety
of biographical, subcultural and spatial features which would precipitate
inter-relations between Hibs casuals and Edinburgh's
more *avant garde* drug subcultures. Hibs casuals, however, more
concertedly reproduce a collective unity by defining themselves
syntactically *against* perceived drug subcultures in Edinburgh and
beyond (Giulianotti, 1994a). The city has acquired the unenviable
title of Europe's Aids Capital, through the delayed effects of
widespread intravenous drug use in the early 1980s. Accordingly,
Hibs casuals tend to reflect a more diffuse and hardened local
antipathy towards the indigenous drug culture than is the case,
for example, with casuals in Glasgow or Aberdeen (Giulianotti,
1994b). It is also rather unlikely that any major player in the city's
narcotics supply would jeopardize his liberty through personal
association with such a public formation.

Through its simplicity and cultural familiarity (especially to
those trapped within it), the protection racket remains perhaps
the most popular metonym of organized crime's money-making
activities. Appealingly, the accessible and naked threat of violence
against those refusing personal and business 'security' is at the
heart of the protection racket (see Gurfein in Tyler, 1962: 181–9).
One case emerged last year of a Hibs casual 'who conducted a
terror campaign against two company directors' (*Evening News*,

18 January 1991) and was sentenced to four years' imprisonment. Although acquitted of two charges of attempted extortion, his defence counsel drew upon accumulating popular knowledge of a criminal organization, to state that his client was merely 'a cog in what may turn out to be a larger wheel'. The spectre of cabal was sustained by the contention of one of the vicims: 'This smacked of the Mafia' (ibid.). The *Sun's* coverage concentrated on the accused's alleged fixation with the Kray Brothers, later recycled by a national broadsheet's appraisal of security policies at nightclubs in Glasgow and Edinburgh (*Scotsman*, 18 January 1992). An earlier feature by the same paper lamented the lack of pacificity at Edinburgh's dance clubs, attributed solely to rapacious casuals, or 'terrorists' in the media-friendly vernacular of one club owner.[7] The 'casual extortion' narrative received its greatest impetus from the prosecution of six alleged 'Hibs casuals' for a series of robbery offences against other youths in Edinburgh's city centre (*Evening News*, 12 March 1991). However, the gang affiliation of those convicted was strongly contested by prominent figures during interview research.

The targeting of Hibs casuals' episodes of 'extortion' by Lothian Police has been ill-defined, and *ipso facto* indiscriminate. Over thirty casuals have at one juncture or another been employed as stewards or security officers at pubs, clubs and shops in and around Edinburgh. Some have been actively investigated by police officers for alleged racketeering. On occasion, these inquiries have been challenged by employer and employee alike, with more sustainable counter-accusations of police harassment. The one conclusion to be drawn is that Hibs casuals' variable control over these spaces is predicated upon a greater collective interest in access to sites of subcultural (stylistic) rather than economic capital. If the profits of racketeering were the objective, surely it would be better to diversify into blackmail or fraud, than simply minding bar doors?[8]

HACKING AWAY BLINDLY: HIBS CASUALS AND CRIMINAL JUSTICE

One important factor feeding into public discourses on Hibs casuals pertains to the evidential limitations of the above speculation, in terms of identifying and prosecuting 'members', most preferably the 'leaders'. The mediated, *finite* visibility of the Hibs

casuals seems to confirm their existence as a criminal organization, most numinously through a tantalizing uniformity, what
may be depicted as a *homology of signs*. Again, the *Evening News*
(22 October 1990) arrives with the message: 'We all know a Hibs
casual – he may be your neighbour or the quiet young man who
drinks in your local; or he may even deliver your letters each
morning.' The purported tearaway is thus coated in a reflective
veneer of normality, sharing everyday pastimes (a drink in the
local) or studiously obeying the Official Secrets Act (delivering
mail). Subjection of the object-matter to an informed gaze for
an unspecified time yields results. Look closely. Read the signs.
Most conspicuously, there is the attire: 'upwards of £400 worth
of fashionable clothing, usually Italian designed'.

The subculture's *disappearance of practices* presents the gravest
danger to prosecution. The authorities' shadowing of the object,
in an endeavour to capture its essence – particularly via the prism
of cabalism, the gang leaders – escalates to what Baudrillard
would term 'the pornography of policing'. The general public
obscenity of police escorts, crowd segregation policies, plain-
clothes uniform officers, the hoolivan, CCTV, and finally the
vicarious hooliganism of covert policing (see Armstrong and
Hobbs, this volume) crystallize as dominant control strategies,
designed to shadow the hooligan's every manoeuvre. Feldman
(1992: 86) has explored the usages of this State strategy in paramilitary policing of Northern Ireland. 'Endocolonization' involves
'the occupation and infestation of insurgent and delinquent communities by systems of surveillance, spatial immobilization, and
periodic subtraction of subjects from homes and communities.'

The track record of prosecuting Hibs casuals is not a good
one, being littered by a catalogue of minor convictions and
acquittals, often mere peccadilloes given the original charges.
Outside their native city Hibs casuals have been arrested in numbers of over fifty on at least four occasions, three times in the
greater Glasgow area and, following a skilfully engineered battle,
in Dundee in 1991. The Glasgow cases netted minor, individual
convictions for offences contained in the catch-all category of
'breach of the peace', such as disorderly conduct, threatening
behaviour, etc. The Dundee case, following raids on Hibs casuals
at home, was not pursued through the courts. Similar numbers
have been arrested in Edinburgh, on at least three occasions.
The most celebrated of these, following a fight between some

Hibs casuals and up to thirty police officers, came to be known as the 'Bristo Square Trial', and collapsed ignominiously due to discrepancies in police evidence. Outwith Scotland, Hibs casuals have been involved in regular soccer-related violence, most notably at Oldham, Birmingham and Millwall, as well as on the continent, in Brussels, Liège and Amsterdam (Giulianotti, 1992). They are also, therefore, the major threat to the political and football authorities' international projection of the Scottish soccer fan as the best behaved in the world.[9]

Early in 1991, a rumour began circulating amongst Hibs casuals that, on the reputed authority of a source in Lothian Police CID, the Home Office had deployed a 26-strong team in Edinburgh with the specified task of inquiring into the gang's criminal concerns. The failure of police prosecutions against Hibs casuals *en masse* – together with the coterminous, mediated discourse of crisis surrounding the formation – provided ready-made referents for the rationale behind this tightening control strategy. In reply, scrapbooks on hooligan escapades were jettisoned and extra-football violence was minimized. Subsequent rumours from other sources indicated that the Home Office team did not dwell long in Edinburgh, pursuing individuals who had reverted to 'disappearance'. But this final development simply adds to the discourses of knowledge constructed by the political, legal and soccer authorities, and the quality and popular media, pathologizing the rather traditionalist, hooligan proclivities of Hibs casuals.

PURSUING THE DISCOURSE OF CRISIS: ANATOMY OF A PROSECUTION

The criminal case which I examine here pertains to the events at a disco in 1990 in Dunfermline, a moderately sized town of approximately 120,000 inhabitants, located about twenty-five miles north-west of central Edinburgh. The incident centres on a public house called The Well, which on the night of the incident was playing host to a nomadic rave disco, The Kronk. This attracted a clientele from as far afield as Edinburgh, and was regularly attended by many Dunfermline casuals, known as the Carnegie Soccer Service (CSS), followers of Dunfermline Athletic FC. At the time of the disturbance, the CSS were capable of mustering between 80 and 100 casuals, and the gang was regarded in rather low esteem by Hibs casuals, as a formation physically

and stylistically more committed to raver than casual identity:
what Baudrillard (1979) might term 'transvestite casuals'. However, the Dunfermline formation did toy with casual-as-pugilist
significations. Court evidence identified a photographed advert
for The Kronk as containing the word 'hooligan'. The disco itself,
of course, is named after the world-renowned boxing gym based
in Detriot.

There had been trouble between Hibs and Dunfermline casuals
prior to The Well incident, outwith match-day contexts. One
Hibs casual had been attacked by Dunfermline casuals on three
occasions, the first two resulting in his hospitalization, the third
(three weeks prior to The Well attack) leading to his wife being
threatened with weapons and the petrol-bombing of the family
home. Following these incidents, a rumour spread that The
Kronk disco was to be attacked by Hibs casuals, as an organized
pursuit of *vendetta*. Half of the thirty witnesses at the disco later
petitioned by the Crown stated that they had heard such rumours,
seven named the Hibs casuals. None was able to disclose the
source of this information.

WELL BOXED IN: THE DOPING OF ATHLETICS

The following account relies on one court document (the judge,
Lord Kirkwood's 'Charge to the Jury') and statements given by
Crown and defence witnesses prior to court proceedings. It also
draws upon newspaper reports of the case, which culminated in
the *Evening News*' front-page screaming '*Riot Terror Pair Jailed,*
Gang Chants: High Court jury told of Hibs Casuals link with pub
trouble' (3 August 1991). From these accounts, it is possible to
depict with reasonable certainty the following scenario.

Some time between 11.00 p.m. and 11.30 p.m. on Friday, 7
September 1990, between thirty and forty youths walked towards
the front entrance of The Well. The first eyewitness to the gang's
approach, an off-duty policeman, puts the time of arrival at 11.20
p.m. approximately. Upon sighting the gang and surmising its
intent, he telephoned his colleagues – their first notification of
possible disorder. Most of the youths were hooded and/or facially
concealed in some way, and armed with weapons, which were
said in court to range from wooden sticks and iron bars to axes
and swords. The front door, the main entrance point for both
The Kronk disco and public bar, was barricaded by the disco's

door-staff, and whilst the gang managed to smash it, they failed to break through an internal door, blocking access to those inside the disco.

The gang then changed its point of attack, smashing through a side door and into The Well's public bar. When running through the bar towards the disco, some attackers picked up missiles and weapons, such as bottles, pool balls and cues from tables, and began throwing these around the bar. Two witnesses stated that they could recall hearing 'gang slogans' being shouted and chanted at this stage, but were unable to elaborate on their exact content. Some of the gang assaulted a man attempting to obstruct their passage, for which charges were later brought.

Failing to break down the internal doors leading to The Kronk disco, the gang went out of the bar and moved around the back of the building to arrive at the rear fire-door to The Kronk disco. The attackers endeavoured to smash their way through, using a variety of weapons. A beer-keg was hurled through the door's glass windows, and some of the attacking gang, most notably a masked individual with long, blond hair, attempted to release the internal door lock from the outside, but failed to do so. A barrage of missiles was released on both sides of the fire-door throughout this mêlée.

At this juncture, many of the 200 or so people at the disco, particularly the attendant women, were in a state of panic. Up to seven 'primary Crown witnesses' (that is, those caught up in the attack) stated that they had understood the attackers outside to be Hibs casuals, although again none had heard the implicating gang slogans being shouted by any of those outside. Three witnesses stated that their personal attributions of the gang's identity were based simply on the shouts of people *inside* the building.

Although the disco music was switched off during the disturbance, audio-visual perception inside was obfuscated by shouting and screaming; by missiles being thrown around the lounge; by the flashing disco lights; by the dry ice which had been emitted throughout the course of the evening; and by the darkness outside where hooded and masked figures lurked. Primary Crown witnesses referred to 'shapes there, people with balaclavas around their face'; 'peoples' shapes, some were masked but I could not identify anyone'; 'figures, some of them appeared to be disguised in balaclavas and scarves but I was unable to identify anyone'. In addition, several of these witnesses confirmed that cocktails of alcohol, cannabis, amphetamines and LSD had been taken within their social group, although they were reluctant in court to identify specific individuals in relation to substances consumed. Given the late time of the attack, between 11.20 and 11.30, and this evidence, it is likely that virtually everyone inside the disco was drunk or had taken illicit drugs in the course of the evening.

While the assault on the rear fire-door continued, some inside the disco attempted to leave through the building's front doors. Before their escape was secured, the attackers had abandoned the fire-door and returned towards the front of the building. Some had peeled off from the main body to reassault the bar, but the majority arrived at the front to confront ten primary Crown witnesses. Three managed to escape, and were pursued unsuccessfully for a short distance; seven others were attacked outside The Well. Three were assaulted to varying degrees of injury. One was badly injured, having been struck between twenty and thirty times by a variety of weapons, the most serious being a blow from an axe which nearly caused total paralysis.[10] After the attack, the victim's back was literally held together by friends until proper medical assistance could be administered, later completed by a four-hour overnight operation. A woman police officer had arrived at the scene of the incident first, but fainted on seeing the wounds sustained. A second man was seriously injured, principally by being struck over the head with a chair, and receiving a four-inch stab wound to the shoulder. A third man, having first punched the third accused at the foyer of the building, was assaulted by a variety of blows from blunt weapons.[11] Total damage caused by the attack on the building was estimated at £4,500; two cars in The Well's car park were also damaged.

THE SOCIAL BASES OF JUSTICE: AN ARRESTING PROCEDURE

Four men were charged with involvement in the disturbance. On the fourteenth day of a month-long trial, one was discharged, his counsel's submission that he had no case to answer being upheld. Inevitably, the three individuals whose prosecution proceeded to a verdict were regarded as prominent members, if not outright leaders, of the Hibs casuals.

The first accused, Andy Blance, was aged 25, lived and worked as a bar steward in the Inverkeithing area, and had forty-one previous convictions, around half of which were football-related. Subcultural knowledge of him was corroborated in court, in that he was noted to have been targeted in the earlier skirmishes with Dunfermline casuals prior to The Well incident. One female Crown witness, although unable to identify him as part of the disorder, qualified her ignorance by actuating local knowledge: 'However, I do know of [Blance] and his friends, they are "Hibs Casuals", and cause a lot of trouble in the Edinburgh area.' Blance was later informed by a source in Lothian Police's crime squad that they considered him 'at the top of the tree' in the imagined casual power pyramid. The accused himself claims that on one occasion he was extracted by police from a crowd of Hibs fans to be theatrically identified to an unfamiliar plain-clothes officer, during the period when Home Office officials were understood to be working in Edinburgh. Adding to this local policing and surveillance 'knowledge', the broadsheet *Scotland on Sunday* (11 November 1990) ran a prominent feature and photographs on Hibs casuals. The article identified one individual, 'Drew', as 'one of the top boys, a leader of the CCS', claiming his position was partially secured by his forthcoming trial for 'an alleged axe attack on a rival from another town'. The article then offered little doubt about whether this charge was congruent with his character: 'he has been inside, serving a two-year term for assault to severe injury. . . . A spell behind bars means others listen.' The article appeared while impending court proceedings rendered reportage of the case and related issues potentially *sub judice*. Andy Blance was found guilty, on a wafer-thin, eight-six majority, and sentenced to five years' imprisonment. His appeal against conviction was thrown out by the High Court; Blance was transferred to an 'open prison' less than eighteen months into his sentence.

The second accused, Ivor Levine, was aged 20 at the time of the incident, and hailed from the West End of Edinburgh. An ex-public schoolboy and business studies student, he was well known in the football and club scenes in Edinburgh (he had attended The Kronk disco before), and was distinctive with his long, blond hair and *avant garde* attire. A diabetic who drinks little and takes no drugs, he had no objective criminal reference points for any association with football-related disorder, a solitary previous conviction being for 'breach of the peace' in 1988. Police and popular constructs of his soccer-related activities would venture to disagree. Levine claims to have seen during his questioning by police a computer print-out reading 'Objective: neutralize the Hibs casuals' to which his name was one of those appended. He also claims to have been asked innocently by a fellow student how, on one occasion, he managed to abseil into the Rangers end at Ibrox, with the aid of a rope ladder! He was convicted and sentenced to four years on a unanimous verdict, and released on parole on his first application. The most serious reservations about this conviction pertain to the prosecution's methods of accumulating evidence against him.

The third accused, aged 20 at the time of the trial and working as a storeman, lived in the Tollcross area of Edinburgh, and was a former regular at The Kronk, at which he had experienced no prior problems. He was installed by the officer in charge of police inquiries into the Well incident, as a 'leader' within the Hibs casuals. In his court evidence, the officer noted:

> Enquiries revealed that Blance and the now [third] accused appeared to be the recognized leaders of the CCS and are known to have travelled to various venues, within and outwith the country to fly the banner of 'The CCS', which stands for 'CAPITAL CITY SERVICES' and is recognized as a collective term for 'FOOTBALL CASUALS'.

The third accused appeared from custody, having been arrested for alleged breach of bail (theft from a boutique, of which he was later acquitted). All charges against him were found not proven by majority verdict.

The trial was held at a specially adapted High Court of Justiciary in Dunfermline, with its jury selected from the town and outlying districts. During the period between the incident and the anticipated trial, the whole affair had been, in the court evidence of the major victim of the attack, 'the talk of the town'. There is no doubt that the subject matter was relevant at a microsocial level within the small and well-knit town of Dunfermline: 'What is gossip-worthy depends on communal norms and beliefs and communal relationships' (Elias and Scotson, 1965: 89). The 'quality' of knowledge about the incident during its ubiquitous discussion was processed through three levels of personal or collective association with the disturbance.

Core, *primary* access to the incident was derived from over 200 witnesses at The Well, or within the building's vicinity, on the night of the attack. At a *secondary* level, other 'witnesses' called to court, and all their peers and relatives (be these inter- or intra-generational) would have broadened the town's first-hand or speculative 'stocks of knowledge' on the disorder. Given that local youths were seriously injured in the incident, the communal impact and interest in its prospective background, causes and effects are guaranteed. However, the epiphenomenal emission of knowledge about the attack – from those present at the disturbance out to those removed from its consequences – encounters an at times dialectically opposed, overlying *tertiary* level of knowledge on the disturbance's social meaning. The tertiary discourse effectively establishes the terms of reference within which the meaning and motives of the disturbance are understood. The authoritative position of police and media is central in defining the meaningful practice of this discourse. Approximately one month after the incident, the *Evening News* (followed with alacrity by the national tabloid press) commenced its prurient 'investigations' of the Hibs casuals, as detailed above. The precipitant discourse of crisis – of cabalism, organized (and organic) crime, the pursuits of violent individual and gang sublimation, and ready prosecutions of *vendetta* – would have gained added nourishment from its secondary refraction within the jury's home locale.

A statement from one witness at The Kronk superbly illustrates how this primary access to the event was refracted by tertiary knowledge of the gang, under the aegis of a populist and communicable discourse of crisis. His immediate involvement in the disorder is recontextualized as that of a citizen harbouring popular assumptions about the identity and machinations of the attacking formation. His experience thus becomes understandable to his townsfolk in the jury.

> The people in the hall were generally panicking, the girls were shouting and trying to hide in order to protect themselves. At that stage I thought the best thing to do was get out the fire exit door, but that was not possible. Mainly because the crowd who were at the rear were trying to get in. I was also aware of people shouting, 'It's the Hibs, It's the Hibs.' It was then that I realized that in actual fact the people from Edinburgh, who are infamous for this type of behaviour were here intent in [*sic*] causing trouble.

MOBBING AND RIOTING: LEADING THE CHARGES?

Four major charges were levelled by the Crown at the three accused, so arranged for a domino-like effect. The central charge was one of 'mobbing and rioting' which, if individually proven, would render each of the accused automatically guilty of attempted murder, serious assault and assault charges. The auxiliary charge of 'possessing offensive weapons in a public place' constituted a compensatory option for the Crown. It would have been rendered redundant if the mobbing and rioting charge had been proven, so a bullish Advocate Depute (for the Crown) withdrew this charge on the trial's thirteenth day. A fourth order of charge was a breach of bail condition against the third accused, which stood or fell with his conviction on any of the other charges arraigned before him.

Although there is some dispute on the legal propriety of conjoining 'mobbing' with 'rioting', following the abolition of the Riot Act 1714 (Gane and Stoddard, 1980: 453), the seriousness of the law's interpretation of this offence is long-standing. Hume considered it to be the 'most eminent' of public order offences (in Christie, 1990: 5), the crowd having 'to inspire fear in the lieges and disturb the public peace. But that disturbance had to be of a sufficiently serious degree' (Christie, 1990: 6). Conversely, there is no requisite crowd size for the charge to be successfully pursued (Gloag and Henderson, 1980: 817; Ewing and Finnie, 1988: 411). A 'common purpose' in the mob's activity is another integral feature of the charge, and this is most effectively secured in prosecutions through indicting 'the ring-leaders' who 'mastermind' the operations (Gloag and Henderson, 1980: 817). This goes some way to explaining the legal-cultural bases of police assertions on 'leadership' of the Hibs casuals in framing evidence against the Dunfermline accused.

Furthermore, and contrary to the established legal principle of individual culpability, the charge of mobbing and rioting renders the accused accountable for *all* of the collective's actions. Defences to charges of 'mobbing and rioting' are at their most propitious in challenging the allegation of individual membership within the mob. Quibbling over the actual common purpose of 'the mob' is unlikely to win many friends among juries more familiar with discourses of crises than the sociology of youth subcultures. In this way, the accused necessarily forfeits claims to

the major court and cultural language of individuality by which
he would normally be held accountable for his own actions alone.

Two classes of defence were offered against the Dunfermline
charges: two accused lodged the special defence of alibi, the two
others stated that they had arrived separately at The Well during
the main incident, but were not part of the mob, their only
intention having been to enter the disco peacefully. Before these
defences could be tested in court, the accused were forced to
negotiate the extraordinary environs of the trial's legal and social
setting.

THE THEATRE OF INTELLIGENCE: THE TRIAL IN CAMERA

The decision to stage the trial in Dunfermline ensured that control and surveillance policing strategies, the 'fatal shadowing of
the criminal object' (see Baaudrillard 1990) intruded regularly
and disturbingly into the public spaces of witnesses, the jury and
the accused. This seemed to confirm local knowledge of the
gang's terrroristic nature and to cast a lengthy shadow over
the criminal justice process's claims to an unprejudiced trial.
Predictably, Hibs casuals lent daily support to the accused, whilst
Dunfermline casuals regularly mirrored this in support of primary
Crown witnesses. Although both groups mapped out informally
boundaried spaces within the courtrooms and waiting-rooms,
there were inevitable episodes of interaction between the two
sides.

Police warnings were regularly dispensed to those guilty of less
subtle machinations against opposite numbers. During recesses
in proceedings, small police escorts were given to both sides, as
they meandered through Dunfermline's bijou shopping centre,
though occasional laxity enabled confrontations between both
sides to occur. Sophisticated policing priorities appeared to be
pitched at a higher level. Intelligence gathering was best exemplified by the barely concealed cameras primed opposite the court
building during the first week of the trial.

The three main accused were each harassed, directly or
indirectly, on at least one occasion in the course of the trial, by
primary Crown witnesses or their peers. On the third day of
proceedings, Andy Blance was surrounded by a dozen local youths
outside the court building; when told to desist by attendant

police, at least one primary Crown witness failed to comply. Ivor Levine was said to have been threatened on the second day of proceedings with a stabbing by another primary Crown witness against him, in front of his own father and solicitor, for which the aggressor was later charged. Throughout the course of the trial, the third accused's mother, who maintained a daily vigil at the court, was said by her son's counsel to have been persistently harassed by local youths, which included the passing to her of threatening notes.

Less substantive evidence of harassment, though more germane to the legal practitioners, were the perceptions of intimidation felt by members of the jury. Some confided in the prosecution team that they were receiving hostile looks from Edinburgh youths in the public gallery. This was seized upon by the Advocate Depute who argued on the second day of proceedings that the court's public benches should be cleared, 'in order to ensure that justice may be done'. The Crown's submission was made without reference to a case authority, save the dictates of Common Law and the protection of national security. The submission was contested by all bar one of the Defence counsels, the dissenting party adding the caveat that the immediate family of the accused should be permitted to attend the court proceedings. Although both suggestions were formally rejected by Lord Kirkwood on this and at least one other occasion (all of which went unrecorded and unreported) according to the Common Law precept that 'justice must be seen to be done', the Crown's wishes were effectively implemented towards the trial's conclusion. Defence counsels successfully sought individual undertakings not to enter the courtroom, to avoid jeopardizing clients' cases. The police also barred large numbers of the public from viewing the verdict and sentencing.

Actual intimidation of the jury was, to my knowledge, limited to two incidents, both of which were almost certainly initiated by those supportive of the prosecution side. One local juror stated that while having a drink in a Dunfermline pub during a weekend break in the case, he was advised to 'Jail the bastards' by an unknown voice behind him. This was not reported to the authorities until after the trial. On the sixth day of the trial, a female juror was discharged amidst rumours that she had been telephoned the evening previously by purported (undoubtedly fictitious) supporters of Blance and advised on the desired out-

come of the trial. Common knowledge of this incident simply
served its intended function: to reinforce the conspiratorial aura
surrounding the Hibs casuals and their identified 'representatives' in the dock. But Lord Kirkwood attempted to direct the
jury: 'You must disregard anything that may be said or any
comments outside the court and you can only proceed on the
basis of evidence given in this court' (*Dundee Courier*, 17 July
1991).

There were more sustainable arguments for the contamination
of the principal Crown witnesses' evidence, most of this being
unattributable to the accused or their erstwhile supporters. The
main victim of the attack admitted he had talked about the case
while proceedings rendered this *sub judice*, although he refused
to name any of his correspondents apart from one: the fabulously
named 'Fairy'. Following this disclosure, Lord Kirkwood made a
point of warning every key Crown witness after giving evidence
that strict silence should be maintained on the court case. It was
also uncovered, in support of the Advocate Depute's submission
for clearing the courtroom, that the witness room had been
entered by an unauthorized member of the public during early
trial proceedings, thus engendering further fears of contaminated
court evidence. Meanwhile, Crown witnesses contended that they
had been harassed in some way by the accused and their supporters. On one occasion, a car was allegedly driven by a defence
witness in a reckless manner at a primary Crown witness; the
fourth accused was held in custody from the first day after he
had allegedly threatened a Crown witness. Neither allegation has
so far been the subject of court proceedings, but each added to
a discernible climate of fear surrounding the proceedings.

Overall, Crown witnesses expressed greater concern at their
treatment by the evidence-gathering and prosecution teams of
police officers, procurator fiscals and the Advocate Depute. Six
Crown witnesses, including four who had been inside the disco
before the attack, expressed concern about the Crown's prospective use of their evidence, before the case had come to court. This
quartet had identified one or more of the accused immediately
following the incident, but later separately sought to qualify heavily these identifications, on the bases of rumours circulating
before and after the disturbance; the mutual sense of anger after
the attack; and the ambiguous framing of identification questions
by police. All of these withdrawals were met with counter-threats

of perjury charges from the Crown, which were realized after further silences in the witness box. Only one witness stated that he had been approached about his position in the witness box, adding that this would not affect his evidence: coincidentally, the same witness was at the centre of the stabbing threat against the second accused (*Dundee Courier*, 18 July 1991). In addition, one primary Crown witness even asked for a lawyer whilst under intense examination. Nevertheless, Lord Kirkwood stated in his charge to the jury:

> The Crown, with a view to testing the credibility or reliability of a witness's evidence, is entitled to put it to a witness that he did say something different to the police but, as I say, what the witness may have said to the police on an earlier occasion is not evidence against any of the accused.

This was to a jury which had lost one of its members to a threatening phone-call supposedly from one of the accused's interlocuters; to a jury which had perceived intimidatory looks from Edinburgh youths on the public benches, as distinct from material harassment by local youths; to a jury which represented a socially and culturally compact town whose major nightspot, housing over 200 local young people, had been terrorized recklessly by a gang thought to be from Edinburgh; all this to a jury which had been ensconsed in a maelstrom of gossip, at primary, secondary and tertiary levels, about The Well incident and its likely perpetrators. All of these knowledge sources had been in circulation long before each juror's civic service had been ordained.

During the course of the trial, the jury also enjoyed the benefit of hearing inadmissible (but evaluatively pertinent) evidence from the Advocate Depute. Rather theatrically, while cross-examining Blance, he produced a document unknown to the Defence, and unrecognized by the court, listing names and addresses of Crown witnesses to be cited. It also contained the names of those in the dock, and thereby implicated each accused in any impropriety, real or imagined. The document was said in court to have been removed from Blance after his arrest in a soccer-related context, and was clearly produced to further calumniate the denial of primary Crown witnesses, who had altered their initial statements, that they had been approached about their evidence. A Motion was put forward by the Defence that the entire trial be deserted on the basis of this severely prejudicial 'evidence'. This submission was merely reported in the press as 'a full day of legal argument' (*Dundee Courier*, 27 July 1991). Lord Kirkwood refused the Motion to desert the trial, upholding his own conviction that this and other irregular speculations on the character and motivations of the accused could remain *ultra vires* to a reasonable verdict from his jury: 'In considering the evidence against Andrew Blance and the other two accused, you must disregard altogether the evidence about that piece of paper and its contents.' The prejudicial document remained the major tenet of Blance's ultimately unsuccessful appeal against conviction. It has also been raised as part of the correspondence between his solicitor and the Scottish Council for Civil Liberties.

GENERALS ON PARADE?: THE ABSENCE OF CORROBORATION

In examining the technical failings, the admissible weaknesses of the prosecution case against the accused, I will concentrate upon the evidence directed against Blance and Levine, who were convicted.

Andy Blance lodged the special defence of alibi, stating that during the disturbance he was working as a bar steward in Inverkeithing, a town which according to Crown and defence witnesses was a car journey of a minimum ten to twelve minutes away from Dunfermline. A Crown witness stated that she saw the accused leaving his work at 11.10 p.m., and returning at about 11.45 p.m. (*Dundee Courier*, 10 July 1991), accepting that he may have been outside chatting, a scenario specifically supported by one defence witness. Five defence witnesses also at the Inverkeithing bar stated that they were unaware of Blance being out of their presence for any significant time, particularly not for over half an hour. A police officer also stated that he had been radioed to attend a disturbance at The Well at 11.20 p.m., indicating that the police were aware of the trouble before this time. This evidence was corroborated by the off-duty officer who had seen the mob *walking* towards the Well at approximately the same time – in other words they had already travelled through to Dunfermline, parked their cars, congregated, and began moving towards The Well. Taking into consideration the time required to drive from Inverkeithing to Dunfermline, the timing of the police radio-message, and notwithstanding the evidence of one defence witness, there are up to five minutes or possibly more unaccountable for in the prosecution depiction of Blance's movements. If time is the major premise for a conviction in this case, therefore, the implicating evidence is barely circumstantial.

The court heard that in their initial police statements, taken soon after the incident, eight primary Crown witnesses present at The Kronk disco had positively identified Blance as being part of the attacking mob. Six of these witnesses later retracted or heavily qualified these identifications, before the case came to court, alternatively prefering to name him as a 'known soccer casual'. Ten other Crown witnesses attending the disco stated that they knew Blance as an individual, but had not seen him at any stage during the mêlée. Furthermore, one Crown witness admitted in a later statement that immediately after the disturbance

I actually encouraged others to make statements naming Andrew Blance and as far as I can remember they did so, some of them named Blance because I named Blance but I don't recollect exactly who I told to take this course of action.

Of the two Crown witnesses whose position on recognizing Blance remained firm, one accepted under cross-examination that he had only been allowed 'a split-second' to catch sight of him, and that he could not be certain that this was a definite sighting (*Dundee Courier*, 13 July 1991). The second Crown witness argued that he recognized Blance as both unmasked and at the front of the mob, but added 'I can't recall how much alcohol I consumed, I had also taken half a tab of LSD'. Thus, conviction by corroborated identification can hardly be said to have been forthcoming either.

The Crown's pursuit of a conviction continued on the lines of quantity of uncorroborated evidence. One Crown witness had initially stated that during the police investigation into the case, he had heard Blance at a police station 'bragging' about the incident at The Well. Under examination, 'He was pressed to explain what he meant by bragging, but said he could not remember' (*Dundee Courier*, 13 July 1991). Another Crown witness, who had been present at a house to which Blance had gone after the disturbance, stated that on several occasions the latter had categorically denied being there, but that a police officer who later interviewed her had been unwilling to record this. There was no forensic evidence against the first accused, nor were there any productions lodged as offensive weapons likely to have been used in the disturbance.

The defence of Ivor Levine accepted that he had been present at the site of the disturbance, but arrived unwittingly in its midst. It was contended that Levine had been to The Kronk on previous occasions, and on the night of the disturbance he and a friend travelled to Dunfermline. The two claimed to have arrived in Dunfermline and parked a short distance from The Well. On approaching the pub, they saw several youths standing outside, one of whom asked where Levine was from and then struck him across the head with a bottle, an assault later corroborated by one Crown witness. Levine then claimed he was threatened by his assailant about 'grassing'.

Six Crown witnesses were called to court ostensibly to identify Levine as part of the attacking mob. Two stated that they had been 'under the influence' during the attack: one was said by a friend to have been asleep for up to fifteen minutes until roused by the disturbance; the second stated that he had seen Levine outside the front of The Well during the incident, but uninvolved in any trouble. A third Crown witness admitted he had read the evidence of others implicating Levine before being called to give evidence himself. A fourth stated that his view of the second accused at The Well had been seriously impaired, and he could give no clear description of him. Two final witnesses against Levine confirmed in court their earlier identifications of him, although this evidence remains highly questionable because of the manner in which it was gathered.

These six witnesses had attended an identity parade soon after the incident, at which Levine was present. The accused objected beforehand to all stand-ins except one, on the grounds that none had 'long, blond hair'. The officers in charge dismissed this objection as 'unreasonable' on the grounds that the stand-ins were the best available: they had decided to conduct the exercise on a Monday afternoon (not a public holiday). Strangely, the officers had documented Levine as having 'long, fair brown hair', when 'long, blond' was a description never challenged or indirectly questioned during the four-week trial. More pertinently, the only stand-in with hair resembling Levine's was known personally by some of the witnesses as a local youth who would definitely not have been involved in the fracas. Up to three stand-ins at the parade were known to Crown witnesses there, one of whom described it as 'a farce' in court. A police sergeant submitted:

> If I had known that witnesses knew the stand-in that would have concerned me. If there was only one other person with long blond hair known to witnesses it would give more force to the objection.

Several witnesses confirmed in court that at the parade some of them had seen and even spoken to Levine before identification, and that this interaction was made known to other witnesses about to participate in the exercise, including one witness who confirmed in court that he was sure Levine had been part of the attacking mob. The other witness to confirm his position in court had in an earlier statement said that this identification was made on the grounds of Levine's hairstyle – which he described as 'permed'. On the interaction between the accused and witnesses at the parade, the same officer commented:

> If I had known that witnesses had seen Ivor Levine prior to the parade, even if accidentally, I would have discussed it with the other officer and decided what to do. It would have given me serious concern in relation to the conduct of the parade and would give substantial grounds for doubting the fairness of the parade, if that had happened.

Levine further contended that his name had been called out by police officers at the station and in front of the parade witnesses, before being objectively scrutinized by them. Clearly, therefore, the Crown purchased this required 'corroboration' against Levine through ignoring its contamination.

CONCLUSION AND POSTSCRIPT

Virtually all of the Crown evidence brought before the jury against the two convicted men can be said to have been undermined and/or contaminated to a significant degree. In the case of Andy Blance, the weakness of corroborating evidence is rather clear-cut, failing to challenge effectively his alibi in terms of space (verifications of his presence elsewhere) and time (the car journey to Dunfermline).

In the case against Ivor Levine, the strongest evidence against him, the identification parade, was clearly undertaken in a most irregular and injudicious manner. The most determined Crown witness against him claimed to recognize him by hairstyle, although three other hairstyles were put forward during the Crown's leading of evidence. Almost all of the primary Crown witnesses against both accused sought to alter their initial statements to police. Some also drew attention to the undue pressure which they felt the prosecution team were exerting in extracting 'admissible evidence'.

The seeds of the prosecution are more accurately found in the various discourses surrounding the Hibs casuals, initiated before the trial. It is possible to trace this process back to the 1980 delegitimation of football hooligan vocabularies of motive, and the subsequent 'discourse of crisis' constructed by the media, and political and policing authorities. This process has rendered the key political agents unable to recognize and rationalize the continuities of Scottish football-related disorder which formations like the Hibs casuals represent.

The arrest and conviction of the two men has not led to their neglect by 'The Family'. A steady stream of letters, visits and donations has characterized their spell in prison. 'Whip rounds' have been held *en route* to away fixtures amongst the main grouping; the proceeds of stylized, Hibs casual T-shirt sales are additional fund-raisers. Meanwhile, the results of the trial appear to have had little effect in threatening the continuation of the Hibs casuals. The gang has been involved in disorder in Europe, during an excursion to Brussels, and at a Madness ska concert which had been attended by Motherwell casuals. They also continue to fare better than any other Scottish opponents in domestic soccer violence. Significant incidents have included a successful battle with Rangers supporters at a 1991 Skol Cup semi-final in Glasgow, involving around 100 Hibs boys. At least 350 turned out for the subsequent Cup Final against Dunfermline, though the latter produced only a handful of opponents. The gang has also precipitated further confrontations with Aberdeen casuals *inter alia*, twice in the 1992–3 football season. On the first occasion, around 50 Hibs boys were attacked and 'backed off' by approximately 70 opponents in Aberdeen city centre. Later, up to 200 Hibs and Aberdeen casuals clashed at Edinburgh's Haymarket, which saw the visitors chased back inside the local railway station. A police plainclothes-led operation saw 19 Hibs casuals arrested for their participation. Reflecting their own division of labour, police 'intelligence' was still retarded by the image of cabal behind the disorder. Some of those casuals arrested at Haymarket were asked in all seriousness by bemused interviewing officers, 'Where were Blance and Levine?' And in a visible tightening of police surveillance strategies, up to 70 were 'detained' following a 'tip-off' that 'an organized gang of Hibs casuals' was planning violence at a local derby (*Evening News*, 23 August 1993). In accordance with established practice, the local media reported police press releases that only 29 had been arrested and no one had been charged. In fact, two individuals were charged with conspiracy; the spectre of cabal continues.

NOTES

1 Featherstone (1991: 61) argues that the ability of a new cultural movement to name itself is a crucial symbolic and sociological device in securing a configurational niche within its field of practice. Self-naming has a political component, 'on the part of groups which seek to legitimate the closure and exhaustion of the old tradition and generate a new space ahead of the established'.

2 Gerry Malone, then Conservative MP for Aberdeen South, asked the Parliamentary Under-Secretary of State for Scotland:

> Does my hon. Friend agree that one of the most important contributions to crowd control is an all-seated stadium? Does he agree that Aberdeen has been able to show an example of crowd control not only in Aberdeen but when Aberdeen clubs have travelled abroad? Aberdeen's supporters are ambassadors for the game, rather than the reverse.
>
> (*Hansard* [Commons], 19 June 1985)

Only three weeks later, Malone presented a Bill, the Criminal Justice (Scotland) (Amendment), to imprison or detain for a minimum of three months anyone convicted of a football-related offence, even if this was a mere breach of the peace near a football ground. In moving the Bill, Malone identified Aberdeen as the main problem area in Scotland:

> We pride ourselves on having avoided it, but unfortunately football violence is again escalating within Scotland. . . . The problem is a real one. During a recent Scottish sheriff court case, a document was provided to the court which showed clearly that Aberdeen soccer casuals were intent, having run riot in Scotland during the past year, on taking the problem south of the border . . . . When the Aberdeen football club sends its supporters abroad to European events, it sends them as ambassadors for Aberdeen and Scot-

land as well. However, unless we stamp out the menace of soccer casuals, that could change.

(Hansard [Commons], 9 July 1985)

3 Jean Baudrillard's 'fatal strategy' emerges from the 'fatal theory' of social relations, which has eclipsed the 'banal theory' of society:

> And doubtless the only difference between a banal theory and a fatal theory is that in one strategy the subject still believes himself to be more cunning than the object, whereas in the other the object is considered more cunning, cynical, talented than the subject, for which it lies in wait. The metamorphoses, the ruses, the strategies of the object surpass the subject's understanding.

(Baudrillard, 1990: 181)

I would suggest that this goes some way to reflecting the publicized banality that Scottish hooliganism is finished, and the subsequent fatalism which infects media and police language when describing the object's unforeseen return.

4 The Kefauver Commission's third interim report into organized crime noted the *Fratellanza* to be the precursor of the Mafia:

> Initiates and new members of this organization took solemn oaths never to reveal the secrets of the group under any circumstances and never to divulge the names of fellow members, even under torture. Each group had a leader. The group leaders were known to each other but not to the members of the various groups. The group leaders reported to the provincial chief who in turn reported to the supreme chief in Palermo, a very wealthy and influential man.

(quoted in Tyler, 1962: 340)

Not even the *Evening News* could suggest that this organization's alleged set-up was duplicated in Edinburgh by the Hibs casuals.

5 A close affine to this popular discourse is the sociological analysis of the lower working classes in 1960s Chicago, and more particularly the tendency of youth gangs to aggregate in confrontations with greater enemies (Suttles, 1968). This thesis has been applied to explain the construction of contemporary football hooligan formations in England, at the local, city, regional and national levels, by Dunning, Murphy and Williams (1988).

6 This condition does not fully square with the 'acephalous' one identified by Armstrong and Harris (1991) among Sheffield United hooligans, although the latter's cabalistic media representation does (Armstrong, 1992). A similarly conspiratorial picture of contemporary hooliganism in Aberdeen was depicted by Moorhouse (1991: 500), on the basis of a self-serving autobiography by a reputed 'leader' (Allan, 1989). Research with this formation confirms the complete opposite – the virtually unanimous recognition among Aberdeen casuals of an abject lack of 'leadership' and 'organization' within their midst (see Giulianotti, 1993a).

7 The pertinent part of the report stated:

But the East Coast rhythmic social scene has been plagued by violence. Especially in Edinburgh, groups of casuals have infiltrated the dancers. One of the main blackspots was at the Calton Studios, which shut at the end of last year – after the owner was stabbed. It is now re-opened under new management . . . . The image stuck. 'We had heard all sorts of rumours about what was going to happen at Slam 3-D,' said one of the party-goers, Andy Cochrane. 'People were saying that the casuals were mounting an assault, they were going to target folk who had been mouthing off about them. Lots of people I know just wouldn't come.'

(*Scotsman*, 23 March 1991)

8 The process of criminalizing street gangs has taken a crude and sinister departure in the United States. RICO, a federal anti-racketeering law, enables social control agents to arrest and charge groupings of youths, some barely into their teens, as members of professional, criminal organizations (Davis, 1992). By contrast, Lothian Police have demonstrated further properties of self-hypnosis when investigating the 'Criminal Underworld'. The 'Fettesgate' affair, for example, saw top-level officers duped into investigating a non-existent, gay 'magical circle' allegedly operating in the Scottish legal system. Ironically, the pointless inquiry was sparked off by the theft of documents from the force's headquarters in Edinburgh.

9 Following the 1992 European Championship Finals in Sweden, the attendant 5,000 Scottish supporters were presented with the 'Fair Play' award by UEFA (Giulianotti, 1993b, 1994c). This caps a decade-long transformation of the Scottish supporter's identity overseas, having been perceived as primarily drunk and violent prior to the 1982 World Cup Finals (Giulianotti, 1991).

10 Medical witnesses at the trial stated that had the blow penetrated a further two millimetres into the spinal cord, the victim would have been rendered paraplegic.

11 The four accused were also charged at the outset with assaulting a fourth person, a young woman who had been inside The Kronk disco throughout the disturbance. The alleged assault concerned striking her on the head with a bottle-like object 'to her severe injury and permanent disfigurement'. The charge related to her being struck during the exchange of missiles whilst the attacking mob had been gathered at the fire-door to the disco. However, as there was no way that the Crown could establish she had been struck by an object thrown from *outside* the building rather than *inside* it, this specific charge was dropped during the trial.

REFERENCES

Abadinsky, H. (1983) *The Criminal Elite*, Greenwood: Westport.
Allan, J. (1989) *Bloody Casuals: diary of a football hooligan*, Glasgow: Famedram.

Armstrong, G. (1992) 'Impartiality and the BBC', in *Flashing Blade*, December.
—— (forthcoming) *Fists and Style*, Ph.D. thesis, University College, London, Department of Anthropology.
Armstrong, G. and R. Harris (1991) 'Football Hooligans: theory and evidence', *Sociological Review*, 39, 3, 427–58.
Baudrillard, J. (1979) *De la séduction*, Paris: Denoel-Gonthier.
—— (1988) *Selected Writings* (ed. M. Poster), London: Polity.
—— (1990) *Fatal Strategies*, New York: Semiotext(e).
Camic, C. (1983) *Experience and Enlightenment: socialization for cultural change in eighteenth-century Scotland*, Edinburgh: Edinburgh University Press.
Christie, M. (1990) *Breach of the Peace*, Edinburgh: Butterworths.
Cohen, S. (1980) *Folk Devils and Moral Panics: the creation of the Mods and Rockers*, second edition, Oxford: Blackwell.
Cosgrove, S. (1991) *Hampden Babylon*, Edinburgh: Canongate.
Crampsey, R. (1990) *The First 100 Years*, Glasgow: The Scottish Football League.
Davis, M. (1992) 'L.A. Was Just the Beginning. Urban revolt in the United States: a thousand points of light', *Open Magazine Pamphlet Series*, 20.
Dunning, E., P. Murphy and J. Williams (1988) *The Roots of Football Hooliganism*, London: Routledge.
Durkheim, E. (1964) *The Rules of Sociological Method*, eighth edition, New York: Free Press.
Elias, N. and J.L. Scotson (1965) *The Established and the Outsiders*, London: Frank Cass.
Ewing, K. D. and W. Finnie (1988) *Civil Liberties in Scotland: cases and materials*, second edition, Edinburgh: W. Green.
Featherstone, M. (1991) *Consumer Culture and Postmodernism*, London: Sage.
Feldman, A. (1991) *Formations of Violence: the narrative of the body and political terror in Northern Ireland*, Chicago: University of Chicago Press.
Forsyth, R. (1990) *The Only Game*, Edinburgh: Mainstream/McEwan's Lager.
Gane, C. H. W. and C. N. Stoddard (1980) *A Casebook on Scottish Criminal Law*, Edinburgh: W. Green
Giulianotti, R. (1991) 'Scotland's Tartan Army in Italy: the case for the carnivalesque', *Sociological Review*, 39, 503–27.
—— (1992) 'Hibs Boys Disturb the Lieges in Casual Fashion', *The Herald*, 13 October.
—— (1993a) 'Soccer Casuals as Cultural Intermediaries: the politics of Scottish style', in S. Redhead (ed.), *The Passion and the Fashion*, Aldershot: Avebury.
—— (1993b) 'A Model of the Carnivalesque? Scottish football fans at the 1992 European Championship Finals in Sweden and beyond', *Working Papers in Popular Cultural Studies No. 6*, Institute for Popular Culture, Manchester.
—— (1994a) 'Keep it in the Family: an outline of the social ontology

of Hibs Casuals', in R. Giulianotti and J. Williams (eds), *Football, Identity and Modernity: fans and players in the world game*, Manchester: Manchester University Press.

—— (1994b) 'Scotland, Drink and Drugs: another generation of casualties?', in P. Lanfranchi and F. Accame (eds), *Gli aspetti sociali del fenomeno della droga nello sport*, Roma: Soc. Stampa Sportiva.

—— (1994c) 'Scoring Away from Home: a statistical study of Scotland football fans at international matches in Romania and Sweden', *International Review for the Sociology of Sport* (forthcoming).

Gloag, W. M. and R. C. Henderson (1980) *Introduction to the Law of Scotland* (ed. A. B. Wilkinson and W.A. Wilson), eighth edition, Edinburgh: W. Green.

Hills, G. (1991) 'Whatever Happened to the Likely Lads?', *The Face*, vol. 2, 39: 71–6.

Holt. R. (1989) *Sport and the British*, Oxford: Oxford University Press.

Home Affairs Committee (HAC) (1990) *Policing Football Hooliganism: memoranda of evidence*, London: HMSO.

Hume, D. (1962) *Enquiries Concerning the Human Understanding and Concerning the Principles of Morals* (ed. L. A. Selby-Bigge), Oxford: Oxford University Press.

Ianni, F. A. and E. Reuss-Ianni (1976) *The Crime Society: organized crime and corruption in America*, New York: Meridian.

Macphail, I. D. (1992) 'Safeguards in the Scottish Criminal Justice System', *Criminal Law Review*, 144–52.

Mills, C. W. (1940) 'Situated Actions and Vocabularies of Motive', *American Sociological Review*, 5.

Moorhouse, H. F. (1991) 'Football Hooligans: old bottles, new whines?', *Sociological Review*, 39 (3).

Redhead, S. (1986) *Sing When You're Winning*, London: Pluto.

—— (1991) *Football with Attitude*, Manchester: Wordsmith.

Redhead, S. and McLaughlin, E. (1985) 'Soccer's Style Wars', *New Society*, 16 August, 225–8.

Roadburg, A. (1980) 'Factors Precipitating Fan Violence: a comparison of professional soccer in Britain and North America', *British Journal of Sociology*, 31.

Stroud, B. (1977) *Hume*, London: Routledge and Kegan Paul.

Suttles, G. (1968) *The Social Order of the Slum*, Chicago: Chicago University Press.

Sykes, G. and D. Matza (1957) 'Techniques of Neutralization', *American Sociological Review*, 22.

Tyler, G. (1962) *Organized Crime in America*, Ann Arbor: University of Michigan Press.

Index